Pragmatic Software Quality Engineer

Software Quality
and
Java Automation Engineer
Survival Guide

(A completely packaged guide with right skills)

500+ Questions & Answers

Basic Concepts + Self Review + Interview Preparation

N = 16, M=550

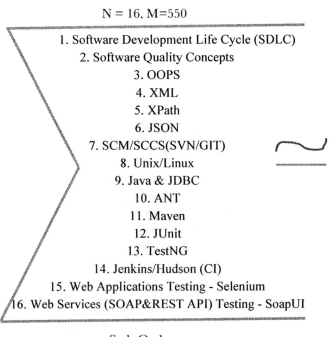

1. Software Development Life Cycle (SDLC)
2. Software Quality Concepts
3. OOPS
4. XML
5. XPath
6. JSON
7. SCM/SCCS(SVN/GIT)
8. Unix/Linux
9. Java & JDBC
10. ANT
11. Maven
12. JUnit
13. TestNG
14. Jenkins/Hudson (CI)
15. Web Applications Testing - Selenium
16. Web Services (SOAP&REST API) Testing - SoapUI

QA & Java Automation Core Skills

S=1, Q=1

Jagadesh Babu Munta

Copyright Notice

Print ISBN-10: 1-63572-000-1
Print ISBN-13: 978-1-63572-000-6

Dedicated to the current and aspiring
Computer Software Engineering Professionals!

Blank Page

How is this book?

"This book provides the best answers to the most frequently asked questions in testing job interviews. It is a unique book that includes all essential information in one single place covering manual as well as automated testing and builds the confidence. Jagadesh Munta is an authority in the testing field, and he has interviewed many candidates at his company. He knows what the hiring manager/team is exactly looking for, and he has distilled all that knowledge into this book. If you are preparing for a software testing job interview, then this is the book that you are looking for!"

-- Satya Dodda
(Senior Software Engineering Director, Oracle America Inc., Santa Clara)

"This book is the reason I was able to become a Test Automation Engineer without having any background in software. Not only did it help me master highly technical interviews and get me a high paying job, but it also instilled principles that have allowed me to excel above my coworkers."

(Systems Integration Automation Engineer, San Jose)

"It is such a wonderful guide and I really liked the way you've covered all the topics. This book is extremely helpful for people like me and also for those who are interested in starting a career as a Quality Engineer."

-- Sindhuri Mutyala
(Software Engineer in Quality, Intuit, Mountain View)

"It will be of real help for interviews."

(Senior QA Engineer, Santa Clara)

"It is an incredible Hands-on guide and helpful for people like those who are interested in starting a career as a Quality Engineer/Testing Engineer. Very beneficial in preparing for the software testing/QA job interviews."

-- Malik MA.
(QA Manager, Acentia Software Solutions, Hyderabad)

"This book is very well done and well organized. There are several good books in the market for Quality Engineering but this book focuses on Quality Engineering concepts from an interview perspective, and I can say this is certainly one of the best books around for Quality Engineers looking for a job. This book is clear, concise and offers much more information. I am confident this book can serve any person looking for Quality Engineering jobs."

-- Praveen Morusupalli
(Software Engineering Director, Oracle America Inc., Frisco)

"Reviewed the book, and overall, it looks pretty good. These questions/answers are truly a bible for anyone entering QA/QE/automation, and you have explained each very well with good examples."

(Automation Engineer, San Jose)

"Content is very practical/hands-on, I liked this fact."

-- Basha Sayed
(Software Development Manager, Oracle America Inc., Redwood City)

"This is a MUST HAVE book for each and every software engineer (DEV or QA doesn't matter). The knowledge acquired by reading this book is practically useful in day to day activities of a software engineer. Though there are some specific chapters relevant to Java/JDBC/Maven etc., this book overall is a great resource to every software engineer whether or not he works on Java. It covers most of the methodologies/technologies we use every day. The book is up to date on present practices (Agile/Scrum/Automation) and also elucidating the pros and cons of it. In a one liner, this book helps one becoming a great Software Engineer."

(Senior Software Developer, Fremont)

"This book provides more help to the people because it is highly informative."

-- Vijaya Bhaskar Tanamala
(Senior Software Developer, Travelers, Hartford)

"As technology keeps changing, we tend to forget the past. This book is like one place for all. Well explained with examples from end to end from all perspectives."

-- Sreenivasulu Naidu
(Lead Software Developer, Hennepin County)

"The concepts explained in this book will help developers handle their day to day job duties effectively. This book is a good starting point reference for the Software Quality Engineers and Developers."

-- Sriramulu Lakkaraju
(Software Engineering Director, Oracle America Inc., Santa Clara)

"I had a chance to review a copy of this book, and I think Mr. Munta has put a broad experience into it. This book is a must read guide for beginners to mid-level experts to prepare themselves for the global market."

– Thirupati Panyala
(Director, VMware, Palo Alto)

"Great attempt to consolidate all the essential and related content for test auto-mation to help developers and QA engineers. Practically, having implemented many test frameworks and worked with many test developers, I can confidently say you will be pleased to have this guide. This book is a go-to guide if you are looking for where to start and as a quick reference for experienced. An excel-lent review guide for those looking for the change of jobs as well and one stop for all testing phase/process and test automation."

-- Hari Prasad Kuppala
(Senior Software Engineering Manager, Oracle America Inc., Redwood City)

Acknowledgements

This book has been made with all supporting of people who interacted with me directly or indirectly.

First of all, I would like to express my indebtedness of gratitude to my parents (*Malakondaiah Munta & Narasamma Munta*) & family for being here on the Earth and growing up. I would like to thank my wife (*Sreelatha Munta*) and sons (*Lokaranjan Babu Munta & Chetan Munta*) for their continuous support in carryout this effort. Special thanks to brothers, *Malik Munta & Jayaprakash Munta* for their extended inputs.

Next, I am grateful with special thanks to *Satya Dodda, Cheuk Chau, Ganesh Kirti, Praveen Morusupalli, Shah Rahman, Chitti Keswani, Shesha Allavarapu, Xiaolin Deng, Luke Su, Ramesh Dimba, Raghav S. Nandhyal, Chandrasekhara Reddy Chennuru, JD Krishnamurthy* for their guidance, support and giving opportunity in gaining the related knowledge.

My sincere thanks to *Sriramulu Lakkaraju, Hari Prasad Kuppala, Tirupathi Panyala, Anjaneyaswamy Varada, Basha Sayed, Venkat Venkatnarayan, Jayanthi Kulkarni, Sujatha Arikapudi, Sudha Pamuru, Padmasri Vallabhaneni, Rika Dodda, Sri Rajesh Ajjarapu, Sarada Kommalapati, Srinivasulu Naidu, Vijaya Bhaskar Tanamala, Sindhuri Mutyala, Venkatesh Apsingekar, Sridhar Dhavara* for their encouragement and extended book reviews.

My apologies to those I have missed mentioning here but deserves to express my gratitude!

Thank you!

Jagadesh Babu Munta

Preface

My book authoring is one of my dreams since the year 2009, and especially I was trying to share my accumulated knowledge to the world of people for their benefit. This book is aimed to help most of the software professions and especially to Quality Engineering folks who don't have much support in terms of books and training compared to developers. This book should be helpful for anyone to understand the basic testing concepts, interview preparation in getting a new QA automation engineer job, or switching from another discipline to Software testing. If you feel otherwise, please feel free to contact at jagadesh.munta@everydayon.com or swqualityautosurvivalguide@gmail.com so that I can improve and take care of it as updates and new editions.

The goal is to help you.

Jagadesh Babu Munta

Contents

SKILL#15. WEB APPLICATIONS TESTING AND SELENIUM

Introduction

The book is about Software Quality & Java automation skills with basic concepts, self-review and interviews preparation related to the Java based projects in a practical sense with questions-answers. This book is targeted mainly at beginners to the software quality and development engineers. It is also useful for experienced quality engineers to do self-assessment and to be on top of relevant automation skills.

In the software industry, the quality related professional role is called as QA (Quality Assurance) or QE (Quality Engineering) engineer. In general, the "Quality Assurance" and "Quality Engineering" roles carry out the similar effort. The QA is a traditional role originated from industrial manufacturing assembly where the final product quality tested by verifying against a checklist, inspected for any damages and finally put a quality sticker. The similar QA role came to IT Software but associated with Engineering background. So, QE role makes sense for Software industry, and it stresses more on the importance of applying the Engineering principles rather than simply repeating the quality assurance actions.

The QA role involves the tasks such as understanding of the software product features & domain knowledge, writing test plans, writing test specifications, manual execution of tests and interpreting results. Later, one has to do the development of automated tests, automated execution and generation of final results summary for release level regression testing. Note that the QA role need average coding skills, but it takes more time and energy than in general as expected by many people. Because, for each product release in the product line, the developed tests should be continuously executed and verified to make sure no regressions at any point in time. The Quality Engineering skills have to be applied all the time during the product development. The quality has to be measured, assessed and concluded to prove that product is meeting the customer expectations. Without the engineering principles, quality testing might be happening and can discover some bugs but it may not ensure the proper proof to justify the on the quality and might leave some gaps. In summary, apply the core engineering principles such as measuring, making consistency, repeatability and correctness during the application of testing techniques.

It is difficult to do the above principles merely with the manual approach because of limitations such as human errors in producing consistent actions & output, testing coverage with quick, agile product development cycles and making sure each build is verified for regressions. The Quality Automation is one of the important things to address this continuous regression testing. The automation effort needs programming skills in the same software domain and relevant skills to achieve the high automation, which saves time and test coverage.

It is hard to survive without having the fundamentals and automation skills in software development and quality as a QA or dev engineer. Also, many skills need references to many other books that were not targeted at QA professions. Now, this book is an attempt to create such survival guide for QA professional with all relevant skills at one place.

This book should help in making sure that you get the basic core concepts, working knowledge and in summary as a survival guide for programming and automation with all required skills. The goal is not to aim at making you an expert at one skill or entirely on these skills. The focus is on finding the needed skills and at what level is being used for 80% of the time (80-20 rule) in the Java programming and Quality engineering profession.

For the Manual QA engineer, this book helps in understanding Quality concepts, SDLC (Software Development Life Cycle), technical terminology, etc. Also, this helps in moving the engineer from manual testing to automation.

This book also helps junior developers working on Java projects in SDLC, OOPS, Java programming, unit testing and most of the other skills are in common with automation. Also, it gives understanding some of the test frameworks and terminologies in the test development.

One of the key thing to observe is that it is not difficult to learn anything but to see what is relevant and why to learn. Learn the things most important to you in the work or life. If someone asserts on what you know, then it builds more confidence in the current profession or newly pursuing one.

At a high level, this book starts with the areas such as processes (SDLC/Quality/OOPS), data (XML/XPath/JSON), code repositories (SVN/GIT), and operating systems (Unix/Linux). Then enters into programming (Java&JDBC), and later build frameworks/tools (ANT/Maven). After that it covers more on unit testing frameworks/tools (Junit/TestNG) and continuous integration tools (Jenkins/Hudson). Next, it includes the functional testing of web applications and web services with frameworks/tools (TestNG/Selenium/SoapUI) covered. Finally, included samples code (for Java/Selenium) to reference offline, and hands-on/getting started in the job.

There are about 500+ questions and answers to ease on understanding the concepts and for review purpose.
The below are 16 core skills covered in this book.
1. Software Development Life Cycle (SDLC): The SDLC is to understand the core methodology of the software development process. This process is one of the essential concept for Dev/QA individual and the teams to collaborate effectively in the creation of the software products or IT services.

2. Software Quality Concepts: The quality concepts are the fundamental knowledge on the testing part of SDLC process that must be possessed by every QA and Dev team for the delivery of a high-quality software product.

3. OOPS: The majority of the software products development has been done with Object-oriented languages such as Java, C++, and other OO high-level languages. OOP concept is very much essential for any Java/C++ programmer to maintain or develop new software in Java.

4. XML: Most of the existing dynamic content, e-commerce sites and many software configurations have been done using XML file format. It is essential to understand this universal XML file format to survive in the Software dev and QA profession.

5. XPath: As long XML is there, the XPath also plays a key role in performing the navigation, extraction of XML, and transformation of the content to various other forms (HTML/text). So better to acquire this skill by developers and QA professionals.

6. JSON: The JSON file format is a newly evolving and modern universal file format. JSON format is being used widely in REST WS, Internet/Web applications, Social sites, etc. Having hands-on with JSON files is crucial for all developers and QA automation professionals.

7. SCM/SCCS(SVN/GIT): The source code is one of the major intellectual property of any software organization. It is essential to collaborate with the developing teams using a source code control system such as SVN or GIT. It is important to understand the SCM concepts and working knowledge on SVN and recently popular GIT software for both developers and QA automation engineers.

8. Unix/Linux: In Today's World, most of the enterprise software, website hosting, and any Internet-hosted software or applications are on the Linux/Unix platform. Having hands-on experience with this platform is fundamental for everyone.

9. Java & JDBC: Most of the existing or new, whether small or larger software projects are still written in Java language. The Java should be at the heart of every software professional and thereby essential to have this language to survive in the software development and QA automation profession.

10. ANT: The ANT is a build framework. Once it was popular and still is being used as Java build framework for both product code and test code in most of bigger software organizations. Having an understanding and hands-on experience for both developers and QA is good.

11. Maven: The Maven is a build framework used everywhere in the recent Java projects. It addresses some of the dependency resolution problems with Java project build process that was a burden with ANT. Maven makes the build process simple by using conventions. Thereby Maven is a significant survival skill for both developers and QA automation engineers.

12. JUnit: The unit testing should be one of core tasks for any Software developer. The JUnit is an old but simple and popular framework for Java projects. This test framework is still being used in many organizations and lot of IDEs support the automatic test code generation and execution. Having JUnit experience is an essential skill for developers.

13. TestNG: The TestNG is one of the common framework used across the unit testing and functional testing. TestNG is being used in most of the recent projects and specifically in Selenium based test projects. Having hands-on with this skill is essential for both developers and QA automation professionals.

14. Jenkins/Hudson (CI): In the Continuous Integration (CI) category, Jenkins/Hudson play a vital role with automated jobs for creating the product builds/bundles and also end-to-end regression test cycles. The Hudon/Jenkins functionality is extendable with plugins, and many of the plugins are already available. It is a widely used tool. Thereby having this skill by both developers and QA engineers gives a real strength.

15. Web Applications Testing – Selenium: The Selenium is a browser-based website testing automation framework. Many of the organizations need this skill to create automated test suites

going through the browser. This framework acts as a remote to the browser. The selenium automation hands-on experience is a must for QA automation engineers.

16. Web Services (SOAP&REST API) Testing and SoapUI: The Web Services are loosely coupled and distributed technology that is widely used. The WS are being used in Service Oriented Architecture (using SOAP-based web services), or with the Internet resources addressed as RESTful WS or REST API or REST endpoints. Nowadays, the REST is very popular and is everywhere. It is essential to understand and test these REST APIs. This skill is a must for both developers and QA engineers to survive in the development of current software and IT services.

Hands-on/Getting started: Once joined the job, many times it will be a confusion where and how to get started the day-to-day work. This section helps to understand those basic expectations from your new company/team and walks through the flow.

Java samples code: Learning by an example is a quick way to learn new things. The Java sample code helps developers and QA engineers to get comfortable in Java programming.

Selenium samples code: The Selenium sample code helps QA engineers in learning the browser-based website test automation using Selenium. Having examples is a good way to quickly getting into coding.

How to read this book?

For beginners and junior software engineers, it is recommended to go from Skill#1 to Skill#16 so that each learned concept or skill would be used in the following skills.

For senior engineers and leaders, just jump to any skill to review the concepts. There is no direct link between the skill chapters rather the previous skills will be used in the later skills.

Overall, these skills review should get you at the level about five years of experience in the Software quality and Java automation profession.

Finally, this book is an attempt to share and build confidence in you with core skills of Software quality and Java automation.

All the best for your journey!

Skill#1. Software Development Life Cycle (SDLC)

The SDLC is to understand the core methodology of the software development process. This process is one of the essential concept for Dev/QA individual and the teams to collaborate effectively in the creation of the software products or IT services.

1. What is Software?
    □ The Software or Computer Software is a set of programs and data that process information and controls underlying hardware. It includes programs, libraries, and non-executable data.
    □ Some of the examples include the following.
        □ Operating Systems such as Windows, MacOS, Linux, Solaris, etc.
        □ Browser software such as Firefox, Chrome, Internet Explorer, Safari, etc.
        □ Office software such as Microsoft Office, Star Office, etc.
        □ IDE software such as Eclipse, NetBeans, IntelliJ, etc.
        □ Any other programs that operate on devices and data.
    □ The main purpose of software is to have the flexibility to control a general purpose solution, business solution or devices such as mobile, desktop or large computers.
    □ The software is everywhere in the Today's evolving technologies. Understanding and gaining of software skills would help in professional advanced technology careers.

2. What is SDLC? Why do you need such models? What are different models?
    □ SDLC stands for Software Development Life Cycle. It is the process of developing any software. There are many processes around from a traditional "Waterfall model" to the latest "Agile" processes. There are many types in Agile itself such as XP (eXtreme Programming), Scrum, TDD (Test

Driven Development), etc.

3. **How is SDLC related to Testing?**
   ☐ Testing is the part of the SDLC and understanding it will help effective testing of a software product. The testing is the process that comes as verification phase in Waterfall model and in testing part of agile Scrum.

4. **What is Waterfall model? What are different phases involved?**
   ☐ The Waterfall model (as the name indicates) is like water flowing from upper ground to next lower ground where development (along with information) passes through different phases as one after the other. It involves five different phases in an order and goes to next phase only after completing the prior phase.
   ☐ The phases are
      i) Inception
      ii) Design
      iii) Implementation
      iv) Verification
      v) Maintenance.
   ☐ It is hard to inject the customer requirements (either with new requirements or changes to old requirements) while development is in progress. It usually takes about six months to 1-5 years to complete such projects and most of the time used in old stable/matured projects and also in larger projects.

5. **What is Agile Scrum process? Can you describe at a high level?**
   ☐ Agile Scrum is an iterative process of developing software with the goal of getting incremental intermediate product delivery. In the agile scrum process, there will be a product backlog, Sprint backlog and short cycles of the development process(typically seven days length of a sprint with the goal

of delivering product in 4-5 weeks) and release. Sprints are repeated until entire product backlog is completed. Every release is towards an improvement or finish towards the end product. Customer requirements can be injected into product backlog and will be picked up by next sprint (through sprint backlog). There will be daily stand-up meetings of approx. 15 mins in length on the scrum sync' up.

6. **When does the testing activity gets started in each development model?**
   - ☐ In the waterfall model, testing is started only in the verification phase after completing the implementation phase.
   - ☐ In the agile model, testing is done in every sprint or scrum cycle. Testing is started since beginning with the features in that sprint and work closely with the dev on the completed features within that sprint.

7. **What is meant by standup meetings in the scrum process? What are the three questions (typically) you need to answer in Agile Scrum process?**
   - ☐ The following three questions are to be answered and should be getting ready for the meeting.
     - i.   What have you done since Yesterday?
     - ii. What are you going to do Today?
     - iii. What are the blocking issues or stumbling blocks (from you)?

8. **Who is Scrum Master? What is his/her role and responsibilities?**
   - ☐ The scrum master is like project manager in the agile scrum software development process. Scrum master handles the sprint schedule, product backlog, sprint backlog and conducts the daily standup meetings with all stakeholders.

9. Are you aware of any Agile tools?
   - ☐ Rally software is one of the tools (http://www.rallydev.com) to used for tracking the Agile process.
   - ☐ Atlassian's JIRA also being used to track the tasks in a sprint and have the epics with JIRA dashboards.
   - ☐ Finally, simple wikis/spreadsheets can also be used as a tracking tool.

10. What is a sprint? What is a typical duration for a sprint?
    - ☐ The sprint is the short cycles of software development lifecycle, and typically it is a weekly or 2 or 3 or 4 weeks period to code, verify, document a set of user stories or fix and verify the bugs.

11. What is meant by product backlog?
    - ☐ The product backlog is the list of tasks and requirements for a product under development. The backlog gives the full list of prioritized requirements or tasks for the product at any given time. If any new or changes in the old requirements, those will be updated in this product backlog and prioritized.

12. What is a sprint backlog?
    - ☐ The sprint backlog is the list of prioritized tasks and requirements to be completed in a particular sprint cycle. It is a subset of top requirements or tasks picked from the product backlog.

13. Where do you add the changed requirements? Whether in a sprint backlog or product backlog?
    - ☐ The changes in the requirements would be added to the product backlog and will not be added to the current sprint backlog. These changes would be picked up in Next sprint cycle (through sprint backlog) from the product backlog.

14. Can you change a sprint backlog during a sprint?
   ☐ No. Not in the current sprint but the next sprint cycle would catch up the sprint backlog derived from product backlog with those changes.

15. What is a use case?
   ☐ Use case is the sequence/flow of actions and events performed by an actor to achieve a business goal. The actor could be an end-user using the system or the system or device itself interacting with some other system. There will be many use cases for a given product under development.

16. What is a user story?
   ☐ The user story, the term used in the agile SDLC process and is a simple description of a software requirement in the end user's perspective and his/her business job function. It should be scoped for an iteration and should provide a business value or add the value to the overall product once implemented.

17. What is Test Driven Development(TDD) process?
   ☐ The Test-driven development is an agile software development process under extreme programming paradigm. In the TDD, the developer first writes an initial, which is a failed automated unit test as per user story and repeatedly modified the code until the test passed. I don't think TDD is that popular or widely used now.

18. What are the advantages and disadvantages of waterfall model?
   ☐ Waterfall model advantages:
      ☐ It can give better project schedule estimation and planning.
      ☐ It provides the re-use of Resources because of sequential phases.

☐ Good for large projects with clear planning, design, architecture before actual implementation. The team is not under time pressure (in comparison with Agile) as there can be sufficient time buffer for planned tasks. Typical project release duration is higher and is between 6 months to 1-5 years compared to Agile monthly project releases.

☐ Waterfall model disadvantages:

    ☐ Customer requirements can't be accommodated in the middle of the project.

    ☐ This takes more time and incurs more cost.

    ☐ There is no incremental product delivery. The final project is available only after the final phase, which is a longer in duration.

    ☐ It is difficult to predict if the project is doomed to failure until the project completion or out of resources.

19. **What are advantages and disadvantages of Agile Scrum process?**

    ☐ Scrum process advantages:

        ☐ Adapt to the changes where customer requirements can be honored in the middle of the project development (that is in the next sprint cycle).

        ☐ It helps in doing incremental product delivery.

        ☐ It takes less time comparing with waterfall model.

        ☐ It gives an early indication of the project status and can be stopped quickly or can be transformed to a different project.

    ☐ Scrum process disadvantages:

        ☐ It can consume more resources because sprint cycles need to cover all dev/test/doc activities at same time.

        ☐ Typically, it is good for shorter projects with less complex projects (where fewer alternatives/architectures to be considered).

        ☐ It demands high productivity and constant effort be done by the team and thereby stress or time pressure felt by the team.

        ☐ Also it will have more quick sync' up meetings.

20. **What is the typical team size in different SDLC models?**

    ☐ A typical number could be viewed as below, and it can very

much be based on the matured SDLC process in the organization.
- ☐ Waterfall model >10 team size
- ☐ Agile model < 10 team size
☐ Nowadays, more team size projects (like more than 50) also
doing well with Agile Scrum process. It is becoming a de-
facto process for most of the startups and new development
teams in larger organizations.
☐ Also, it could be some kind of mixed as waterfall and agile
together in the development process.

21. **Which SDLC model suits for rapidly changing requirements?**
☐ Agile SDLC process (say scrum) is most suitable because
the changes can be uptaken in the next sprint cycle. Thereby
customer requirements can be considered during the product
development time itself rather than waiting till the product
release.

22. **Which model suits for incremental product delivery?**
☐ Agile SDLC process (say scrum) because it is an iterative
process contributing to the overall product in each sprint cycle. Thereby product progress can be seen as sprints in progress and can be demo-ed or given to the sales and trial customers before the final release of the product.

23. **What is meant by refactoring? Where do you typically do?**
☐ Refactoring is the general software engineering process in
coding and is to make code changes in such a way that it can
improve readability, structure and optimization while keeping the use case/behavior intact.
☐ This refactoring process is very typical in the software programming and also especially in the agile process as it is
iterative because getting the perfect code is not possible with
all optimizations at a time.

24. **What is meant by alpha and beta products? Who are the consumers? What is the main objective?**

    ☐ The Alpha product is the very initial product available after code completion but exists with many bugs (all features might not work as expected).

    ☐ The Beta product is the next milestone product after Alpha release with more bugs fixed but some bugs can still exist in the end-user functionality and also still the quality improvement should be done.

    ☐ Few Alpha customers would be selected for Alpha testing, which is done at the customer site to get the very initial feedback on the features understanding.

    ☐ Few Beta customers would be selected for Beta testing, which is done at the customer site to get the feedback so that those can be fixed before the release of the RTM (Release to Manufacture) product.

    ☐ The main objective of these intermediate releases is to make sure that the customer acceptance is in-line with the product development and make corrections with their feedback.

25. **What is a PRD (Product Requirements Document) or BRD (Business Requirements Document)? What it contains and who owns this?**

    ☐ PRD is the product requirements document with the list of customer features gathered and the documented by the product management (PM) team. The PMs interact with customers on the product requirements and acceptance criteria later.

    ☐ BRD is the Business requirements document, which is similar to PRD but used in the context of IT projects or consumer projects (like retail or financial) than Product research projects.

26. **What is a functional specification? What it contains and who owns this?**

    ☐ The Functional specification document is a detailed requirements analysis document created by the senior development

team for each feature listed in the PRD/BRD.
☐ This document contains a detailed specification of features and owned by the Dev team.

27. **What is meant by soft code freeze (SCF)? When does it happen in the SDLC process?**
☐ Soft code freeze or Feature complete is a considerable milestone that occurs after completing the implementation of all the features during the development process.
☐ After SCF, no more features would be added, and instead, only critical, high and medium bugs would be fixed.
☐ A separate branch or tagging of source code repository would be created for this SCF milestone and keep using this branch until release is completed.
☐ QA team would continue to test and file bugs as Dev team continue to fix the bugs (but no new feature).

28. **What is meant by hard code freeze (HCF)? When does it happen in the development process?**
☐ Hard code freeze is a milestone and happens after SCF milestone when most of the critical/high/medium bugs fixed and ready for final QA test cycle to find any showstopper bugs (that can stop the release).
☐ After HCF, only show stopper (customer impact is very high) bugs would be fixed.
☐ Please note that these show stopper bug fixes are allowed only with product management approvals.

29. **What is product release candidate (RC)? What is a release?**
☐ Release Candidate (RC) is the final milestone in the product release cycle timeline.
☐ RC is created after HCF is completed and QA would do the final test cycle before RTM release.
☐ RC would be released as RTM product when no show stopper bugs found on this final build.
☐ The product release is nothing but bits are ready to handover

for manufacturing (i.e., to cut the CD/DVD) or download from the internet by the customers.

☐ For the release bits testing, QA and dev teams would do the final sanity testing like checking binary sizes, documentation links, basic installation, downloads check, etc., so that customers don't see any basic issues.

30. What is release notes? Who drives this?

☐ Release notes is a document that is made available to the customer along with product release where customer is aware of such as basic version, features summary, critical known issues with workarounds, documentation references etc.

☐ Release notes document is integrated into the product bundle and also downloadable from the internet. Any updates in future would be updated in the online documentation.

☐ Release Engineering (RE) team drives the release notes but contributed and reviewed by all the project stakeholders.

31. What is a release criteria? Who sets this up and who has to follow?

☐ The Release criteria are the minimum checklist or goals to be achieved to release the product. This effort is driven by RE team, and all the project stakeholders would contribute to making this release to happen.

☐ Below is a sample release criteria/checklist and can be taken as a template if none is available.

   ☐ Bugs criteria
      • No P1, P2, P3 open bugs
   ☐ Quality criteria
      • 100% feature coverage and test development
      • 100% test execution
      • 95-100% pass rate
      • >90% automation for regressions
   ☐ Stress/Load/Concurrency criteria
      • 100 users/sec

1. Software Development Life Cycle (SDLC)

☐ Performance criteria
- Minimum throughput numbers related to the product.
- Comparison to other competitive products
☐ Code coverage
- >90% class level
- >50% method level
- >40% instruction/statement level
☐ Internationalization (I18N) & Localization (L10N)
- Internationalization support
- Specific languages to translate
- NOTE: I18N is short form as there are 18 characters between I and N in the "InternationalizatioN". Similarly, L10N is short form as there are 10 characters between L and N in the "LocalizatioN".
☐ Documentation (books/online)
- Release notes
- User Manuals
  - o Installation Guide, Admin Guide, Developer Guide, Troubleshooting guide, etc.
☐ License and license text
☐ Support/Maintenance plan

32. What is meant by a release showstopper? When does it happen?
☐ The showstopper is a bug that has a visible & high impact to the customer and must be fixed before the product release. If the fixes are not possible within the release time, then corresponding bugs and workarounds should be added to release notes.
☐ This kind of bug fixes should go through focused reviews and approvals to minimize the regressions (if any) in this final release of the product.
☐ The showstopper happens after the HCF and RC milestones or during the final sprint of the development process.

☐ The regressions tests should be selected based on the bug fixes instead of running all the tests because of the need for quick turnaround time.

33. **Who are all project stakeholders? What are those teams?**
☐ In general, below are the Project stakeholders in a product development organization.

   ☐ Product Manager
   - Acts as a bridge between product and customers
   - Responsible to create PRD (Product Requirement Document) or BRD (Business Requirement Document).

   ☐ Project Manager/Dev Manager/Dev Director
   - Owner of the product execution (who creates and executes the Project Plan)
   - Acts as a driver for successful project release.

   ☐ Program Manager
   - Co-ordinates with all stakeholders during the project execution and helps project driver.
   - Conducts release meetings

   ☐ Architects
   - Responsible for performing product architecture considering the big and strategic goals like scaling, availability, performance, security, technology, etc.
   - Creates architectural diagrams and documents.
   - Work closely with the design/development teams for making the implementation successful.

   ☐ Designers
   - Responsible for the product design and work closely with Architects and developers.
   - Creates FSD/FS (Functional Specification Document)
   - Please note that sometimes Architects can act as designers or senior developers can be designers.

   ☐ Developers

- Responsible for implementation (coding) as per FS.
- Do bug fixes
- Conducts unit testing

☐ QA/QE
- Responsible for Testing (tasks like write test code, execute tests, file bugs, create Test Plan and Test Specification).
- Review documents - release notes, manuals/guides

☐ Doc writers
- Responsible for all sorts of documentation like user guides/manuals/help content.

☐ Release Engineers (RE)/Devops
- Responsible for doing the integration of modules and creating the builds.
- The DevOps would host and monitor the stage and production sites.

☐ Support Engineers/Front-end support (customer facing)
- This team would triage the customer issue and pass on to backend support if needed.

☐ Support Engineers/Backend support
- They would triage and fix the customer issues escalated by front-end support engineers.

34. **What is a test cycle at product level?**
    ☐ A test cycle is the duration of time, where all the test activities can be completed on a given product binary/build.
    ☐ A typical cycle could be varied from 1 week to 4+ weeks.

35. **How does the QA team track the weekly status or progress?**
    ☐ Typically, QA team representative (Director or Manager or Lead) would prepare the answers to the following questions while tracking the status summary.
      ☐ How many open bugs and list of these bugs?
      ☐ How many blocking bugs (P1)

☐ How many tests are failing (count and %)? Example: 30% failing

☐ How much test development is pending? Example: 40% tests

☐ When will be the test automation is going to be completed?

☐ What are the bugs inflow (new bugs came since last reported time) and outflow (fixed bugs since last reported time)? (Example: Weekly)

☐ What are the total number of bugs fixed and bugs opened? Bugs trend.

☐ How many bugs yet to be verified?

  • Please note that the bugs verification & closing usually done by the bug filer.

☐ Get all the answers in a wiki or document and update in the email for the weekly status report and send to stakeholders.

36. What is Go/No-Go for product release?

☐ "Go/No-Go" is the decision voting conveyed/sent after their respective release criteria met by each project stakeholder participated in the release meeting.

☐ Once all votes of GO received, then RE would take it as the GO for release. Any No-Go voting should be discussed and mitigated or fixed before release.

☐ Once it is a GO, then it is a celebration time for the entire project team;)

← End: Skill#1. Software Development Life Cycle (SDLC) ←

Good!
Keep going and never give up!!
Please re-read again for more clarity and feel free to contact for help!!!

→ Start: Skill#2. Software Quality Concepts →

Skill#2. Software Quality Concepts

The quality concepts are the fundamental knowledge on the testing part of SDLC process that must be possessed by every QA and Dev team for the delivery of a high-quality software product.

37. What is meant by software Testing?
    - ☐ Software testing is a matured process of verification or validation of software against the features, requirements or specifications, which are both functional as well as non-functional. It involves creating test plans, test specifications, test code development, execution of tests and checking the documentation. Also making sure that the product code changes doesn't cause the regressions, which means failure of earlier working features.

38. What is meant by software quality?
    - ☐ Software quality means the expected level of meeting the specifications or requirements, which are both functional as well as non-functional. The different levels of low, medium and high represent overall quality. In general, high-quality products will have higher customer satisfaction and recognition in the same line of low-level products. Software testing contributes to determining or assess the product quality.

39. What is a software bug or defect?
    - ☐ Bug is nothing but an unexpected or deviation from expected behavior in the product. It could be detected during either positive or negative testing. That means either no errors or exceptions or missing things in the positive cases or an expected errors during the negative cases where the user should receive it. Bugs are recorded with all the relevant information to re-produce the observation or test scenario in a

bug software like bugzilla tool.

40. Why do you need to Test the software? What happens if you don't test separately than the developer?
- ☐ In general, the product customer is important for any of the product producer. Higher quality of the customer satisfaction better to the company. It would be too expensive if customer experiences the bugs both in-terms of fixing those bugs and credibility. The quality assessment can be done through software testing. Thereby, every product has to be tested and assessed for quality before delivering to the customer. Typically, the developer testing is minimal and limits to the unit code. Also covered only few peripheral units but not at the customer focused functional, end to end integration at a system level. So, it has to be tested separately than the developers and typically done by software quality group.

41. How Quality Engineering different from Quality Assurance or simply execution?
- ☐ Quality Engineering is to apply engineering principles such as consistency and repeatability in the software development processes and whereas Quality Assurance is more of monitoring activity of processes. Many times, these are interchangeable, but the key is to apply consistency and repeatability in the testing than simply running a scenario once.

42. What is the need for having a separate Quality Engineering Team?
- ☐ Developing code and verifying by the same coder might make some of the bugs under cracks and need a team who would use the product as if like customers. That's why QE engineers are like first customers.

43. Can we eliminate all bugs in a given product through extensive testing? What should we do?

☐ Because of the complexity of software programming algorithms and code, it is impossible to eliminate all the bugs in
a given product. It would need unlimited resources, time and
even then no guarantee for zero bugs. Thereby, typically
quality is assessed as per planned criteria and customers can
view the quality at different levels such as low, medium and
high.

44. What are functional requirements and nonfunctional requirements?

☐ The functional requirements are the use cases relevant to the
end user visible features of the product. For example, bank
transactions in an online banking site.

☐ Nonfunctional requirements are the ones that needed to have
the system/software functioning correctly. The examples are
security, performance, reliability, availability, and scaling,
etc.

45. What are the different types of Testing? Can you list some?
Some of the testing types are as below:
  ☐ Unit testing
  ☐ Functional testing
  ☐ Integration/System testing
  ☐ Security testing
  ☐ Performance testing
  ☐ Stress and Longevity testing
  ☐ High Availability testing
  ☐ Exploratory testing
  ☐ Installer testing
  ☐ Regression testing

46. What is meant by white box testing? List down some testing
types for white box testing. Who does this type of testing?

☐ White box or unit testing is nothing but testing by looking at

the actual or product code and focus on the units of the code to verify for basic code health.
- ☐ It is also called Unit testing.
- ☐ Typically performed by product developers.
- ☐ Example test frameworks used are JUnit, TestNG for Java and nUnit family frameworks.

47. **What is meant by black box testing? List down some of the testing types for Black box testing. Who does this type of Testing?**
- ☐ Black box testing is nothing but testing of the product without looking at the developed code and focuses on the customer functional use cases or scenarios.
- ☐ It is also called functional testing.
- ☐ Typically performed by QA team
- ☐ Example test frameworks used are TestNG, Selenium, Load Runner, etc.

48. **Differentiate white box vs. black box testing.**
- ☐ See the above two answers.

49. **What is Unit Testing? What is its relation to whitebox and black box testing.**
- ☐ Unit testing is units of the code to verify the basic code functioning and done by developers while developing the product code. It is related to White box testing.

50. **What is Functional Testing? What is its relation to whitebox and black box testing? Who does this testing?**
- ☐ Functional testing is the testing with more focused on the functional specification or customer use cases and features testing without looking at the product code itself.
- ☐ It is related to black box testing because the test scenarios are viewed simply as whole without going through the code while testing.

☐ Typically, functional testing is performed by QA team.

51. **What is Security Testing? Is it functional or nonfunctional requirement testing?**
   ☐ Security testing is focusing on the security aspects of the product including security penetration testing.
   ☐ Security is a nonfunctional requirement of a product.

52. **What is Regression Testing? When and how often do you run these tests?**
   ☐ Regression testing is the execution of already created test suite or executing manual scenarios again. The goal is to make sure that already-existing features continuing to work while code changes are happening. Typically, these tests executed on hourly, daily, weekly or bi-weekly on different platforms and test matrix based on the product release cycles. Also performed regression testing at the time of build creation and developer check-ins.

53. **What is Performance Testing? Who does this testing - QA or separate team?**
   ☐ Performance testing is the measurement of speed (time per transaction or request process time) and throughput (number of users per second served) under adequate infrastructure that customers use.
   ☐ Also teams performance comparison analysis with competitive products.
   ☐ Typically, performed by a separate team (Performance team) than QA team in a larger organization.

54. **What is a Test Plan? Describe briefly the contents of a Test Plan. Have you ever written a Test plan?**
   ☐ The test plan is a testing artifact in the planning process to plan the testing with details like scoped, non-scoped requirements to test, test strategy, resources, matrix and schedule

(estimates) created by the QA team.

☐ At a high level, there are two types of plans based on the scope on the project/module level.

    ☐ Master test plan, which is for the entire product/project.

    ☐ Module test plan, which is for the individual modules.

☐ Master test plan is based on Market requirements document (MRD)/Business requirements document (BRD)/product requirements document (PRD)/Architecture & Design document.

☐ Module test plan is similar but focused on a module/component under test based on the Master test plan and component functional specification.

☐ A typical module test plan content is shown as below. You can take this as a template for the test plan even though some variations might exist in the organizations.

    ☐ Introduction or Overview

        • Add brief introduction on the component or module to be tested.

    ☐ Objectives

        • High level ideas on the component testing goals.

    ☐ Features Covered (in Scope)

        • High level list of feature names to be tested

        • Prioritized features

    ☐ Features NOT Covered (relevant but not in scope)

        • Certain nonfunctional features like any other team is going to cover such as performance; other testing can't be covered such as localization (l10n) or internationalization (i18n).

    ☐ Test Methodology

        • Framework selection

        • Tools to be used

        • Manual or Automation testing strategy

        • Regression testing strategy

        • Bugs - tools/infrastructure details

        • Security testing

        • Code coverage

    ☐ Entry Criteria

        • Add conditions that are needed to be met before testing can start.

- NOTE: Usually this will be covered in the Master test plan (MTP) and add the variations only here and refer others to MTP.
- ☐ Exit Criteria
  - Add conditions that need be fulfilled for signoff, like bugs (severity) to be deferred, %of pass tests,
  - Note: Usually this will be covered in the Master test plan.
- ☐ Test Certification Matrix
  - Note: Usually this will be covered in the Master test plan and add the variations only here and refer others to MTP.
  - Add Platforms/OS/JDK/Browser types and versions and any other software needed for the certification.
- ☐ Schedule, Responsibilities, Deliverables
  - Schedule
    - o Task|Owner|Duration|Start   Date|End Date|Comments
  - Responsibilities
    - o Team's individual owned areas
  - Deliverables
    - o TS/TDS (Test Spec/Test Design Spec)
    - o New Tests
    - o Automation scripts
    - o CI setup
    - o Results Analysis
- ☐ Risks and Mitigations
  - What are the possible risks - like delay in builds can cause testing delayed, features integration late can cause late test cycles etc.
  - Any assumptions should be added here.
- ☐ Reviewers and Approvals
  - Add Development counter-parts(corresponding dev engineers), Leads, Managers
- ☐ References
  - List of referenced docs - like PRD, Design doc, Functional specs, Master test plan doc etc.
- ☐ Revision History
  - Maintain the history of high-level changes on the test plan to track.

☐ Yes. In the past, created both master and module test plans.

55. **What is a Test design and specification? Describe briefly contents of Test Spec or Test Design spec. Have you ever written a Test Spec?**

☐ Test design process is more of thinking of the test scenarios and their priority. The Test Specification (TS or TDS) is documenting those scenarios as test cases before actually testing as either manually or automating the tests.

☐ A typical test specification content is as below and can be taken as a template to create the document.
  ☐ Introduction
  ☐ Prioritized list of Test Scenarios for each requirement in the functional spec to be covered pointing to the below details
  ☐ Details
    • Requirement
      o Add requirement id and summary of use case or user scenario
    • Test scenario
      o Add Test scenario id (to reference back in your test code and bug if needed).
      o Add description on test scenario, i.e., end-to-end flow for the above requirement including the pass/fail criteria.
        • Test steps
          o Add a list of exact steps to be followed in the testing of the use case.
          o Add expected result and pass/fail criteria.
        • Input
          o Data to be used for the above test scenario.
        • Expected Output
          o Expected output after completing the steps.
          o Add pass/fail criteria.
  ☐ Test Environment Setup
    • Configurations covered (add references from Master Test Plan if existed or else refer those here).
    • Specific setup and versions needed for different test scenarios.
  ☐ Reviewers and Approvals

- It is similar to Test plan approval.
☐ References
- Add links to test plan, functional specifications, etc.
☐ Revision History

56. What is meant by a Test scenario? Where do you put test scenarios?

☐ The Test scenario is nothing but a sequence of steps to be performed with a goal of verifying a user story or use case or requirement. These scenarios are going to become the test cases or tests and grouped as test suites.

☐ Test scenarios are going to be created during the test design process and will be documented in the test specification.

57. Can you describe the bug life cycle? What are different states of a bug?

☐ The bug life cycle is the process managing the events starting from creating a new bug until it is closed.

☐ Below are the typical bug lifecycle states but might have different named states based on the bug tool:

☐ New (state) → sets when filed a bug by QA or re-opened.

☐ Assign → sets when assigned to a developer by QA/QA manager/Dev Manager/Developer.

☐ Evaluate and in-progress → sets by the developer during evaluation.

☐ Fixed → sets by the developer when code change happened for bug fix.

☐ Duplicate bug → sets by the developer if already that bug exists.

☐ Not a bug → sets by the developer if it is not a bug.

☐ Not reproducible → sets by the developer if it is not reproduced.

☐ Verified → sets by QA after verified as OK.
- Re-open to New → sets by the developer
- Re-open to New → sets by clarifying how to reproduce again by QA

☐ Closed → by QA/Filer after verification.

58. What is meant by bug Priority? Who sets the priority of a bug? Can we change it after filed the bug?
- ☐ Bug priority is nothing but an indication of how important or urgent to get the bug fix.
- ☐ Typically divided into five levels: P1 (highest), P2, P3, P4, P5 (lowest).
  - ☐ P1: Need immediate fix (tests blocking) within 24hrs
  - ☐ P2: Need by next build (major functionality is not working)
  - ☐ P3: It is ok to wait but fix before release
  - ☐ P4/P5: It is not mandatory, it is ok to fix or not in the current release.
- ☐ The bug filer would determine the priority and set while filing the bug. The thumb rule is to set the same priority as severity while filing the bugs. Example: P1/S1, P2/S2, P3/S3, P4/S4, P5/S5.
- ☐ Yes. Anyone can change the bug priority and bug tools would allow that. Typically, changed after the conversations with stakeholders like release managers and product managers. Example: QA can file a bug, but Dev manager or product manager can change the priority.

59. What is meant by downgrading a bug and upgrading a bug?
- ☐ Downgrading the bug means lowering the priority of a bug. That is the change from higher to lower the priority of the bug (in bug tool).
  - ☐ Example: P1 → P2/P3/P4/P5, P1/P2 → P3/P4/P5, P3 → P4/P5
- ☐ Upgrading the bug means increasing the priority of a bug. That is the change from lower to higher the priority of the bug (in the bug tool).
  - ☐ Example: P2/P3/P4/P5 → P1, P3/P4/P5 → P2/P1, P4/P5 → P3/P2/P1

60. What is meant by bug Severity? Who sets the severity of a bug? Can we change it after filed the bug?
- ☐ Severity (S) is the indication of bug's effect and impact on the customers. For any new bug, this is the first thing to be

determined while filing the bug.
- ☐ Typically, severity is divided into five levels and are: S1 (Highest), S2, S3, S4, S5 (Lowest)
  - ☐ S1: means that the feature can't be tested or blocking further testing
  - ☐ S2: majority features are not working, and many tests are failing
  - ☐ S3: some cases are not working
  - ☐ S4, S5: very corner cases and not impacting the major functionality
- ☐ The bug filer would determine the severity and set while filing the bug.
- ☐ No. Typically, once set the severity in the bug, then no changes can be done. Typically, bug tools will not allow changing the severity.

61. How do you file a bug? What details would be added? Give an example.
- ☐ The bugs would be filed using the organization's bug tool and follow the bug guidelines. Adjust the above terms based on the tool being used.
- ☐ The below information is needed before filing any bug.
  - ☐ Which product id, component id/name
  - ☐ Which scenario or test
  - ☐ What is the result/output
  - ☐ What are its priority and severity
  - ☐ More details like console output or screenshot etc. to add in description
- ☐ Typically, bug tools are web tools and filling the forms and later editing as needed. Below is the example snapshot to create a new bug.

    Bug state: new/duplicate
    Product:___
    Product version:__
    Component/module:___
    Sub Component/sub module:___
    Priority:__
    Severity:__
    OS/HW/DB/JDK:___

    Subject: <u>Login failure - invalid password error even with</u>

<u>correct password</u>
Description: (text area with limited size, say 3000 chars)

It has been observed that there is a login failure on Today's latest build b20 dated 12/22 even when entered the right password. The following error noticed on the UI screen.

……..

Also, the below error message/stack trace/exception noticed in the server log file, server.log

……..

Steps to reproduce:
1. Go to URL: http://....
2. Click login button
3. Enter user name: user1
4. Enter password: password1
5. Click Go button

Now you can notice the error on the screen. Double checked the user name in the database, and it worked fine during user creation.

Also attached the screenshots. You can also find the entire log file at /home/jmunta/error_logs/bug12221_server.log

Attach: upload the UI screenshot.
upload the log file.

Click submit and see the successful message as below and get email notifications to the filer and default assignee. The bug number is used in the conversations with stakeholders.

Bug <number> created successfully.

62. What is Stress or load testing? What is longevity testing? How does stress and longevity testing are related? What kinds of bugs can be found? Who does this testing - QA or Dev or any other team?

☐ The stress or load is the number of concurrent or simultaneous users or requests (say 100 users/second) sending to the system under test. The stress or load testing is to find the limits of those concurrent users/requests without breaking the system or within the acceptable behavior under the load.

☐ The longevity is the period, and longevity testing is the where continuously running of the tests for 24x7 a week or 3 days or a day under the load to make sure system doesn't break when it is serving the requests for a long time.

☐ Typically, stress and longevity testing are done together. It means that load test (say 100 users/second sending to the system under test) is running continuously (no stoppage) for seven days to test the overall reliability of the system under test.

☐ The bugs in the stress/longevity testing are difficult to find and difficult to reproduce and fix. Below of few types of issues that can be seen.

   ☐ Resource leaks such as memory leaks and file leaks
   ☐ Deadlocks
   ☐ Process hangs

☐ Typically, tested by a separate Stress testing team under QA group or by a System Reliability team.

☐ In general, the tests are complex to reproduce and verify because of time and complexity.

63. What is System testing? Who does this testing? What are the key elements in system testing?

☐ The system testing is the end-to-end use cases testing with all the infrastructure and environment in place for the system under test to be tested.

☐ The system testing is initiated when most of the product under test is available, and it is also called integration testing where all the modules integrated into a product. In fact, system testing is a big umbrella covering many test areas.

☐ Most of the time, big test apps and the infrastructure related tests would be considered here. Sometimes the system testing might be covered only the Reliability testing (Longevity and Stress).

☐ Under the system testing, some of the major areas included are Security Testing, Performance Testing, Reliability Testing (Longevity and Stress or Load testing), Installer Testing, Interoperability Testing, Compatibility Testing, Upgrade Testing and User experience Testing.

64. What is a topology? How does it relate to testing?

☐ Topology is the reference architecture of the product deployment with reference to customer scenario. These topologies typically documented in the deployment user guide like enterprise deployment guide (EDG). Customers would use these topologies as a reference at their sites.

☐ The common topologies and reference configurations would be used in the system testing to mimic the customer use cases with big apps testing, stress/longevity testing, performance testing, etc.

65. What is High Availability(HA) testing? What are different types of failures? Who does this testing?

☐ High availability testing is where the product to be tested for the continuous availability based on the product defined technology such as clustering, load balancing and redundant components or systems, self-recovery, etc. It involves multiple instances of the same application on different machines so that a single failure (please note that multiple simultaneous failures use cases are typically expensive and hard to implement/support) of a software component or hardware component should not bring down the system.

☐ In this testing, different kinds of failures would be injected while testing of the regular use case is in progress. In fact, the test should work even when a failure occurs under HA requirement.

☐ One of the major activity in the HA testing is the injection of failures. Some of the failures include as below.
  ☐ Software/Process failure
    • Kill a process or stop gracefully
  ☐ Hardware or node failure
    • Proper shutdown or power off
  ☐ Network failure
    • Pull the ethernet cable or turn off the OS level eth

        interface
- ☐ Other subsystems of the SUT (System Under Test)
- ☐ Typically, tested by a separate HA testing team or System testing team under QA group.

66. **What is meant by code coverage? What is its main purpose? When does this activity happen during the product life cycle? Is it a testing activity? Who lead this? What kind of tests executed?**

- ☐ The code coverage is the measurement of how much the product code has been exercised with all unit/functional/system tests.
- ☐ A typical code coverage tool would produce metrics like how many or % of Java classes covered, methods covered, loops and instructions covered.
- ☐ The significance of code coverage is to help in identifying the gaps in testing and also to assess the test coverage. Also, 100% code coverage should not be viewed as a high quality of the product. Instead, the results can trigger some more testing or optimization of the code.
- ☐ Many times, code coverage is done after fully tested the product to see if any dead code or to find the missed testing coverage. Most of the times, the code coverage can be taken at the class level but at least method level is important. Usually, the QE team will report code coverage reports on regular basis.
- ☐ The QA engineer should co-ordinate with all relevant test teams in carrying out such effort. The major tasks include understanding of the tool and automation of the enabling the tool with the installed product, gathering the results, merging of results from different runs and publishing of the collective report. The report will be distributed to the stakeholders by a Java package name or by module. Each module-level QE engineer can see if the results are appropriately covered or not and add the tests if required to cover all the classes and methods in that module. The feedback should be taken into the developer team to add unit tests or remove the dead or unused code for the product. Usually above 40-50% code coverage is considered as high coverage.
- ☐ Why not 100% coverage target? It is all about human resources invested for testing of the product and thereby 100% means that enormous test engineering resources requirement

and practically is not feasible. Achieving higher code coverage can be aimed for any product as part of the quality testing of the product.

67. What are different code coverage tools for Java?
- Some of the free and open source code coverage tools are
  - JaCoCo (now a days more popular and originally developed from Emma)
  - JCov
  - Emma
  - Cobertura
  - Clover
  - PIT

68. How does the Quality is being tracked? What are different levels?
- The quality is being tracked on the convergence of meeting the release criteria such as a number of tests executed/passed/open P1/P2/P3 bugs, Stress/Longevity criteria, Performance targets, code coverage, etc.
- To track the quality, below are some of the measurements done on each build or sprint or weekly basis.
  - Test Execution metrics: track the dev code changes and testing progress since the last build or tracking period.
  - Bug Metrics/Defect Tracking: the number of open bugs and closed bugs since last build or tracking period.
  - Code Coverage: %class, %method, %line coverage since the last build or tracking period.
  - Performance Numbers: throughput numbers since the last build or tracking period.
- Bugs metrics containing incoming and fixing of bugs would be plotted as graphs and tracked on a weekly basis. A bell curve is what expected for the period of product testing cycle. That means initially, incoming or new bugs would be

low and later in high and then later goes down again as fixing bugs. If deviated from this bell curve, then there might be the possibility of low quality as bugs keep coming, and convergence of release is not meeting the criteria.

☐ The quality is assessed and projected at different levels than in absolute numbers. These are -
  ☐ High quality
  ☐ Medium quality
  ☐ Low quality

☐ The high-quality product should be the target of any good product and of course, it would cost more compared to a low-quality product.

69. **What is meant by testing artifact? What are different artifacts?**

☐ The testing artifact is anything that is produced as part of the testing process or methodology.

☐ Below are some of the typical testing artifacts:
  ☐ Test Plans (TP)
  ☐ Test Design Specifications (TDS) or Test Specifications (TS)
  ☐ Test Frameworks/Harnesses
  ☐ Test Scripts
  ☐ Test Cases
  ☐ Test Suites
  ☐ Test Results
  ☐ Test Reports
  ☐ Bugs

70. **What is the test development process? What are key steps?**

☐ The test development process is the part of SDLC with strategy, methodology, frameworks and tools, etc. to be applied in the product testing.

☐ The below are the key steps involved in the process.
  ☐ First is to understand the component/module or integration of the product functionality expected behavior.

It means that one should go through the use cases/user stories/features and discuss with developers for any clarifications. For this, use functional specification or JIRA tickets for user stories or tasks.

☐ Second is to think and brainstorm with the team about all test scenarios for a particular use case. That means to create the exact sequence of steps to be performed for each use case as if like testing manually. Put of those scenarios incrementally in the Test Spec (TS) based on agile process or waterfall SDLC process.

☐ Third is to execute the tests manually and file bugs if any deviation from the expected behavior. In summary, for all test scenarios (based on priority) from TS

- Run it manually if possible (example: going through web pages navigation/flow)
- Write the test code/test script
  - o Typically, it is done in the same language that code has been developed, like for java project is java based test code.

☐ Fourth is to create a Test Development Framework, which is a set of utilities/tools to help in the following tasks:

- Execution engine/driver to trigger test cases runtime/execution. Otherwise one has to run manually, say using simple java command line.
- Supply input data as properties or CSV or other data files. Otherwise, one has to run manual supplying of arguments.
- Generate Result/Report document (say HTML or XML). Otherwise, one has to look at the console for results.

☐ Fifth is to select or create a custom Test Tool/Driver

- Identify and select an open source/free/commercial right tool that helps in the testing or automation of tests. For example, Selenium for web site test automation or SoapUI tool for web services testing.

☐   Six is to design and implement a Reporting mecha-
    nism
    • Design the final reports like TestNG or any cus-
       tomer HTML reports with basic system under test
       details, number of tests executed, tests passed, tests
       failed, tests skipped, etc.
☐   Seventh is to setup SUT (System Under Test) envi-
    ronment.
☐   Eighth is to run test scenarios manually and file bugs
    if any.
☐   Ninth is to automate the tests for regression testing.
    • Create the test scripts/test code along with a base
       build framework (as dev used in their builds) like
       Ant or Maven or Gradle build tools.
    • Review the test code with team (peers/dev).
    • Check-in the scripts/code into SCM repository (say
       git and along with product code).
☐   Finally, perform regression testing
    • Execute the automated tests build by the build of
       the product.
    • Schedule automated execution jobs using tools
       such as Jenkins/Hudson CI.
    • Send the daily test result reports
    • Analyze the failures
    • File regression bugs
    • Verify and close bugs

71. What is the difference between manual testing and auto-
    mated testing?
    ☐ Both manual and automated testing would need in under-
       standing the use cases/user stories.
    ☐ Manual testing process
       ☐   It is a simple process of manually testing of scenarios
           by executing interactively (like performing clicks &
           form submissions) and making decisions for pass or
           fail.

☐ Required to understand the basic user interfaces and has less learning curve.

☐ It is the basis for initial testing of use cases and file bugs.

☐ A lot of time and human resources cost involved in performing each build regression testing by repeating the tests.

☐ Hard to execute and scale if many test scenarios existed

☐ Potential to have inconsistent results and human errors

☐ General test steps
  • Clicks on the browser
  • Look at the logs
  • Run commands
  • Look at the console output.

☐ Automated Testing process

☐ It is a process of testing the scenarios using automated code (using single command or scheduled process) with pass/fails reports generated.

☐ It is hard to create automated tests and requires high learning curve compared to manual testing.

☐ More skills and knowledge is required to automated tests. Sometimes hard to automate or complex to automate some cases.

☐ Easy to run and scale for large number of tests

☐ Less cost and effort in performing build to build regression testing.

☐ Less error prone once properly automated.

☐ Different test areas
  • GUI automation
    o Web, Java Swing
  • CLI automation
    o commands
  • Interactive tools automation
  • Debugging
  • Integration with continuous build systems (like Hudson/Jenkins)

72. What is the test execution process? What do you need to focus?

- ☐ The test execution is the process of executing the tests/test scenarios and file bugs or verifies the bugs on each product build. It is called "test cycle".
- ☐ First time, execute the test scenarios during test development process.
- ☐ Perform regression testing involves the below actions.
  - Execution of manual tests (if any) on each build (or weekly basis)
  - Execution of automated runs on daily/nightly builds.
  - Performing bugs verification
- ☐ Please note that avoid inconsistency in test results so that one can rely on the results. This can be achieved by repeating the tests many times with negative cases like software processes are down or network down or connection to the db/remote systems down etc. and fix the tests.
- ☐ Archive Results and Reports for audit purpose in future.
- ☐ A typical execution process flow is as below with multiple stages of testing:
  - ☐ Gate 1 - Dev Gate: Run sanity/quick tests locally when development code is ready for integration. If any code failures, then analyze and fix or else if any test failures, then fix the tests. In any case, until all tests passed, dev code should not be integrated into the repository. After quick tests passed then, development code integration can happen.
  - ☐ Gate 2 - Release Gate: Execute Smoke tests on the integrated build using CI and typically executed by RE (Release Engineer). If any failures in the smoke tests, then build should not be promoted for any further testing. Fix code or test failures and rebuild the integrated code and release the build.
  - ☐ Gate 3 - QA functional Gate: Execute all BAT (Basic

Acceptance Tests) to on core platforms. If BAT tests passed, then carry out the full test suite on all core platforms and BAT on other secondary platforms.

☐ Gate 4 - System Gate (Stress/Longevity/HA/Performance): Once the BAT tests passed and gave thumbs up by QA team, then System testing teams can pick the build to continue on their testing including Performance testing.

☐ There might be variations on the names of the tests categories like used in the above such as Quick or Sanity, Smoke Tests or BAT tests, SRG (Short Run Group), LRG (Large Run Group), Large suite, Short suite, etc.

☐ For each build cycle, the above gates would be opened in the build testing process.

73. **What is smoke testing? When do you run? Who run these tests?**

☐ The smoke tests are of a short number of P1 use cases to check the basic functionality of the integrated product is ok or not. The purpose is to have this gate in promoting the good builds to avoid the waste of time by other teams when basic functionality is not working.

☐ Typically, these tests executed when a build is being created (integrating of code) and also dev check-ins can use smoke as gate keeping on the regressions from the code changes.

☐ These tests are created by QA team by adding selected tests from each module or core integrated test scenarios.

74. **What is Basic Acceptance Testing (BAT)? Who and when do you execute BAT tests?**

☐ BAT tests are the functional test scenarios covering the customer acceptable use cases. These are used to verify the code before executing Full test suites and System/Integration testing.

☐ BAT tests also executed as per test execution matrix (smart test matrix) to cover some of the secondary platforms to save the execution time with appropriate test coverage.

☐ These tests also used by lower stack components as a basic check to make sure no regressions introduced for the upper stack components. For example, App Server BAT tests given to JDK QA for validating different JDK version changes.

☐ BAT tests are developed by the QA team and are a subset of the whole functional test suite.

75. How do you sign-off from QA? What do you do?

☐ The below simple checklist can be done followed to signoff from QA on the testing before releasing the product.

☐ QA should make sure all the committed/planned tasks as in the Test Plans of all modules have been completed. The checklist should include all bugs verification, no P1/P2/P3 open bugs, 100% tests execution and expected pass rate, code coverage measurement with targeted % of numbers etc.

☐ The test engineers should send the email to Dev/QA lead and Dev/QA manager with signoff message or update the dashboards/wiki on the release status update.

☐ Finally, QA representative - lead/manager should send or update the signoff status from QA to Release Manager and all project stakeholders.

← End: Skill#2. Software Quality Concepts ←

Good!
Keep going and never give up!!
Please re-read again for more clarity and feel free to contact for help!!!

→ Start: Skill#3. Object Oriented Programming & System (OOPS) →

Skill#3. Object Oriented Programming & System (OOPS)

The majority of the software products development has been done with Object-oriented languages such as Java, C++, and other OO high-level languages. OOP concept is very much essential for any Java/C++ programmer to maintain or develop new software in Java.

76. What are OOP and OOPS?
- [ ] OOP is short form for Object Oriented Programming;
- [ ] OOPS is a short form for Object-Oriented Programming and System.
- [ ] It is a programming paradigm with core concept of programming completely on the objects, which are analogous to real world objects. It means everything (thinking and programming) is around objects.

77. What are fundamental principles or characteristics or properties of OOP?
- [ ] Abstraction
- [ ] Encapsulation
- [ ] Inheritance
- [ ] Polymorphism

78. What are the benefits or advantages of using OOP?
- [ ] Modularity
- [ ] Reusability
- [ ] Pluggability

79. What is an Object? What it contains?
- [ ] It is analogous to real world object where it contains State

(or attributes or properties or data) and Behavior (or actions or services) together. The object's state is controlled by its behavior and NOT by other external objects directly.

80. **What is a Class? Why do we need?**
   - ☐ The Class is a blueprint or prototype or type or categorization for objects. The common state and behavior are put-together as Class.
   - ☐ It is the basis for creation or instantiation of new objects of that class type.

81. **What is an instance?**
   - ☐ It is merely an object that has been created from a class (a thing created at some point in time or at that instant).

82. **What is a method?**
   - ☐ It is the behavior/logic encapsulated in the object (as a block of statements), which can do the actions on behalf of the objects. It acts on the data that the object contained.
   - ☐ Objects communicate via methods.
   - ☐ It is similar to a function in procedural programming.

83. **What is meant by object state?**
   - ☐ It is the data of the object. The attributes or data of the object will be added as variables to store the data. The data type or type of the data it contains depends on the class or data types. The methods act on this state or data. For best practice, protection (who can access) of the state is important and should only manipulate by the methods in its object.

84. **What is Interface? Why do we need?**
   - ☐ An interface is a external view or contractual agreement between class and external world without exposing the internal

state & internal behavior. When a class is going to implement the interface, then external objects would rely on the interface for bindings of that class. Without interfaces, managing the external dependencies (making sure bindings are ok) would be hard and more work.

85. What is Abstraction? Generalization? Concreteness?

☐ Abstraction is nothing but the hiding of the details, which helps in reduction of the complexity. It is like analogous to an abstract (summary) of a project report. The abstract classes will be having none or partial implementation. Interfaces can be realized as pure abstract classes.

☐ Generalization is looking at higher levels and very common characteristics among the objects. It is opposite to the specialization. It is like till 10th grade everyone reads similar courses but after that goes into specialization (into doctor, engineer etc.). Generalization gives the advantage of loosely coupling system and replaceable.

☐ Concreteness is specialization and has all the implementation details. It is a complete class to create objects.

86. What is Encapsulation? How can be achieved?

☐ Encapsulation is nothing but data hiding or sealing of the object's internal state. It is achieved by making the fields as private and provide appropriate methods for any access or modifications to the external objects.

87. What is Polymorphism? How can be achieved?

☐ Poly means many and morphisms means forms or shapes. It is nothing but invoking same behavior/method name but acts differently based on the different types of input parameters or overriding of behavior in a subclass or during the inheritance.

☐ Polymorphism is achieved through overloading, overriding or inheritance.

88. **How do you differentiate Object Oriented Programming with Procedural Programming?**

    ☐ See the differences between procedural and object-oriented programming.

Procedural Programming	Object-Oriented Programming
The Procedural programming is a programming paradigm that divides the problem into logical modules that are procedures/functions, which are a sequence of steps.	The Object-oriented programming is a programming paradigm that focuses on the abstraction and real world objects.
In this, procedure /functions and data are separated.	In OOP, the data and the methods are bound together as classes/objects.
In this, some level of re-usability and modularity can be achieved.	OO programming follows certain principles: Abstraction, Encapsulation, Inheritance, Polymorphism and benefits more re-usability, modularity and pluggability.
In procedural, it might raise more runtime errors and difficult to maintain the large code.	The OOP is in general to address the issues with procedural programming, also have less runtime errors and easy to maintain the large code.
Example languages: BASIC, C, Pascal etc.	Example languages: Java, C++ etc.

89. **What are the differences between Object-Oriented vs. Object-based programming**

    ☐ OOP paradigm has the core principles such as abstraction, encapsulation, inheritance, polymorphism defined to call object-oriented whereas Object-based programming para-

digm doesn't have all principles such as inheritance, encapsulation, polymorphism but merely working with objects (instances, constructors, methods, properties).
☐ OOP have inbuilt real world objects constructed from classes/blueprints. Object based uses prototyping concepts and adding members to the objects.
☐ OOP example: Java, C++ languages
☐ Object-based example: JavaScript language

90. What is Abstract Class?
☐ Any class with partial implementation, in which some of the methods are abstract (i.e., with only declaration but no implementation) and some of the methods could have implementation is called Abstract class.
☐ Please note that real objects can't be created directly from Abstract classes and can be only be done after creating the concrete class by extending the Abstract class with remaining abstract methods implementation.

91. What is Inheritance? What are the benefits? What are different types of Inheritance? Describe them.
☐ The inheritance is one of the core OOP principles where a class inherits from the parent or multiple parent classes to leverage the behavior/methods and data/properties.
☐ It could be a single inheritance (inherit from single class) or multiple inheritance (inherit from multiple classes) type.
   ☐ Example: Java supports only single inheritance for classes and supports multiple inheritance for interfaces. C++ supports multiple inheritance for classes.
☐ The current class is called Subclass and the parent call is called Superclass. In the inheritance tree, a child is called as a subclass and parent is called as a superclass.
☐ The process of inheritance can be viewed as making a generalization/generic object and to bring specialization/specific object.
☐ The analogy is like going from abstraction to concreteness.

☐ The inheritance helps in reusing of the existing code.

92. What is the difference between Abstract class and an Interface?

☐ The below are the differences at a high level.

Interfaces	Abstract classes
Interfaces form a contract to the external world/client.	Abstract classes provide the abstraction/generalization and thereby form the class/object relationships.
An interface is a complete or full abstraction without any implementation.	Abstract classes provide a partial implementation (at least one method is not implemented).
Interfaces must be implemented by Concrete or Abstract classes.	Abstract classes must be extended by other classes to provide concrete/full implementation. Otherwise (if few more methods implementation left), still it has to be an abstract class.
Interfaces goal is to impose the required behavior by saying what all the objects can do instead of how the object is doing.	Abstract classes goal is to provide common behavior at super/parent classes so that sub/child classes can inherit.
Can't instantiate objects	Can't instantiate objects
Java supports multiple inheritance for interfaces.	Java supports only single inheritance for abstract classes.

93. How do you create Objects?

□ Objects can only be created from concrete class constructors.

□ Create the objects using "new" keyword in the Java.

□ General syntax:

   □ <ObjectType> object = new <Constructor>

□ Examples:

   □ HelloWorld w = new HelloWorld("JD");

   □ Car c = new Car("Toyota", "Sienna", 2006);

94. What is a constructor? What is a destructor?

□ The constructor in OOP is a special method in class, which is invoked automatically during the construction of objects from the class.

□ Java class constructors can be declared similar to methods but as a special type of method with name same as the class name and no return type.

□ The destructor in OOP, again it is a special type of method/function and used when objects are no longer needed, those objects would be deleted. In Java, there is no destructor to be written, and instead, unreferenced objects would be collected automatically by the garbage collector.

95. What is default constructor? What is parametric constructor?

□ The default constructor is a no-argument constructor in the class.

□ The parametric constructor is an argument constructor in the class.

□ In Java, if none of the constructors defined in class, then there will a default constructor provided automatically (from the top level parent class, Object class). If any constructors (default or parametric constructor) defined, then Java doesn't provide any other default constructor.

96. What is overloading? What are different types?

☐ The concept of having the same name but does different actions (or different behavior) is called "Overloading".

☐ Using below two types or ways, one can achieve the overloading.

  ☐ Method overloading

   • Write the same method names but with different parameters in a class.

   • Example: In the below class, "sum" methods are overloaded.

   ```
   public class Calculator {
           public int sum(int x, int y) { }
           public int sum(int x, int y, int z) { }
           public int add(int x) { }
   }
   ```

  ☐ Operator overloading

   • Use the same operator but with different operands.

   • Examples:

     o a+b = int value when a and b are ints.

     o a+b= string concatenation if a or b is a String object.

97. What is overriding? How to do?

☐ The concept of having the same method signature (method name and parameters) with different implementations during the inheritance of classes is called Overriding.

☐ The overriding is achieved through inheritance in the derived or child or subclass.

☐ In this, superclass's method would be overridden in the subclass with a different implementation (note that it can't be done within the same class).

☐ Use optional @Override annotation in the subclass's method while overriding the method so that compiler check can happen and can throw an error if Override rule (same method signature) is not happening.

98. What is data hiding? Why do you need it?
- ☐ Data hiding is the general concept in computer science to hide the data or implementation from the external world.
- ☐ The goal is not to leak the implementation details to the user.
- ☐ Data hiding is to prevent the unexpected changes and also make changes in future if required.
- ☐ Use the data access modifiers to achieve this.
- ☐ Data hiding in the OOP is accomplished through Encapsulation.

99. What is "this" and "super" keywords w.r.t objects?
- ☐ The keyword "this" refers to the current object reference and "super" reference to the super class's object reference.

100. What is meant by method signature? Does it include return type?
- ☐ The method signature is the method name, parameters of a method.
- ☐ It doesn't include the method return type.
- ☐ Example:
  - ☐ In the below method, "main(String [] args)" is called the method signature.
  - ☐ public void main(String [] args) { ..}

101. Can an abstract method be private? Why or why not?
- ☐ No. The abstract method can't be private as the abstract class has to implement this method by extending the super abstract class.

102. What are the class relationships?
- ☐ The class relationships are the weak (other object can exist without current object), strong (other object can't exist without the current object), shared and non-shared types.
- ☐ The following are some of the major relationships among the classes.

☐ Association
- Is 'a' relation between 2 objects.
- One object instance causes another object to perform an action on its behalf.
- This is simply a form of relationship either weak or strong with 1-1, 1-many or many-1 relationships.

☐ Aggregation
- Is 'the' relation between 2 classes.
- It is a special type of association. This forms a shared relationship among the objects.
- One object 'has' another object (containment/has-a relationship).
- Example: A Car object has Wheel object, which can exist without than Car as Wheel can be created ahead of time and can be shared with other objects.

☐ Composition
- Mutually dependent relationship.
- It is a special form of aggregation and has the strong association where one object can't exist without the other object.
- Define one class inside another class.
- Inner class and outer class relationship.
- Example: A Car object can have Engine object, which can't exist without Car.

103. What is UML and why do you need?
☐ UML stands for Unified Modeling Language.
☐ It is for documenting the architecture or design of the programs with classes, interfaces, relationships, etc.

104. What is UML notation for relationships?
☐ The below are the simple notation to understand the relations.

3. Object Oriented Programming & System(OOPS)

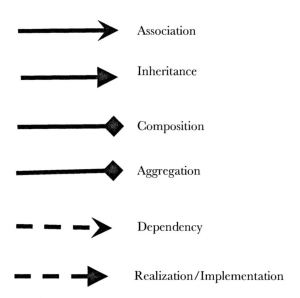

← End: Skill#3. Object Oriented Programming & System (OOPS) ←

Good!
Keep going and never give up!!
Please re-read again for more clarity and feel free to contact for help!!!

→ Start: Skill#4. XML →

Skill#4. XML

Most of the existing dynamic content, e-commerce sites and many software configurations have been done using XML file format. It is essential to understand this universal XML file format to survive in the Software dev and QA profession.

105. What is XML? Is it a standard?
- ☐ XML stands for eXtensible Markup Language. It is derived from SGML family, originally used to do electronic publishing.
- ☐ It is a W3C standard.
- ☐ XML is a flexible human readable text file to have the data exchange format that is independent of platform, protocol and language.
- ☐ Example:
  ```
  <?xml version="1.0" encoding="UTF-8" ?>
  <software>
      <titles>
          <title id="12345" vendor="abc">ABC1</title>
      </titles>
  </software>
  ```

106. What are the main objectives of XML?
- ☐ The following are some of key objectives of XML:
  - ☐ It should be flexible and simple text-based human-readable data exchange format.
  - ☐ It should support structured data.
  - ☐ It should be an extensible and self-describing document.
  - ☐ It should be independent of operating platforms or protocols or computer languages.

107. **What is the structure of XML?**
- ☐ XML structure is more of a tree structure with parent/child/siblings relations.
- ☐ XML starts with a root tag and contains elements with open tags and corresponding closing tags.
- ☐ XML files are used in creating portable documents to transfer among different systems, system/software configuration files, and software builds creation, etc.

108. **How do you define the structure of XML? How do you write XML?**
- ☐ The XML structure is based on the DTD (Document Type Definition) or XSD (XML Schema Definition).
- ☐ Based on the DTD/XSD, XML is going to be created by following the doctype, elements, and the order of those elements in the document.

109. **What are the differences between XML and HTML?**
- ☐ XML is mainly for data exchange whereas HTML is mainly for data viewing or display.
- ☐ XML has no built in tags whereas HTML have built-in tags (such as html,header,body,h1,div,center etc.) with specific purpose/meaning.
- ☐ XML should have closed empty tag whereas HTML can skip.
- ☐ XML is processed by backend code whereas HTML is processed by front-end tools like browser and javascript.

110. **What is meant by well-formed XML?**
- ☐ Well-formed XML is an XML, which meets the following conditions for correct syntax.
  - ☐ Having only one root tag.
  - ☐ All open tags must have to be closed.

111. What is meant by validation of XML?

- ☐ XML validation is a check for the following and is valid XML if and only if (iff).
  - ☐ Well-formedness of XML
  - ☐ Semantics matching against corresponding the DTD or XSD.

112. What is DTD? What is XML Schema or XSD? What are the differences?

- ☐ DTD stands for Document Type Definition.
- ☐ XSD stands for XML Schema Definition.
- ☐ Both DTD and XSD are for defining the structure definition to write or process the XML files. These metadata definition files define the list of allowed elements & structure in the XML document.
- ☐ DTD or XSD is required only if the entities need to agree for communication otherwise simple XML is ok without DTD/XSD (like for testing or experimenting).
- ☐ XSD is newer than DTD for defining the structure definition for actual XML file to follow with much more powerful than DTD.

113. What are some of the popular techniques to parse XML files?

- ☐ There are three well-known parsing techniques.
  - i) DOM parser
    - ☐ Entire XMl doc is being loaded into memory.
    - ☐ Traverse the Nodes and NodeList.
  - ii) SAX parser
    - ☐ It is different than DOM parser and is based on events.
    - ☐ Not all the XML document is loaded into the memory but instead read line by line based on events triggered like open tag, closed tag, characters, comments, etc.
  - iii) StAX parser

☐ StAX stands for Streaming API for XML.

☐ SAX parser pushes the data based on events whereas StAX parser pulls the data by maintaining a cursor position instead of events generation.

114. What are XML declaration and processing instruction in XML?

☐ The XML declaration is as below with first line having version and other details between <?xml and ?> tags. Note that this is not a processing instruction and instead to indicate as XML.

    `<?xml version="1.0" encoding="UTF-8" ?>`

☐ The processing instruction is enclosed between <? and ?> and optional target like guide the instructions for application.

☐ The PI can be anywhere in the document.

☐ General processing instructions

    `<?PITarget PIContent?>`

☐ See more details on processing instructions at

    http://www.xmlplease.com/xml/xmlname/pi#s6

115. What is namespace in XML?

☐ XML namespace (NS) is mainly to avoid the conflicts on the names/tags in the XML documents.

☐ It is to have the same names from different URLs but different definitions without collision among those names.

☐ This can be achieved by prefixing the namespace to the name. You can see with xmlns:<prefix>="URL" in the root element attribute.

☐ Default namespace will not have the prefix.

☐ Example:

    `<root xmlns:m="URL1" xmlns:n="URL2">`

        `<m:tag1></m:tag1>`

        `<n:tag1></n:tag1>`

    `</root>`

116. **What are real applications of XML?**

☐ XML is being widely used since the evolution of the internet. Some of the applications include -

☐ XML files as portable documents

☐ XML configuration or metadata for tools/servers

☐ XML files as exchange of data/catalog in the automated processing

☐ XML also the basis for Universal Business Language (UBL) and electronic publishing.

☐ ANT, Maven build files are XML files.

☐ XML files can be used places where custom structured data needs to be defined.

← End: Skill#4. XML ←

Good!
Keep going and never give up!!
Please re-read again for more clarity and feel free to contact for help!!!

→ Start: Skill#5. XPath →

Skill#5. XPath

As long XML is there, the XPath also plays a key role in performing the navigation, extraction of XML, and transformation of the content to various other forms (HTML/text). So better to acquire this skill by developers and QA professionals.

117. **What is XPath? Why does it matter?**
   - ☐ XPath is an expression language for addressing/defining/extracting parts of the XML document.
   - ☐ XPath is used to identify or select and extract the parts.
   - ☐ XPath uses path expressions/predicates to navigate in XML and contain libraries for standard functions.
       - ☐ There are more than 100 built-in functions to handle strings/numeric values, date and time comparison, node manipulation, boolean values, etc.
   - ☐ XPath is mainly designed to be used by XSLT and XPointer. It is based on the tree representation of XML. It helps in transforming or extracting the data from XML/HTML.
   - ☐ There are many XPath implementations in Java, C#, Python, JavaScript, etc.

118. **Is it a standard specification? Who defined?**
   - ☐ XPath is defined and recommended by W3C.

119. **How do you represent XML for navigation?**
   - ☐ XML navigation is represented and viewed as a tree of nodes.

120. **What are different node types in XPath?**
   - ☐ The following are the different types of nodes:
       - ☐ Element
       - ☐ Text

☐   Attribute
☐   Namespace
☐   Preprocessing-instruction
☐   Comment
☐   Document

121. **What are different node relations?**
☐ Below are different node relations:
     ☐   Root
     ☐   Parent
     ☐   Children
     ☐   Siblings
     ☐   Ancestors
     ☐   Descendants

122. **What is meant by atomic node value or value?**
☐ Atomic node is a node that has no parent or children.

123. **What is the XPath expression for selecting an element from root node?**
☐ To select the node from the root node, use / and then add nodes path to reach the desired node in the tree.
☐ Example: /parent/nodename

124. **What is the XPath for selecting any node under the tree?**
☐ To select a node anywhere in the tree, use prefix //.
☐ Example: //nodename

125. **What is the XPath for selecting a node with an attribute?**
☐ To select node elements with attribute name use the below expression - //nodename[@attributename]

126. **What is a predicate? What is its purpose?**
☐ The predicate is a condition, and its purpose is to filter

nodes from the list of nodes.
☐ Predicate is embedded in the brackets [].

127. **What is the XPath for selecting the first node? And also last but one node? Or at a particular position?**
 ☐ The below are the XPath expressions with different inbuilt functions.
  ☐ //nodename[1] : selects first nodename of nodenames
  ☐ //nodename[last()] : selects last nodename
  ☐ //nodename[last()-1] : selects last but one nodename
  ☐ //nodename[position()<3] : selects first 2 nodenames

128. **What is the XPath for selecting nodes with expected attribute value?**
 ☐ To select matching nodename elements with attributename's value, use the following expression.
 ☐ //nodename[@attributename=value]

129. **What is the xPath wild characters to match any node and nodes with any attribute?**
 ☐ Use "*" wild character for matching any node(s).
 ☐ Example://book[@*] : all elements that have any attribute
 ☐ //*[@attributename=value] : to select all elements to match attributename matching value.

130. **How to select several XPaths in a single selection/expression?**
 ☐ Use "|" operator to combine several XPath expressions.
 ☐ Example: To select all title and author nodes, use //title | //author

131. **What is axis? Why do you need? Please provide few expressions with axes.**
 ☐ Axis is the name that defines a node-set relative to current

node using relationships. It is useful to reference nodes without going through root node and instead with a relative in reference to the current node.

☐ General syntax is Axis::nodename[predicate]
☐ Different Axes:

  ☐ ancestor : selects all ancestors in the node hierarchy of the tree.
  ☐ ancestor-or-self : selects ancestors and the current node itself
  ☐ attribute : selects all attributes of the current node
  ☐ child : select all children of the current node
  ☐ descendant : selects all descendants of the current node
  ☐ descendant-or-self : selects all descendants of the current node and current node itself
  ☐ following: selects everything after the current node
  ☐ following-sibling : selects all siblings after the current node
  ☐ namespace : selects all namespace nodes of the current node
  ☐ parent : selects the parent of the current node
  ☐ preceding : selects all nodes the current node
  ☐ preceding-sibling : selects all siblings before the current node
  ☐ self : selects current node
  ☐ Examples:
  ☐ child::store → selects all store nodes that are children of the current node
  ☐ attribute::value → selects value attribute of the current node
  ☐ child::text() → selects text node children of current node
  ☐ child::node() → selects children nodes of current node
            ☐ Examples:
      ☐ child::store → selects all store nodes that are children of current node
      ☐ attribute::value → selects value attribute of current node

☐ child::text() → selects text node children of current node

☐ child::node() → selects children nodes of current node

132. What are different XPath operators?

☐ Below are the operators. These are semantically similar to other programming operators.

    ☐ Arithmetic operators: +, -, div, *, mod

    ☐ Conditional operators: =, !=, <, >, >=,<=

    ☐ Logical operators: or, and

133. What are some of the inbuilt/standard functions in XPath?

☐ Below are the some of the functions available in XPath expressions.

    ☐ contains(mainstring,substring) : returns true/false based on substring existence in the mainstring.

    ☐ count(nodeset) : returns total number of nodes.

    ☐ last() : returns the last node index.

    ☐ position() : returns the contextual position index from current.

    ☐ substring(string, start, end) : returns a part of a given string starting from start index to end.

☐ More functions and details can be found at https://developer.mozilla.org/en-US/docs/Web/XPath/Functions

134. What are different XPath evaluators?

☐ Some of the XPath evaluators are

    ☐ Browsers - Mozilla, Chrome, IE

    ☐ XSLT (eXtensible Stylesheet Language Transformation) processors.

135. Where do you use XPath in real applications?

☐ The major application is of the XPath is to convert XML

to another XML/HTML/Text format. That is Conversion of XML → XSLT (XPath expressions) → XML/HTML/Text

☐ Browser HTML DOM element references with XPath in selenium automation.

← End: Skill#5. XPath ←

Good!
Keep going and never give up!!
Please re-read again for more clarity and feel free to contact for help!!!

→ Start: Skill#6. JSON →

Skill#6. JSON

The JSON file format is a newly evolving and modern universal file format. JSON format is being used widely in REST WS, Internet/Web applications, Social sites, etc. Having hands-on with JSON files is crucial for all developers and QA automation professionals.

136. **What is JSON? How does JSON format look like (snippet)?**
- ☐ JSON stands for Java Script Object Notation.
- ☐ JSON is a lightweight data-interchange text format.
- ☐ JSON is a subset of JavaScript (JS) programming language.
- ☐ It is language independent, and many high-level languages have libraries to create and parse the format.
- ☐ The JSON format is human readable, faster and easier than XML.
- ☐ There are no reserved words/keywords and support structure/hierarchical (values within values).
- ☐ The JSON file is a collection of JSON objects and the object contains name/value pairs. The typical extension is ".json".
- ☐ The JSON object is {"name":"value",..} and ordered list of values arrays like [value,..]. See more at json.org. See more details at json.org.
- ☐ A JSON file format example is as below.
```
{ "employees": [
    { "firstName":"Michael" , "lastName":"J" , "address":""},
    { "firstName":"Jagadesh" , "lastName":"Munta",
"address":"Fremont, CA" }
]
}
```

137. Is JSON a programming language? Or a protocol? Or a message format? Is it language dependent?

☐ No. JSON itself is not a programming language nor a protocol. It is simply a data or message format.

☐ The JSON files are independent of the high-level programming languages. These JSON files can be generated and parsed by many programming languages.

138. What are the key advantages with JSON over XML format?

☐ The JSON format is human readable, compact, lighter, faster and easier than XML.

☐ There are no reserved words/keywords and supports structured/hierarchical (values within values) data, and thereby the same data size is going to be less.

☐ The processing of the JSON is much simple compared to XML.

☐ Also, the implicit (no additional libraries) data parsing can be done using JavaScript and thereby it is easy to present on UI.

139. Where do you use JSON?

o JSON format can be used in any application where data serialization and deserialization along with some structure is required.

o JSON is extensively used in RESTful Web Services/REST APIs for the data embedding in requests and responses.

140. What is the HTTP header used for passing the JSON data?

o In the HTTP, below header and value is used to indicate that JSON content is available in requests or responses. Set this header while sending the HTTP request or response.

Content-Type: application/json

141. How do you process (parse, transform, generate, query) the JSON text?

- o The parsing of the JSON text can be done using APIs provided by different languages.
- o In JavaScript itself, JSON.parse(text) can be used to get the JS object and then simply reference the names with dotted notation and arrays.
- o In Java, there are many APIs available. Some of the free and popular APIs and references in use are as below.
  - JSON-P (Java API for JSON Processing) - https://json-processing-spec.java.net/
  - Jackson Library - https://github.com/FasterXML/jackson-databind/
  - GSON (Google's) library - https://github.com/google/gson
- o Overall, the Jackson library is very simple and highly performed APIs to use for JSON processing.

142. How do you query the data from JSON file from shell command or in a simple script?

- o In many occasions, it is required to parse the JSON file quickly and also to use in a shell script to cover the primary use cases. For this, there is a tool called "jq" and it is a handy utility just like sed on Unix/Linux.
- o The jq tool can be downloaded from https://stedolan.github.io/jq/.
- o Example:
  - Below is to just get all JSON data in a nice formatted way, use as '.' As filter.

  jq '.' filename.json

← End: Skill#6. JSON ←

Good!
Keep going and never give up!!
Please re-read again for more clarity and feel free to contact for help!!!

→ Start: Skill#7. Source Coe Control System (SCCS)/SCM -
SVN&GIT →

Skill#7. Source Code Control System (SCCS)/ SCM - SVN & GIT

The source code is one of the major intellectual property of any software organization. It is essential to collaborate with the developing teams using a source code control system such as SVN or GIT. It is important to understand the SCM concepts and working knowledge on SVN and recently popular GIT software for both developers and QA automation engineers.

143. What is source code control system (SCCS) and SCM? Why do you need?
   □ The SCCS stands for Source Code Control Software and SCM stands for Source Code Management. In a practical sense, both are referring the same and SCM is more widely used.
   □ The main purpose of SCM is to have the source code versioning, collaboration, and sharing with others local or geographically dispersed teams or open source.

144. Describe the key elements in SCM such as repository, workspace, versioning?
   □ Repository is the storage that is being used to store the project source files/code. Also termed as source code repository. The repository (repo) is typically referred to URL using HTTP or client specific protocol.
   □ Workspace is the tree structure of the project source files organized to work with various build systems like ANT/Maven.
   □ Versioning is the change management to keep track of all prior changes.

7. Source Code Control System(SCCS)/SCM - SVN & GIT

145. What do you store in the repository?

☐ The project source files will be saved in the SCM repository and typically the text files like .java, .html, .properties, .xml, etc. files and NOT any binaries or generated code or other generated artifacts. This way the versioned sources can be downloaded quickly and also saves the space. Besides, losing binaries is not a big deal as such, unless only third party binaries are only available and can be stored.

146. What is source code? Why is it important? What happens if you keep the code at individual machines?

☐ The source code is the set of program files and related files developed by the developers or QA teams to program for the desired requirements. These are the text files and typically read and modified by more than one engineer as a team.

☐ The source code is important to preserve because it is the actual IP (Intellectual Property) of any software project.

147. What are the primary functions of SCCS software?

☐ The standard functions of SCCS software include the following.
  ☐ Atomic operations like commits to be consistent state
  ☐ Concurrent access and file locking
  ☐ Versioning and merging
  ☐ Branching, labeling, tagging, and the snapshot of the source trees.

148. What are different popular SCCS software available?

☐ Below are some of the popular free/open source software:
  ☐ CVS - Concurrent Versioning System (oldest)
  ☐ SVN - Subversion
  ☐ Mercurial
  ☐ Git (Latest and distributed architecture)
☐ Below are some of the popular commercial software:

☐   Visual SourceSafe(Microsoft)
☐   ClearCase (IBM)
☐   Perforce
See more at https://en.wikipedia.org/wiki/List_of_ver-
sion_control_software

149. **What is meant by the checkout, check-in or commit, merge, delete, log, status?**
☐ Checkout is the operation to retrieve (or) pull sources from the repository to the local directory, called work-space (or working copy).
☐ Check-in is the operation to store or commit the sources or changes from local working workspace to the files in the repository.
☐ Merge is the operation to apply two sets of changes on a single file or multiple files.
☐ Delete is the operation to remove the sources from repos-itory.
☐ Log is the operation to show the history of changes on a single file or multiple files.
☐ Status is the operation to determine commit status of the local working copy of files w.r.t the files in the repository.

150. **What is meant by the trunk or mainline? Branching? And tagging?**
☐ The trunk or mainline is the main trunk of code tree path in the repository that is not a separate branch. It is also called master or tip. From this trunk or master, the branches can be built so that parallel code paths can exist.
☐ Branch is a forked tree path that is to build a different code path. This way, it is easy to develop and release the prod-uct independent of other branches including mainline or master in parallel with the same set of files.
☐ Typically, before stabilizing of a product release, new branches would be created and allowed only changes re-quired for that release. In Git, the common practice is to

create branches for their module code and later merge to
the master or other top level branches.
☐ Tagging is labeling of master or a branch at that time to
retrieve the versioned files at that point. It is like taking a
snapshot.
☐ Please note that one can only check-in the files in a branch
or mainline but not in a tagged label itself.

151. **What is meant by merging conflicts? What happens if you
don't resolve the conflicts? How do you resolve the conflicts?**
☐ Merging conflict is a checkin error raised when the local
workspace is not in sync with remote repo before applying
the changes and the same lines of the files got changed in
the remote repo. In this state, the tool can't reconcile the
changes.
☐ If conflicts can't be resolved, then one can't commit the
changes directly. The client will not allow the files check-
in to the remote repository.
☐ In such cases, before check-in, one has to resolve by selecting in-favor-of one change (either local or remote)
than the other change. Otherwise, manually merge each
change in those files to get the unified changes and then
override in the repo.
☐ Merge conflicting resolution: there are 3 options
    ☐ manual resolution
    ☐ first changes replace the second changes
    ☐ second changes replace with first changes

152. **Can you describe SVN? What are the supported protocols?**
☐ SVN stands for Subversion. It is one of the free/open
source SCM used by enterprises. It is kind of older but
still being used in bigger companies.
☐ SVN supported protocols are svn:// and http:// or https://.

153. What kind of architecture/design used in SVN? Any other architectures?

☐ SVN is based on client/server technology with centralized server architecture.

☐ The other alternative is distributed protocol with a decentralized architecture where developers have their own development or work repositories and only shared when published. Example: Git.

154. What do you need for interacting with SVN server?

☐ One should have repository URL with svn or http/https protocol and svn client or browser.

155. What is the svn command for checkout workspace?

☐ To checkout the existing source code from SVN repository, use svn client software (to be installed before using on your laptop/desktop) and then project URL.

☐ The general svn command line syntax is below.

svn <cmd> <repourl>

☐ Use the below command style where host and port refer to the SVN hostname/IP and port number; <repo> is the repository name; trunk or branch name;<projectdir> refers to project directory.

svn co http://host:port/<repo>/<trunk-or-branch>/<projectdir>

156. What are the svn commands to do a fresh checkout, check-in or commit all files in the current directory?

☐ To do fresh checkout the workspace, use similar to the following command.

svn co http://host:port/<repo>/<trunk or branch>/<projectdir>

☐ To add the files or directory:

svn add <file/dir>

☐ To commit the files/directories:

svn commit <files/dir>

Example: *svn commit* . (this will commit all the files in the current dir)

157. **What is the command to see the list of files modified locally?**
    □ Use the below to check the status:
    svn status <file/dir>

158. **What is the svn command to see the history of changes done on a particular file?**
    □ *svn log <file/dir>*

159. **What is the svn command to see the differences between the locally changed file vs. file in the repository?**
    □ The command to see the differences to the remote revision is as below.
    svn diff –r <revision> <file>
    □ For more help on commands, reference the free online book at http://svnbook.red-bean.com/en/1.7/svn-book.pdf

160. **Which svn plugin used in Eclipse?**
    □ Subclipse plugin in Eclipse IDE - http://subclipse.tigris.org/

161. **Can multiple users checkout and check-in in parallel? Is there any lock?**
    □ Yes. Multiple users can do the checkout and check-in without any issue in parallel, but if there is a change on the same file at the same time, internally SCM software maintain the locking mechanism.

162. What are the key features that you need for any version control systems like Git?

☐ A typical sequence of operations with any SCM is as follows.

   i) Checkout a project from repository

   ii) Create new files or subdirectories or edit files

   iii) Update from repository

   iv) Check-in or commit

   v) Go to or repeat from above step 2

   vi) Check status

   vii) Push to master in case of Git or distributed SCMs.

163. What are the typical steps to work with Git?

☐ To create a new git project or start a new repository for an existing project, use below 3 steps

   git init --> which creates .git folder

   git add .

   git commit .

☐ First time to get the code from remote repository/git server

   1. *git clone https://github.com/jagadeshmunta/myproject1.git*

☐ Add files to the workspace

   2. *git add .* ---> adds all files and directories in the current directory

☐ Check status w.r.t remote repository

   3. *git status* →

                  (shows untracked/to be committed files)

☐ Update the workspace from a remote repository

   4. *git pull*

☐ Commit (to the local workspace)

   5. *git commit -m " message" <files/dir>*

☐ Send the files to remote repository.

   6. *git push origin master (or) git push origin*

       branchname

☐ Repeat #2 to #5 for further modifications.

☐ Operate with branches with below commands.

- ☐ git branch --> lists the branch names and * for the current branch
- ☐ git branch <branchname> --> if no branch exists, it will create a new branch
- ☐ git checkout <branchname> --> switch the branch to given branchname

☐ Use below commands to do modifications in the workspace:

☐ --Checkin--
  - ☐ git add .
  - ☐ git commit -m "message" <files/dir>
  - ☐ git push origin <branchname>

☐ Merging to master
  - ☐ git checkout master
  - ☐ git pull
  - ☐ git merge <branchname> (NOTE: if conflicts occur, then resolve manually and do the commit - git commit -m "")
  - ☐ git push origin master --> push the changes to the remote master

← End: Skill#7. Source Code Control System(SCCS)/SCM - SVN &
Git ←

Good!
Keep going and never give up!!
Please re-read again for more clarity and feel free to contact for help!!!

→ Start: Skill#8. Unix/Linux OS →

Skill#8. Unix/Linux OS

In Today's World, most of the enterprise software, website hosting, and any Internet-hosted software or applications are on the Linux/Unix platform. Having hands-on experience with this platform is fundamental for everyone.

164. **What is an Operating System (OS)? Brief on its typical functions.**
   □ The Operating system is the software that manages or controls the underlying hardware or machine and other software resources. Most of the computing devices are programmable with the help of OS.
   □ Typical functions of OS are:
      □ Process Management
      □ Memory management
      □ I/O management
      □ File Management
      □ Network management
      □ Applications Management
      □ User management

165. **What are the different OS architecture types?**
   □ OS architecture is of broadly 2 types.
      □ Monolithic OS and is a single bundle that does all the management.
         • Example: Windows (a single application crash the entire OS, like bluescreen)
      □ Kernel/Micro OS is the layered operating system (like onion) with a small footprint of centered nucleus or kernel that does some core OS to machine interaction functions. In this, the kernel is going to separate the other top level activities and user applications. Because of this kernel style, the program

that effects can only cause that process go down/hang and can not impact/crash entire OS.

- Example OS: Unix or Linux OS.

166. What is meant by a Platform?

☐ Platform means Hardware + Operating System and sometimes referred with OS only or HW only.

☐ Examples: Intel x86 Platform, Apple Mac Platform, Windows platform, Linux platform, Solaris Sparc platform, IBM mainframe, HP Hardware etc.

167. What is Unix/Linux and how is it different from Windows?

☐ The Unix and Linux are the multi-user, multi-task, kernel based operating systems (OS) widely used on server side hosting of enterprise applications and websites. Typically, users would do remote login to these systems. These OSes support command line terminal mode and GUI also.

☐ Unix OSes are mostly commercial. Some of the examples are Sun Solaris, HP-UX, IBM AIX, Mac OS, etc. that are tied to hardware platforms.

☐ Linux OSes are typically free and open source. Some flavors of Linux OSes are commercial for support and having more security. Example Linux OS are CentOS, Ubuntu, RedHat Enterprise Linux (RHEL), Oracle Linux, SuSE Linux, etc.

☐ The Windows operating system is a single user desktop-based operating system where the user is going to interact with machine physically. Windows is widely used and easy to use GUI OS, which is commercial from Microsoft.

☐ Windows platforms are typically used for client-side computing whereas Linux used for server side computing. Some of the latest Windows versions are Windows 7, Windows 8 and Windows 10.

168. How do you see Linux and windows differences at usage level?

☐ Windows --> It is case insensitive (lower/upper case treated as same)
   ☐ Path separator is ; (semi-colon)
   ☐ File separator is \ (back slash)
   ☐ Prompt : >
   ☐ super user: Administrator account
☐ Linux --> It is case sensitive (lower and upper cases are different)
   ☐ Path separator is : (colon)
   ☐ File separator is / (forward slash)
   ☐ Prompt: $
   ☐ Super user: root (#)
   ☐ Everything is a file

169. What are different parts of linux OS?

☐ Linux kernel + Utilities and libraries + Shell
☐ Shell is the user interaction program in the unix/linux OS. Below are the popular shell programs:
   ☐ sh (Bourne Shell)
   ☐ bash (Bourne Again Shell)
   ☐ csh (C Shell)
   ☐ ksh (Korn Shell)
   ☐ tcsh (Turbo C Shell)
☐ Selecting a particular shell is more of preference with regular usage. Recently bash is popular.
☐ Comparison of various shell programs can be found at https://en.wikipedia.org/wiki/Comparison_of_command_shells

170. How do you connect to a remote unix/linux machine?

☐ To log in to a remote host, one can use the below protocols or client/server programs:
   ☐ ssh (secured shell) is to make a secured connection to the server using ssh protocol and is widely used

   & recommended.

   ☐ telnet and rlogin are less secured. These are not being used lately because of security concerns.

   ☐ VNC (Virtual Network Connection) software is to
connect to a remote server GUI.

  ☐ On linux, use the ssh program.

   ☐ It uses ssh protocol

   ☐ Credentials as one or the other as below:

    • username & password.

    • public/private key certificates

   ☐ VNC for GUI connection to the remote server

  ☐ On windows, use the SSH client such as putty.exe and can
be download from http://www.putty.org/. Also, VNC can
be used for GUI access on remote linux/unix server.

  ☐ From mac or another linux, use the following way and enter the username and password at the prompt.

   ☐ Usage: ssh <hostname or IP address>

   ☐ VNC can be used to connect to the remote server
VNC for GUI access.

171. How do you search given string or word in a file?

  ☐ Use grep or egrep command.

   ☐ Case sensitive

    • grep <word> <filename/filenames>

    • Example: grep import "*.java" (NOTE: this
prints all import found files.)

   ☐ Case in-sensitive (use -i option)

    • *grep -i <word> <file/filenames>*

   ☐ Enclose the word in quotes "" or ' ' if spaces are
there.

**172. How do you run a command or process in the back-
ground? How do you bring it to the foreground?**

  ☐ To start a command in the background, enter that command and then append with an ampersand (&).

  ☐ Type "bg" command in the same terminal to send it back

to the background.

☐ Type "fg" command in the same terminal to bring it to the foreground.

☐ Example:

☐ *cp -r dir1 /home/jmunta &*

☐ *fg*

☐ *bg*

173. **What is the command to find running processes and process ids (PID)?**

☐ Use "ps" command.

☐ Example: *ps -ef* (NOTE: prints all running processes including command file name)

174. **What is the command to kill a particular process id?**

☐ Use "kill" command to shutdown/stop a running process. Also, apply -9 option if process does not respond (to normal kill command) and to do forcefully.

☐ Example: *kill -9 <pid>* (replace <pid> with actual pid shown in the ps command)

175. **What is the command to list the hidden files?**

☐ Use "ls" command with -a option to get all the files including hidden ones.

☐ Example: *ls -a*

176. **What is meant by file permissions? How to set the permissions? What is meant by 644?**

☐ File permissions are the attributes for files to authorize read, write, execute by different users, groups or all public. Also note that in Linux/Unix, everything is based on files.

First, have an understanding of the binary numbers, conversion to and from decimal to binary. Binary means 2 and actual values are either 0 or 1 only.

Example: decimal 5 as binary and 8 as binary.
5 --> 0101 (binary form)
5/2 -- 1 (remainder)
2/2 -- 0
1   -- 1

5--> 101

8 --> 8/2 --> 0
   4/2 --> 0
   2/2 --> 0
   1/2 --> 1
1000 (binary form)

When you do long listing of the files (ls -l command), then
you would see the permissions in the first column.
The symbols rwx stands for read write execute permission. 1 means permission is there (represented as 1) and -
means not there (0).
   1 1 1
- : 0

The permissions for a file is represented as 3 octal fields
as below.
(owner) (group) (others/world)
 rwx   rwx   rwx

111 : is 7 (as decimal)

rw- : 110 --> 6
   $1x2^2 + 1x2^1 + 0x2^0$ --> 4+2+0 = 6

rwx------
111 000 000
7 0 0

700 --> permission

currently 775 (111 111 101)

b) To change the permissions, use chmod command.
Example: chmod 700 <file/dirname> (or) chmod a+x
<file/dirname>
Examples to see the final octal value for the permission
to use in the chmod.
111 001 001 : 711
100 000 000 : 400
110 000 000 : 600

c) 6 4 4 : permission means that owner can read and write,
group and world can only read. 110 100 100

177. **Why do you get the error 'command not found' while executing a command/file (with right directory path)? How to make it work?**
   □ When the command program file is not in the PATH environment variable or if the command file doesn't have the executable permissions for the current logged in user (or group it belongs to), then 'command not found' error would be thrown by the shell.
   □ To fix the above problem, make sure it is set in the PATH or enter full path or make sure executable permissions given to the users/groups/owners.
   □ Example:
      chmod a+x <command/filepath>
      export PATH=${PATH}:<command/filepath> where
      <command/filepath> is the actual path of the program.

178. **What is the command to see the contents of a file? How to pause after each page filled?**
   □ Use "cat file" command to display all contents of the file.
   □ Use "more file" command to view the file page by page

and click enter button to display next line or click space-bar button to display next page.

179. **What is the command to get first 10 lines of a file? And getting first 5 lines?**
    ☐ Use "head file" command to show first 10 (default case) lines from the file.
    ☐ Use "head -5 file" command to show first 5 lines from the file.

180. **What is the command to get last 10 lines of a file? And getting last 5 lines?**
    ☐ Use "tail file" command to get last 10 (default case) lines of file.
    ☐ Use "tail -5 file" command to get the last 5 lines of file.

181. **What is the command to monitor a running log file (such as a tomcat server.log or other file where content is getting modified all the time)?**
    ☐ Use "tail -f file" command to monitor (display contents as it gets updated) a running/continuously updated file.
    ☐ Example: tail -f server.log

182. **What permission to be set to a directory so that 'cd dir' command would work?**
    ☐ Set executable permission to the directory along with other permission or as below to give executable permission to everyone.
        chmod a+x dir

183. **What is meant by pipeline (|)? Where do you use?**
    ☐ The pipe or pipeline is to pass the output of a command to the next command as input.
    ☐ It is used to get the chained actions together in a single

command.

☐ Example: to get the count of the java files in the current directory.

ls *.java |wc -l

184. What is meant by symbolic link and the command to create a symbolic link to a file or directory?

☐ The symbolic link means creating a new file name referencing to another file or inode (i.e., underlying structure pointer of a file) of a file. If the link file pointed to a filename, then it is called soft link else if it is pointed to the inode, then it is called hard link. The hard link will follow the name (even if it is moved to a different file) whereas soft link will not move if the original file moved to a different file.

☐ Use "*ln -s frompath topath*" to create a soft link as topath for frompath file. That means topath is simply a reference to the frompath and both refer to the same content.

☐ Use "ln frompath topath" to create the hard link as topath for frompath file.

185. How do you find given file and directory sizes?

☐ Use "du" command to find the size. The below will give the size in MB/GB.

du -sh fileordir

186. How do you find a file in a given directory?

☐ Use "find" command to find the file in a directory.

☐ The below command is used to find all java files under the dirpath.

☐ *find   dirpath   -name "*.java"*

187. What is 'vi' editor? Describe on how to edit files (insert mode, save, copy lines, paste lines, delete lines, etc.)?

☐ The vi is default editor on unix/linux and stands for "visual instrument".

☐ Type vi at the shell prompt and follow below shortcut keys to edit the files.

Press Esc key to enter into escape mode to activate the shortcut keys.

press i --> for insert (before inserting any characters)

press o --> Inserts a new line below your current line

press O --> Inserts a new line above your current line

press : --> enter into command

    w --> save and be there in the editor

    q --> quit

    wq --> save and exit

    x --> save and exit

press <n>yy --> Yanking of n lines (copy of n lines into buffer)

    p --> print below the cursor line

    <n>p --> prints n lines below cursor line

    u --> undo

    dd --> delete current line

    <n>dd --> delete n number of lines (it is a like cut operation and you can paste like above p command)

    A --> insert at the end of line

    I --> insert at beginning of line

    x --> delete a single character at cursor position

    <n>x -> delete n number of characters from your cursor position

    w --> word by word move the cursor

    dw -> delete a word at cursor position

    <n>dw --> delete n words starting at cursor position

    /<word> --> search for word

    n --> next in the search

    N --> reverse in search

    :set number --> display line numbers

    ctrl + g --> display the current position

:$ -> go to bottom line

:1 -> go to first line

:<n> --> go to nth line

:1,$:s/Hello/Hi/g : replace Hello with Hi entirely in the file

r : mark for replace and press whatever letter you want

188. **What is an alias? How do you set an alias and how to remove alias?**
   □ The alias is setting a name for a command. The main purpose is to have a short name for a long command or with different options command.
   □ To set alias, use "alias <aliasname> <command>" command.
   □ To unset an existing alias, use "unalias <aliasname>"
   □ Examples:
   □ alias l "ls -lrt" → after this command execution, running just l as the command would give the long list with reverse in timestamp.
   □ unalias l → after this command execution, l command would not found.

189. **How do you count lines, words, and bytes in a file?**
   □ Use "wc" command would give the number of lines, words, and bytes.
   □ Usage: wc filename
   □ Example:
   $ wc test2.txt
         34   240   1429 test2.txt
   (#lines #words #bytes)

190. **What is the command to check which user being used in the prompt?**
   □ Use "id" command. Run "id" to check the username.

191. What is a 'touch' command do? Where do you use?
- ☐ Usage "touch file" command is to update the timestamp of an existing file to current time or to create a new file if the file doesn't exist.
- ☐ It is useful for creating an empty markup file for some events to track.

192. What is the file separator character and path separator character in unix/linux?
- ☐ In Unix/Linux,
  - ☐ path separator is : (colon)
  - ☐ file separator is / (forward slash)

193. What is the kernel? What is the command to see the kernel version?
- ☐ Kernel is the nucleus of the unix/linux, which is set of core programs that interact with the hardware and other software resources.
- ☐ The "uname -a" command would give the kernel version along with other details.
- ☐ Example:
  $ *uname -a*
  Linux jdcloudapps 3.2.0-24-virtual #37-Ubuntu SMP Wed Apr 25 12:51:49 UTC 2012 i686 i686 i386 GNU/Linux

194. What is the command to see the machine name or hostname?
- ☐ Use "*hostname*" command to find the hostname of the machine.

195. How to find the OS release version?
- ☐ One way is to check the OS version using the files /etc/*release*. See below.
  $ *cat /etc/*release**

```
DISTRIB_ID=Ubuntu
DISTRIB_RELEASE=12.04
DISTRIB_CODENAME=precise
DISTRIB_DESCRIPTION="Ubuntu 12.04.3 LTS"
NAME="Ubuntu"
VERSION="12.04.3 LTS, Precise Pangolin"
ID=ubuntu
ID_LIKE=debian
PRETTY_NAME="Ubuntu precise (12.04.3 LTS)"
VERSION_ID="12.04"
```

196. How do you see the system details like total memory(RAM), processors and monitor the processes?
   □ Use "*cat /proc/meminfo*" command to get the memory information.
   □ Use "*cat /proc/cpuinfo*" command to get the cpu/processors information.
   □ Use "top" command to monitor/refresh the memory, running processes, cpu utilization, etc. on the console until ctrl+c pressed.

197. How do you redirect the output of a command to a file (such as log file)?
   □ To redirect output to a file.
      □ Use "*tee*" command to write output to a file while displaying on the console.
         • Usage: command | tee filename
      □ Use "> filename" to write to a file (if file exists, then its contents would be overwritten).
         • Usage: command > filename
         • Example: ls -l > file.txt

198. How do you append text to a file without overwriting the existing content?
   □ Use ">> filename" to append output to an existing file.

    ☐ Usage: command >> filename

    ☐ Example: ls -l >> files.txt

199. **What is the command to pause the screen scrolling temporarily and resume again?**

  ☐ Process ctrl+s to pause scrolling on the shell console screen.

  ☐ Process ctrl+q to resume scrolling on the shell console screen.

200. **How do you suspend a running process? And then send to the background or bring to the foreground?**

  ☐ First, process ctrl+z to suspend a running process on the shell console.

  ☐ Then type "bg" command to send the suspended process back to the background.

  ☐ Later type "fg" to bring back the background process to the foreground.

201. **What is a 'tar' command? How to use it and how to untar a file?**

  ☐ The "tar" stands for "Tape Archive" and is used to package a set of files as a single file with .tar extension.

  ☐ The below tar command with option "-c" is to create a new tar with all files in dir. NOTE: If the extraction should not have the dir name, then go to that directory and do the tar on the current directory.

    tar -cvf filename.tar dir/

  ☐ The below tar command is to peek through for list of files/dir in that tar file.

    tar -tvf filename.tar

  ☐ The below tar command is to extract/untar the files/dir from tar file.

    tar -xvf filename.tar

202. Write a single command to count all java files in a given directory and have a word 'test'.
   - ☐ The below is the required command with subcommand and pipe.

   grep test `find dirpath -name "*.java"`|wc -l

203. Write a command to get the 3rd word (separated by comma) of a string in a variable.
   - ☐ Use "cut" command. Below is the syntax:

   cut –f<wordnumber> -d'<separator>'
   - ☐ To get the 3rd word with comma separation, use the below example (mainly cut –f3 –d','). See the 3rd word "result" in the output.

   $ export VALUES=val1,val2,result,comments
   $ echo $VALUES|cut -f3 -d','
   result
   $

204. What is a sudo command? Why do you need?
   - o The sudo command is used to run a command with another user than the currently logged-in user.
   - o Typically, sudo is used to run commands that need more privileges (root privileges) than the current user (say jmunta). From the security point of view, this is the best practice. For example, run a command such as packages installation without login as root user or without getting to root user with su command. Depending on the configuration, the root privileges will be used for administrative commands/files with sudo access.
   - o Typically, current user's password should be entered during the sudo command run. Without sudo command, one has to login with root or su (super user), which might be a bad practice due to potential security hacks.
   - o Examples:
       ssh jmunta@host

> $ sudo vi /etc/hosts → to edit the root only accessible file with current user.
> $ sudo rpm –iv xxx.rpm → to install rpm packages with current user.
> $ sudo -u jagadeshbmunta ls ~jagadeshbmunta → to list the files of a different user than current user.
> $ sudo su → to enter into root.
> #

205. **What is a ping command and how it helps in checking the host reachability?**
   o The ping command is a basic utility to check if a network interface works locally or a connection works between the current machine to another machine. It is used to check if a machine is reachable and alive over the network.
   o The ping command is to send packets to and receive from another machine over ICMP protocol and also determines how much time it takes. If the machine is not reachable, then ping will time out or else give the time taken to receive back the response. Note that if ICMP is blocked, then ping doesn't work.
   o General syntax and examples are as below:
   ping <ip or hostname> → press ctrl+c after few responses because it is continuous check and provide statistics after ctrl+c.

   ping <ip or hostname> -c 1 → for 1 time check and provide statistics at the end.

   ~jagadeshmunta$ ping localhost
   PING localhost (127.0.0.1): 56 data bytes
   64 bytes from 127.0.0.1: icmp_seq=0 ttl=64 time=0.042 ms
   64 bytes from 127.0.0.1: icmp_seq=1 ttl=64 time=0.063 ms
   ...
   64 bytes from 127.0.0.1: icmp_seq=9 ttl=64 time=0.073 ms
   ^C

--- localhost ping statistics ---
10 packets transmitted, 10 packets received, 0.0% packet
loss
round-trip min/avg/max/stddev =
0.042/0.056/0.073/0.010 ms
~ jagadeshmunta$ ping localhost -c 1
PING localhost (127.0.0.1): 56 data bytes
64 bytes from 127.0.0.1: icmp_seq=0 ttl=64 time=0.061
ms

--- localhost ping statistics ---
1 packets transmitted, 1 packets received, 0.0% packet
loss
▪ *round-trip min/avg/max/stddev =*
0.061/0.061/0.061/0.000 ms
~ jagadeshmunta$ ping facebook.com
PING facebook.com (31.13.77.36): 56 data bytes
64 bytes from 31.13.77.36: icmp_seq=0 ttl=85
time=24.945 ms

...
^C
--- facebook.com ping statistics ---
3 packets transmitted, 3 packets received, 0.0% packet
loss
o *round-trip min/avg/max/stddev =*
24.945/25.396/26.098/0.503 ms

206. **What is curl command and why do you need?**
   o The curl is a simple command line utility to retrieve the contents of a given URL. There is no need for browser to get the Web content because the browser requires graphical terminal whereas curl can work on non-graphical terminal or at command prompt.
   o The curl can be used to quickly check URL responses, download files, and also automating them through shell scripts. Recently, the curl is being used heavily to test the REST APIs/endpoints in a quick way.
   o The curl supports different protocols such as http/https/ftp/ftps, etc. and have lot of options. Run "*man curl*" command to see more details.

○ The below are some of the frequently used options, especially while working with HTTP/REST endpoints.

- -o *filename* → Use this option to store the response or output in this given filename.

- -X *requestmethod* → Use this option to specify the HTTP URL request method such as GET/POST/PUT/DELETE etc., otherwise it will be GET by default.

- -H *"headername: value"* (or) --header → Use this option to specify the required HTTP headers in the request. Supply multiple –H options to send multiple headers.

- -u *"username:password"* → Use this option to supply the authentication credentials such as username and password in the URL request.

- -d *@filename (or) --data @filename* (or) –d *name@filename* → Use this option to send the data in the file (after URL encoding) to the HTTP POST request. Also, multiple –d options can be specified. This causes the header to include as *application/x-www-form-urlencoded.*

- -F *"fieldname=value"* (or) --form *"fieldname=value;content-type"* (or) –F *"name=@file"* → Use this option to supply the HTTP form data POST to the URL. Multiple field name/values can be specified by multiple –F options.

- -k or --insecure → Use this option to ignore the certificate check and do non-secure https request.

○ Some of the examples to understand the usage:

- curl http://www.mycompanyinc.com/files/file1.zip

- curl –o file.zip http://www.mycompanyinc.com/files/file1.zip

- curl –X GET –u "username:password" –o file2.zip http://www.mycompanyinc.com/securefiles/file2.zip

- curl –X POST –u "username:password" -H "Content-Type: application/json" –d @prod.json http://www.mycompanyinc.com/api/v1/products

- curl –X POST –u "username:password" -H "Content-Type: application/json" –H "prodchannel=social" –F "prodtitle=Prod1" –F "file=@prod.json;filename=listfile" http://www.mycompanyinc.com/api/v1/products
- curl –k –u "username:password" –o file3.zip https://www.mycompanyinc.com/secure-files/file2.zip

207. How do you write associative arrays in bash?

☐ Use the below statements in the bash shell script to use associative arrays (to reference with a name instead of index numbers).

  ☐ declare -A myarray
  ☐ myarray[${VARNAME}]=${VAL}
  ☐ Referencing the value as ${myarray[${VARNAME}]}

208. How do you run a command on the terminal without terminating when the shell closed or terminal closed?

☐ Use "nohup" also called "no hangup" command. Usually used along with & to start background.

☐ Example: The below command starts the Jenkins process and stays without hanging-up even after the terminal closed.

nohup java -jar jenkins.war &

209. How to see the help for commands in unix/linux?

☐ Use "man" command.

☐ Typical usage is "man commandname".

210. What is a shell script? Write a script to do 1) Given Java code compilation and execution of class 2) Print hostname and how many java files are there in a given directory.

☐ The shell script is an executable text file with inbuilt shell statements, and other executable commands put together to perform desired logic. It is usually having .sh or .csh extension and should have the executable permission.

☐ The shell provides the most of the programming constructs like if, while, for etc. to do branching of code or conditions or loops etc. and can be used in the shell script.

☐ The first line of the script indicates which interpreter or shell to use, and it starts with #!.

    ☐ Example: #!/bin/bash or #!/bin/sh

☐ The input arguments to the script can be read using below variable references ($0 gives the filename itself)

    ☐ $1 - first argument value

    ☐ $2 - second argument value

    ☐ ..

    ☐ $9 - ninth argument value

    ☐ ${10} - 10th argument value (note the curly braces and is to avoid the conflict with $1).

☐ Program#1: compileandrun.sh

```
#!/bin/sh
####################
# Description: Compilation and run
####################
        FILE_NAME=$1
javac -d . $FILE_NAME
# HelloWorld.java --> HelloWorld
CLASS_NAME="`echo $FILE_NAME | cut -f1 -d'.'`"
java $CLASS_NAME
```

☐ Program#2: countjavafiles.sh

```
#!/bin/sh
##############################################
##
# Description: A simple program for printing hostname
##############################################
##
echo "*** Hostname is `hostname` ***"
DIR=$1
NUM_FILES=`find $DIR -name "*.java" | wc -l`
echo $NUM_FILES java files found in $DIR
```

← End: Skill#8. Unix/Linux OS ←

Good!
Keep going and never give up!!
Please re-read again for more clarity and feel free to contact for help!!!

→ Start: Skill#9. Java →

Skill#9. Java

Most of the existing or new, whether small or larger software projects are still written in Java language. The Java should be at the heart of every software professional and thereby essential to have this language to survive in the software development and QA automation profession.

211. **What is Java? What are benefits of Java language?**
   □ Java is a high-level, general-purpose and robust object-oriented programming language that is widely used programming language in this internet era. The first Java release happened in May 1995 by Sun Microsystems Inc., and James Gosling is known as the father of Java.
   □ Java language is platform independent with one of the core principles of WORA (Write Once Run Anywhere), which means the same compiled code can be executed on many operating systems (like Linux, Windows, Mac, etc.) without any source code changes.
   □ Java supports many commonly needed programming features such as inbuilt automated garbage collection, security, networking and multi-threading features, etc.

212. **What is Java Platform? Why it is called a platform?**
   □ The Java itself is referred to as a platform because of its virtual machine (JVM), where the compiled code is executed. The JVM creates an environment in similar to the operating system for the programs to execute.
   □ The JVM (Java Virtual Machine) is a specification (JSR336 for Java7) and can be implemented by anyone. The Sun's/Oracle's JDK (Java Development Kit) is the Reference Implementation for a given JVM specification. The specification and reference implementation are governed through JCP (Java Community Process). Please

note that any new specification related to Java should go through Java Specification Request (JSR) and there should be Reference Implementation (RI) to show as working specification.

☐ Java has 3 types of platforms.

　☐ Java SE or J2SE (Standard Edition)

- Java SE is the bundle that contains the core language support, Swing UI library classes, AWT libraries, JDBC library classes, JAX- WS web services library classes and other related basic classes.

- The end users using the JavaSE can develop or run the Standalone desktop applications/games or to create the servers or remote programs.

- The latest version is Java SE8.

　☐ Java EE/J2EE (Enterprise Edition) Standards/Specification

- This is at enterprise level feature specification such as Web (JSP, Servlets), EJB (Enterprise Java Beans), JMS(Java Messaging Service), JSF (JAva Server Faces) etc.

- The Java EE implementation can be realized through Java EE Application Servers or Web Containers software.

- The end users can develop the Java EE applications (bundled as .ear, .war, .jar files) and then deploy on to these JavaEE supported web containers or Application Servers.

- The web applications (bundled as .war file) with JSP and Servlets can be deployed on Web Containers (WC) Server such as Tomcat web container or any Java EE compliant Application Servers like WebLogic, GlassFish, WebSphere, etc.

- The enterprise applications (.ear, .jar) can be deployed on to any Java EE compliant Application Servers such as (JavaEE RI SDK) GlassFish AS

(v3 for JavaEE6, v4 for JavaEE7), WebLogic Application Server, WebSphere Application Server, JBoss Application Server, etc.
- The latest version is Java EE 7.
☐ Java ME (Micro Edition) → Mobile and devices
- The Java ME is meant for mobile devices. It is a stripped version that is aligned with devices compared to the Java SE.
- It is used to create mobile applications such as games, utilities, etc. on devices like Symbian OS, BlackBerry OS, etc.
- The latest version is Java ME 8.
☐ Get more details from Oracle's Java technology site - http://www.oracle.com/technetwork/java/index.html

213. **What are key features of Java?**
☐ Here is the summary of key features list.
- ☐ Java is a simple, high-level and general purpose object-oriented programming language
- ☐ Java itself is a platform and technology.
- ☐ Java is cross-platform with WORA (Write Once and Run Anywhere) support.
- ☐ It is secured and distributed language.
- ☐ Java is a network-centric language used for Internet applications.
- ☐ It supports multi-threaded coding to achieve high performance.
- ☐ Java is a highly robust & reliable platform with automated garbage collection and fewer runtime errors without memory pointers like in C++.
- ☐ Java is a static type checking language.
- ☐ Java is extensible technology with lot of additional packages available.
- ☐ It supports internationalization (i18n).

214. **Is Java language cross-platform?**
- ☐ Yes. One of the key features of Java is this cross platform support. That means once the Java bytecode is generated from the source code on one platform, then it can be executed on other platforms without porting/changing the code.

215. **What is JVM? Describe more on this.**
- ☐ JVM stands for Java Virtual Machine.
- ☐ The JVM can be expressed as a collection of the specification, implementation, and runtime instance. The specification is about the bytecode specification, and the implementation is the JRE, and the runtime is the instance of VM whenever Java code is executed.
- ☐ There are multiple implementations from different vendors.
  - ☐ HotSpot VM from Oracle(acquired Sun Microsystems, Inc.)
  - ☐ JRockit VM from Oracle(acquired BEA)
  - ☐ IBM's J9 VM
  - ☐ Other VMs
- ☐ JVM mainly does the following operations.
  - ☐ Loads the bytecode using the bootstrap classloader and then apps classloader
  - ☐ Verifies the bytecode
  - ☐ Executes the bytecode
  - ☐ Provides the runtime environment.
- ☐ The Java HotSpot JVM is the latest and has the below features.
  - ☐ Adaptive compiler, which loads and analyzes the code for performance bottlenecks (hotspots) and takes the appropriate action to boost the performance.
  - ☐ Rapid memory allocation and garbage collection with fast and efficient collectors.
  - ☐ Thread synchronization with multithreaded code

designed to scale with shared memory multi-processors.

☐ Two types of HotSpot VMs

- Java HotSpot Client VM, which is tuned to reduce startup-time and less memory footprint. Invoked by using -client option to the java command.
- Java HotSpot Server VM, which is tuned to provide a maximum speed of execution.

216. **What is JRE? Describe more on this.**

☐ JRE stands for Java Runtime Environment.

☐ It contains the JVM and other core libraries/APIs required for java bytecode/class file execution.

☐ JRE is a must for any Java program/.class file execution.

☐ Please note that JRE alone is not sufficient for Java code development.

217. **What is JDK? Describe more on this.**

☐ JDK stands for Java Development Kit.

☐ It contains the JRE and other development tools like javac, jar, keytool etc., and other libraries/APIs to provide the java development environment.

☐ It is required for any java code development (compilation, bundling, using supported libraries, etc.)

☐ Also include other integration technology APIs/libraries such as JDBC, JAX-WS, etc.

218. **Does JVM know about Java language? If yes, how much or what API it knows? If not, then what it can do?**

☐ No. JVM doesn't know the Java language itself. It only knows about the particular binary .class format, which contains the instruction bytecode, symbol table, and other ancillary information.

☐ See more details from Java Virtual Machine specifica-

tion (Java SE 8) https://docs.oracle.com/ja-
vase/specs/jvms/se8/jvms8.pdf

219. What is the relation between JDK, JRE and JVM?
- [ ] JVM instance is created when java process gets executed (as simple as java command is invoked) and it is always part of JRE. Note that JVM can't be separated out from JRE.
- [ ] JRE contains JVM + Core APIs/libraries to get java program runtime environment (JRE=JVM+Core libraries).
- [ ] JDK contains the JRE, tools and other integration APIs/libraries (JDK=JRE+Tools+other jar files)

220. Where to get the Java or JDK?
- [ ] JDK can be downloaded freely from https://java.com/en/download/ (or) from http://www.oracle.com/technetwork/java/javase/downloads/index.html and install on the machine that you are going to develop the software.
- [ ] Or download free versions of Eclipse or NetBeans or IntelliJ or any other favorite IDE etc.

221. Could you describe in general how is the Java code development process or lifecycle?
- [ ] At a basic level, the Java coding process goes like this.
    - [ ] Source code (step 1) → Compile (step 2) → Run class (step 3)
        - .java file → .class file → Launch .class file through JVM
- [ ] Start with source code writing as a text file with .java extension and it should be coded from top to bottom (in such a way that code is getting executed and in general from top to bottom unless control statements needed).
    - [ ] Use IDE like Eclipse, NetBeans, IntelliJ, etc. or vi, vim, notepad or any text editor.

- ❑ It is recommended to have the filename (<file-name>.java) with camelcase style, i.e., capital letter at beginning of the word and lowercase letters in all other places. Example: HelloWorld.java
- ❑ Next, do the compilation of the code as below.
  - ❑ javac <filename>.java
  - ❑ It generates the .class file with same file name with .class extension (<filename>.class). Example: HelloWorld.class
- ❑ Now, ready to run the class with java command, which launches the JVM to execute the class bytecode. Please note that don't supply the .class extension. The below command executes the class bytecode in the launched JVM.
  - ❑ java <filename-no-class-ext>
- ❑ Finally, the developed classes can be bundled as jar file. That means all project related multiple classes can be packaged as .jar (called java archive) using jar tool. Later, these jar libraries can be given to customers or reuse in other projects.

222. **What is meant by compilation? Why do you need to do?**
- ❑ The compilation is the process of converting the human-readable machine independent source code into the machine or binary code (instructions to the OS).
- ❑ The compilation process is required to create an executable and low-level machine understandable programs. Examples to compiled languages: Java, C++, C, FORTRAN, etc.
- ❑ The compiled code is much faster and high performance than interpreted programs.
- ❑ The interpreted program means some other program interprets the source code directly without converting to any intermediate binary form (Example interpreted languages: Perl, Python).
- ❑ Java uses java program as an intermediate program to create a virtual platform so that cross-platform execution can

happen without re-compile/re-create the code.

223. **How do you compile the Java code?**
   - ☐ The following is the general command syntax for compiling java code
     - ☐ javac -d <outdir> -cp <classpath> <filename>.java
     - ☐ This generate the .class file at outdir directory if no compilation errors otherwise prints list of errors/warnings.
   - ☐ One can use the IDEs to compile java code in the projects.

224. **What is the file extension to be used for Java source code?**
   - ☐ The Java source code file name should have the .java extension. Example: FeatureXValidation.java

225. **What is meant by WORA?**
   - ☐ The "WORA" stands for Write Once Run Anywhere.
   - ☐ It is one of the core objective of Java technology where cross platform/portability of code is the key. That means writing of code should not be repeated for every OS/platform, and instead it should work without repeating the developer effort.

226. **What is the Java program's runnable format?**
   - ☐ The Java program's runnable file is a special binary formatted file called class format. It is a bytecode file with .class extension corresponding to same source .java filename. This binary code is executed by JVM to run on the machine.

227. **What is the class file structure?**
   - ☐ Each java class file contains instructions about a single class or interface.
   - ☐ Class file structure as specified in the Java Specification

as below.

```
ClassFile {
    u4          magic;
    u2          minor_version;
    u2          major_version;
    u2          constant_pool_count;
    cp_info     constant_pool[constant_pool_count-1];
    u2          access_flags;
    u2          this_class;
    u2          super_class;
    u2          interfaces_count;
    u2          interfaces[interfaces_count];
    u2          fields_count;
    field_info  fields[fields_count];
    u2          methods_count;
    method_info methods[methods_count];
    u2          attributes_count;
    attribute_info attributes[attributes_count];
}
```

☐ The magic code identifies the file as class file for-
    mat and is 0xCAFEBABE
☐ See more details at https://docs.oracle.com/ja-
    vase/specs/jvms/se7/html/jvms-4.html

228. How to determine the java and javac versions?
☐ Run the the java/javac command with -version option.
    $ java -version
    java version "1.7.0_71"
    Java(TM) SE Runtime Environment (build 1.7.0_71-b14)
    Java HotSpot(TM) 64-Bit Server VM (build 24.71-b01,
    mixed mode)

    $ javac -version
    javac 1.7.0_71

229. How do you run Java programs using the command line?
- ☐ Run the java programs using the command line (CLI) is as below.
  - ☐ java -cp <classpath> <full-classfilename-no-class-extn>
  - ☐ The full classname means prefixing the package name (the name used in the code with package statement) and dot (.) to the class like <package>.<classname>
  - ☐ Examples:
    - • java ClassX (NOTE: run like this when ClassX doesn't have a package)
    - • java com.jd.ClassX (run like this when ClassX has the package com.jd)
- ☐ Or run the program with IDE. Typically during the development time for high productivity.

230. How do you resolve classes dependency during compilation and runtime? What are different ways?
- ☐ There are two ways to resolve the class dependencies from javac/java commands:
  - ☐ Add all the dependent class paths (called setting classpath) using an environment variable called "CLASSPATH".
  - ☐ Or add all dependent class paths using -cp or -classpath option of javac/java command.
- ☐ Please note that IDEs might do in different ways from UI by adding jars or classes into the project build settings but would do internally one of the above.

231. What is a Java package? Why do you use?
- ☐ The Java package is a technique to organize and manage the classes in similar to directories in the filesystem. The package name is followed by reverse domain name (com.jd) notation and specified as "package <pkgname>" statement at beginning of the java program.

☐ The primary purpose of the package is to resolve the namespace conflict for classes where the same class name (with different code) can be used while developing software(by the same company or different companies).

232. How do you package the classes into a single file? What is the format of the file?
☐ The packaging of multiple Java classes into a single file can be done with jar tool and the jar file format is similar to zip format.
☐ In general, the jar files are the java libraries with class files and related resources bundled together. There is a manifest file with details about jar is also included.
☐ Below are some of the key operations with jars.
   ☐ To create the jar file from set of files
     jar -cvf <filename>.jar <files-or-dirs>
   ☐ To extract the jar file contents
     jar -xvf <filename>.jar
   ☐ To see the jar file contents
     jar -tvf <filename>.jar

233. What do you set in the CLASSPATH (or) -cp (or) -classpath options? Like class file path/class files directory path/jar files directory path/exact jar file path?
☐ Set the directory path in CLASSPATH or -cp <classpath> (=<directory>) to include all .class files and <package>.<classfile> classes in the classpath. Please note that jar files if any available in that directory will be not be included. Also, multiple directories can be specified in the classpath with path separator (: on Unix or ; on Windows) to include all classes from all those directories.
☐ Set specific jar files path in CLASSPATH or -cp <classpath> (=<jarfilepath>), then all classes in the jar files will be included. Also, multiple jar file paths can be specified in the classpath with the path separator (: on Unix or; on Windows platform).

☐ Set both directory and jar paths together to cover all dependencies (all classes from directories & jar files) in the classpath. Please note that this way in general used in the java command.

234. What is JVM stack? When does this be created?
☐ The JVM stack is the LIFO (Last In First Out) short lived fast memory allocated while executing the java program.
☐ The stack gets created whenever a method is getting called to store the parameters, local variables (method level), and references to the variables in the heap.
☐ The stack memory size can be specified using -Xss jvm option while running the java program otherwise uses default size (512k on 32-bit VM on Solaris and 312k on 32-bit VM on windows; 1024k on 64-bit VM).

235. What is StackOverflowError? When do you get it and how to resolve?
☐ The JVM throws java.lang.StackOverflowError, whenever it's stack is full.
☐ Typically, the stack full can happen in the below situations.
    ☐ When the recursive function doesn't have a termination condition and goes into infinite loop.
    ☐ When many variables and large size data structure is being used in the default or lower stack sized JVM.
☐ To resolve the above error, check the following.
    ☐ Fix the recursive method termination condition
    ☐ Increase the stack size or reduce the size for variables.

236. What is OutofMemoryError? When do you get this and how to resolve?
☐ The java.lang.OutofMemoryError occurs when JVM heap is full during the runtime. Please note that the physical memory can be more than the actual size available to JVM.

☐ The typical reason for this error could be spikes in the data usage by the java application or memory leaks from the application.

☐ The memory leaks can happen when leaving behind the allocated memory (not cleaning up) every time the application logic gets executed and thereby filling up all heap in the JVM.

☐ The error can be resolved after analyzing the objects in the heap and performing the one or all of the below.

☐ Reduce the data size

☐ Address the memory leaks

☐ Increase the heap

☐ The heap size available to JVM can be customized (increasing/reducing) by specifying -Xms (for initial size) and -Xmx (max size) JVM options while running java program.

237. **What is ClassNotFoundException? When do you get this and how to resolve?**

☐ The java.lang.ClassNotFoundException is a checked exception in Java and is thrown by the JVM when the given class can't be loaded by its classloader.

☐ Typically it happens when the application tries to load the named class and can't load in the following.

i) forName() in Class

ii) findSystemClass() in the ClassLoader

iii) loadClass() in the ClassLoader

☐ The root cause for this exception is that the given class is not in the classpath (not in either CLASSPATH system variable or -cp or -classpath options don't have the class or jar file path or not specified the full classname with package name).

☐ To resolve the above issue, make sure the classpath is appropriately set in the CLASSPATH environment variable or -cp or -classpath JVM options.

238. What is JVM heap? When does it gets created?

☐ The Java heap is the main memory used by all parts of Java application during execution.

☐ The heap is going to be created whenever JVM launched/started. That is when java command is issued.

☐ All Java objects are going to be stored in the heap, and that means whenever an object is created, it is always stored in the heap and is globally accessible across the JVM.

☐ The heap memory is going live since the start to the end of the application runtime. The heap memory itself is divided into different generations like young generation, old generation, etc., and is cleaned up by automatic Java garbage collector.

☐ The default JVM heap size is 64MB even when the machine has more RAM.

☐ The Java runtime throws the java.lang.OutOfMemoryError when the heap is full.

☐ The heap size available to JVM can be customized (increase/decrease) using -Xms (initial size) and -Xmx (for maximum size) JVM options. Example to set 1G initial and 2GB max JVM heap, then use -Xms1G Xmx2G while running java program.

☐ If more Java objects and data structures are being constructed in the Java program, then it is required to tune (increase) the heap size of the JVM.

239. What is Garbage Collection? What is its role in JVM?

☐ The Java Garbage collection is the automated process of recovering the unused objects from the Java heap memory. These unused objects are the objects without having any references from other parts/objects of the program.

☐ The programmer doesn't need to worry about allocating the memory for data structures/variables and also deallocating or to release or clean up those objects from the program itself. Internally, Java will automatically do this process. The deallocation is handled by this Java Garbage Collector (GC).

☐ It is not guaranteed when GC will do this. The Java will automatically determine the right algorithm based on the goal of the optimized performance of the program execution.

☐ The GC can be triggered forcibly but again not guaranteed and might impact the program performance. So, it is not recommended to take the GC control in the application program.

☐ Below are the few Garbage Collector types to understand better on the available options.

i) Serial GC

- The Serial GC is a single-threaded GC on a single processor and multiple processors. It is the default GC on any single processor machine.
- It is the choice for most of the applications that don't have the low pause time requirements.
- To enable serial GC, use -XX:+UseSerialGC JVM option.

ii) Parallel GC

- The Parallel GC is a multi-threaded high performance GC. The number of threads can be controlled with below JVM option and have the 'n' value based on the number of processors. -XX:ParallelGC-Threads=<n>
- This GC is also called Throughput collector.
- Some of the flavors in Parallel GC are as below.
  - o Parallel young generation and Serial Old generation
    - ■ To enable, use -XX:+UseParallelGC JVM option
  - o Parallel young generation and old generation
    - ■ To enable, use -XX:+UseParallelOldGC
  - o Concurrent Mark Sweep (CMS)
    - ■ To enable, use -

   XX:+UseConcMarkSweepGC and -XX:Par-
   allelCMSThreads=<n> where n=number of
   processors.

- ■ It is used for applications that require low
  pause times.
  - o G1 Garbage Collector
    - ■ It is available since Java 7 and it is kind of
      replacement for CMS.
    - ■ To enable, use -XX:UseG1GC
- ☐ See more details on using the Java options for parallel or
  serial GC at http://www.oracle.com/webfolder/technet-
  work/tutorials/obe/java/gc01/index.html

240. Does the heap storage have to be contiguous?
- ☐ The JVM specification (link) says that the memory for the
  heap doesn't need to be contiguous. The default Sun/Ora-
  cle JVM is contiguous and other JVMs might not be contiguous like IBM's.

241. What is a variable? Where do you define?
- ☐ Variable is a named memory data pointer to hold data in
  memory. The values (size and layout) of the variable
  would be in the range of the defined by the data type.
- ☐ Variable has an associated data type like int or object data
  type such as String.
- ☐ Variables are defined either in the scope of class level and
  method level.
- ☐ The variable definition syntax can be seen like
  <datatype> <variablename>;
- ☐ Example: int numberOfItems;

242. What is meant by variable assignment and initialization?
- ☐ Variable initialization is the definition and assigning
  value in a single statement.
  - ☐ Example: int maxNumberOfItems=1000;

   □ Variable assignment is nothing but setting value after defining the variable in a different statement. <variablename>=<value>.

      □ Example: maxNumberOfItems=2000;

243. **What are different types of variables?**
   □ Below are different types of variables.
      □ Instance or Non-static or Object variables/fields
      □ Non-instance or Static or Class variables/fields
      □ Local variables

244. **What is a static variable, and its scope? How do you reference it?**
   □ The static variable is a variable defined with "static" keyword and defined at class scope level or in a static method of a class.
   □ These variables belong to the class (not to the specific objects) and thereby called class variables (not instance variables).
   □ Below is the syntax for variable definition.
      □ static <datatype> <variablename_id> = <value>;
      □ Example: static int counter = 1; // the counter value is same irrespective of number of objects created.
   □ The static variables are referenced using <ClassName>.<variablename> Ex: Hello.counter;
   □ The static variables get initialized during the class loading and initialized with values.
   □ All instances share the same copy of the variable.

245. **What is an instance variable and its scope? How do you reference?**
   □ The instance variables are the variables that are defined at class scope level without static keyword. Also called non-static variables or object variables.
   □ The instance variables are belong to class instances, i.e., objects. That's why these variables are called instance

variables.

☐ The general syntax for instance variable definition is like:

   ☐ <datatype> <variablename/id> = <value>;

   ☐ Example: int i = 10;

☐ The instance variables referenced using <objectreference>.<variablename>; Example: h = new H(); h.i=20;

☐ The instance variables are initialized by default.

246. Are all non-static variables are instance variables?

☐ No. The non-static variables defined in the method scope called local variables and not instance variables. Also, note that the instance variables should be defined at class level.

247. What is a local variable, and its scope? How do you reference?

☐ The local variables are the variables defined within a method i.e, scope is at method level.

☐ The local variables should be referenced with the variable name and only within the defined method (local to the method).

☐ Local non-static variables are not initialized by default, and one has to assign before use. Otherwise, there will be compilation error like "variable x might not have been initialized".

248. What are the differences between static variable and instance variable?

☐ The static variables defined at the class level or within a static method with special keyword 'static' whereas instance variables are the variables without keyword 'static' defined at same class level. Note that both are called fields.

☐ The static variables are belong to class and thereby called class variables whereas instance variables belong to object and thereby called instance variables.

☐ The class variables dereferenced with <classname>.<variablename> whereas the instance variables dereferenced with <objectname>.<variablename>.

☐ If the requirement is to have a single copy of the variable throughout the class, then define as static variable (like a counter to keep track of visited pages) else if each object should have a copy of its own data, then define as an instance variable.

249. What is a field? How is it same or different (or same) from other types of variables?

☐ The field is an attribute or an instance variable or class variable that is defined at the class scope. It is same as the static or instance variable but not the local variable.

250. What is a data type? Where do you use?

☐ In static type programming languages such as Java, the type of the data also must be specified before storing the data. Thereby compiler can do the static type checking to reduce the runtime errors.

☐ The datatype is used as a part of a variable definition. The supported data types depend on the language.

☐ The Java data types are as below.

☐ Primitive data types or primitives

- byte : stores 8-bit signed 2s-compliment number (min value: $-2^7 = -128$ max value: $2^7-1=127$ inclusive)
- short : stores 16-bit signed 2s-compliment number (min value: -2^{15} max value: $2^{15}-1$ inclusive)
- int : 32-bit signed 2s-compliment number (min value: -2^{31} max value: $2^{31}-1$ inclusive)
- long : stores 64-bit signed 2s-compliment number (min value: -2^{63} max: $2^{63}-1$ inclusive)
- float : stores 32-bit IEEE 754 single precision floating point number
- double : stores 64-bit IEEE 754 double precision

floating point.

- boolean : stores 1 bit (as 0 or 1 to indicate false or true)
- char : stores 16-bit unicode character (min: '\u0000' max: '\ffff')

☐ Object data types

- String
- Primitive wrapper objects like - Byte, Short, Int, Long, Float, Double, Boolean, Char
- Other Java supplied classes or user application classes

☐ See more details at https://docs.oracle.com/javase/tutorial/java/nutsandbolts/datatypes.html

251. **What are the default values for instance or static variables?**

☐ Below are the default values assigned automatically when the instance/static variables declared with corresponding data types.

    ☐ byte : 0
    ☐ short : 0
    ☐ int : 0
    ☐ long : 0L
    ☐ float : 0.0f
    ☐ double: 0.0d
    ☐ boolean: false
    ☐ char: '\u0000'
    ☐ String or any object type: null
    ☐ Examples:
       int i; // i=0
       String n; //n=null

252. **What is meant by Parameter? How is it different from a variable or field?**

☐ The parameter is the variable used within the method signature as METHOD argument. It is declared same as variables without any initialization. So, parameters can be classified as variables but should not be treated as fields. The similar kind of parameters is used in the constructors.

☐ Example:

> *public void main(String [] args) {} // here args is the parameter*

253. **What are different techniques to pass the parameter values from caller to callee method?**

☐ The values of the parameters passed from the caller to the callee is usually determined by the way the language supported. There are two main techniques.

i) Pass by value

ii) Pass by reference

254. **What kind of parameter passing technique is supported in Java?**

☐ Java supports only "Pass by value" and doesn't support "Pass by reference".

255. **How does the "Pass by value" works?**

☐ In the "Pass by value" technique, the value of the method parameter to be passed is going to be first copied and then assigned to the actual method's argument value.

☐ Here, the value is going to be passed than actual memory reference even if it is the object. In this case, its object reference value will be copied and then send to the called method.

☐ By this, the variable value passed to the method can't be modified through the method. If an object is passed to the method and its object's instance variable changed within the method, then it gets reflected after method execution is completed.

☐ Example: Java supports this technique.

256. How does the "Pass by reference" works?
- □ In the "Pass by reference", the actual reference of the parameter value is going to be passed to the method than as a copy.
- □ In this, the variable or object passed to the method can be modified through a method.
- □ Example: C++ supports but Java doesn't support this technique.

257. What are the differences between "Pass by value" and "Pass by reference"? Please give an example.
- □ In the "pass by value", the parameter value is going to be copied and then passed to the method whereas memory reference is passed to the method call in the pass by reference.
- □ See the below example and output to notice the difference between these techniques.

Public class Test {
   String x = "Hello";
   method1(x);
   System.out.println(x);
   ...

   Employee e1 = new Employee("Test1");
   method2(e1);
   System.out.println(e1.getName());
   ..

   public void method1(String s) {
      System.out.println(s);
      s = "hi";
      System.out.println(s);

   }

   public void method2(Employee e) {
      System.out.println(e.getName());

```
        e.setName("ModifiedName");
        e = new Employee("JD1");
        e.setName("JD2");
    }


}
```

Console o/p w.r.t "Pass by value" or "Pass by reference".

Hello

hi

hi --> It is not right for "pass by value" but it is correct for "pass by reference".

hello --> displayed with "pass by value" (in Java).

-

Test1

ModifiedName (not "Test1" for "Pass by value" and "JD2" if it the "Pass by reference".)

258. What is a literal? Any examples?

☐ The literal is a fixed value that is specified in the source code and can be assigned to a variable.

☐ Example:

```
    byte b = 50;
```

☐ Integer literals

```
    int n = 20;
```

☐ Floating-point literals

```
    float pi1 = 3.1415f;
```

☐ Character and String literals

```
    char c = 'x';
    String description="This is a test case for feature x";
```


259. What is an expression?

☐ The expression is a combination of variables, operators,

and methods to produce a single value that depends on the data types of the variables and values used in the expression.

☐ Examples:

int x=10;

int y = 20;

double z = (x*3.14+y)/10;

260. **What are the unary & binary operators?**

   ☐ The unary means single, and the unary operator is associated with a single operand in the expression.

   ☐ Below are the unary operators with simple examples.

   ☐ + : makes the expression as positive.

   ● Example: int i=+10; // positive 10. By default positive without + but it can be used for expressions.

   ☐ - : makes expression as negative

   ● Example: *int i=-n; // negative n value.*

   ☐ ++ : increment by 1

   ● Example: *++i; // i=2 if i=1 before this statement.*

   ☐ -- : decrement by 1

   ● Example: *--i; //i=0 if i=1 before this statement.*

   ☐ ! : logical inversion or negation

   ● Example: *boolean s = false; boolean s1=!s;// s1=true*

   ☐ Examples: *i++; (or) i--; (or) ++i; (or) –i;*

   ☐ Binary means two and the binary operator is associated with two operands in the expression.

   ☐ Operators : +, -, /, *, %

   ☐ Examples: x = y + 20;

261. **What are prefix & suffix unary operators? What are the differences?**

   ☐ The prefix unary means the operation (either increment or

decrement) performed on the operand first and then evaluated (value is substituted) the value in next. In the expression, the operator going to be specified first and then operand.

- ☐ Syntax example: ++i or --i
☐ The suffix unary means that operand is going to be evaluated (value is substituted) first, and the later operand is going to be incremented or decremented. In the expression, the operand is going be first and then the operator.
- ☐ Syntax: i++ or i--
☐ Examples:
    - ☐ i=5; system.out.println(i++);//prints 5 and i=6
    - ☐ i=6; system.out.println(++i);//prints 7 and i=7
    - ☐ i=7; system.out.println(--i);//prints 6 and i=6
    - ☐ i=6;system.out.println(i--);//prints 6 and i=5

262. **What is a statement? What are different kinds of statements?**

☐ A statement is a unit of execution that is expressed in the high-level language with syntax supported by the language.
☐ At a high level, statements can be classified as below.
    - ☐ Assignment expression statements
        - Example: *i=10;*
    - ☐ Prefix or suffix unary expression statements
        - Example: *i++;*
    - ☐ Object creation expression statements
        - Example: *Employee e = new Employee("JD","1");*
    - ☐ Method invocation statements
        - Example: *System.out.println(e.getName());*
    - ☐ Block statements
        - Example: *{ }*
    - ☐ Control statements
        - Examples: if, for, while, do-while

263. **Can we have an empty statement? How do you write an empty statement?**
   - ☐ Yes. Empty statements are ok in Java.
   - ☐ It is kind of no operation (no-op).
   - ☐ Simply write open curly braces and close curly braces ({}).

264. **What is a block? Can we have an empty block? Do we need to have ";" at the end for a block?**
   - ☐ A block is a group of zero or more statements together with statements inside open and close curly braces with appropriate balance (not crossing with other blocks/braces).
   - ☐ Yes. An empty block is allowed. It is kind of no-operation (nop).
   - ☐ No ';' after the block statement.
   - ☐ Example:
     if (status){ //block1 open
            System.out.println("PASSED");
     } //block2 close
     else { // block1 open
            System.out.println("FAILED");
     } //block2 close

265. **Where do you use block statements?**
   - ☐ Blocks are used in following statements.
     - ☐ if and if-then-else statements
       if (condition) { .. } else { .. }
     - ☐ Loop statements - for, while, do-while
       for (;;) { ..}
       while (condition) { .. }
       do { .. } while (condition);
     - ☐ Static blocks (loaded as part of class loading)
       static {

       ..

       }

266. What are looping statements? Could you briefly explain?

☐ The "for" loop statement: It is a control flow statement where the block (a group of statements) is going to be iterated through a range of values.

☐ The general syntax is as below.

for (initialization-expression; termination condition; increment/decrement expression) {

// statements

}

☐ Here is the flow of execution.

- First, initialization expression is going to be executed (only once for the entire for loop)

- Second, the termination condition is going to be evaluated and if value is false, then for statement terminates. Otherwise, it will continue to execute the block.

- Last, it evaluates the increment/decrement expression.

- Then execution will go back to Second and third and will be repeated.

☐ If the termination condition never finishes (when increment/decrement expression is not getting closure to the termination condition), then it will be in the infinite loop.

☐ Example:

```
//Print 10 hello words
for (int i=0; i<10; i++) {
System.out.println("hello");
}
```

☐ The "while" loop is a another control flow statement and the while block gets executed until the condition expression is evaluated to false.

☐ General syntax is as below.

```
while (condition) {
// statements
}
```

❑ Example:

```
// Print 10 hello words
int i=0;
While (i<10) {
    System.out.println("hello");
}
```

❑ The "do-while" loop is a control flow statement and the block executed at least once and until while condition is evaluated to false.

   ❑ General syntax as below.

```
do {
    // statements
} while (condition);
```

❑ Example:

```
// Print 10 hello words
int i=0;
do {
    System.out.println("hello");
} while (i<10);
```

267. How do you represent infinite loops with "for", "while" or "do-while" statements?

❑ Infinite "for" statement can be done by simply not having any initialization/termination/increment expressions. If required to terminate the infinite loop, then add if condition and use break statement.

```
for (;;) {
    //statements
}
```

❑ Infinite while can be achieved by having true in condition.

```
while (true) {
    //statements
}
```

❑ Infinite do-while can be achieved by having true in condition.

```
do {
```

//statements
}while (true);

268. What is meant by branching? What are different branching statements? Where do you use?
- ☐ The branching is to get out of the normal execution flow. Below are 3 main statements.
  - ☐ break
  - ☐ continue
  - ☐ return
- ☐ break : It is used to come out of the loop or block. Used frequently with a switch statement.
  - ☐ Unlabeled break - use simply "break"
  - ☐ Example:
    int i=0;
    for (; ;){
    // statements
    if (i==10) break;
    //statements
    i++;
    //statements
    }
  - ☐ Labeled break - use break with label.
    - • Example:
    label:
    for (; ;){
    //statements
    break label
    //statements
    }
- ☐ continue : It is used to continue next iteration by skipping the current iteration in the loop.
  - ☐ Unlabeled continue: simply use "continue".
    - • Example:
    int i=0;
    for (; ;){
    // statements

```
if (i==10) continue;
//statements
i++;
//statements
}
```

☐ Labeled continue: use continue <label>.
  • Example:
```
label:
for ( ; ;){
    //statements
    continue label
    //statements
}
```

☐ return: It is used to come out of the executing method to the caller.
  ☐ Usage without return value: simply use "return".
  ☐ Usage with return value: return <variable/value>;
    • Example:
```
public int computeVal(int val) {
    // statements
    if (val>100) {
        return val;
    } else {
        return 100;
    }

}
```

269. **What is the purpose of switch statement? How do you write switch statement?**
  ☐ The switch statement is used when many execution paths arise in the program logic. The same use case can be done with the if-then-else statement, but there will be many if-else conditions.
  ☐ Switch works with byte, char, int primitive data types and

wrapper data types, enumerated data types, String objects.

☐ The switch syntax:

```
switch (data) {
    case <value>: //statements
                break;
    case <value>: //statements
                break;
    case <value>: //statements
                break;
    default: //statements
            break;

}
```

☐ Example as code snippet:

```
/*
 * Guess my vehicle based on given seats
 */
public String guessVehicleType(int seats) {
String vehicle = null;

switch (seats) {
case 1:
        vehicle = "Bicycle";
        break;
case 2:
        vehicle = "Motor Bike or Sedan";
        break;
case 3:
        vehicle = "Autoriksha";
        break;
case 4:
        vehicle = "Car";
        break;
case 5:
            vehicle = "Mini Van";
            break;
case 6: case 7: case 8:
            vehicle = "Van";
            break;
```

default:
>   *vehicle = "Bus or Train";*
>   *break;*

}
return vehicle;
}

270. **How do you write an interface? Can you implement multiple interfaces from single class?**
□ In general, an interface is for establishing a contract with outside clients.
□ The interface is a reference type in similar to class with few restrictions.
□ The interface can contain only contain method declarations/signatures, constants, static methods, default methods, etc.
□ The interface should not contain any implementation (there should not be {} for methods) except for default and static methods.
□ Interfaces can't be instantiated and can only be implemented by classes or extended by other interfaces.
□ Multi-inheritance for interfaces (extending multiple interfaces) in Java is allowed.
□ Multiple interfaces can be implemented ("implements" keyword) by a single class.
□ Use the interface reference type (i.e., return type) than implementation class while used by the clients.
□ Example interface and implementation: Here Vehicle is the interface and Car is the implementation/concrete class. Notice the method differences.

/**
* Vehicle.java
*
*/
package jd;

```java
/**
     * Vehicle interface/contract
 * @author Jagadesh Babu Munta
 *
 */
public interface Vehicle {
    int seats =0 ;
    boolean isAuto = false;
    int speed = 0;
    void moveForward(int speed);
    void moveBackward(int speed);
    void applyBreak();
}
```

☐ Class to implement the above interface

```java
/**
 * Car.java
 *
 */
package jd;

/**
 * @author Jagadesh Babu Munta
 *
 */
public class Car implements Vehicle {

    /**
     * @see jd.Vehicle#moveForward(int)
     */
    @Override
    public void moveForward(int speed) {
        // TODO
    }

    /**
     * @see jd.Vehicle#moveBackward(int)
     */
```

```
@Override
public void moveBackward(int speed) {
    // TODO
}


/**
 * @see jd.Vehicle#applyBreak()

 */
@Override
public void applyBreak() {
    // TODO
}


/**
 * @param args
 */
public static void main(String[] args) {
    // TODO
}
}
```

271. **How do you write abstract class? Can you extend from multiple classes?**

☐ The abstract class is a class that is declared with abstract keyword. At least one of the methods should be declared as abstract, i.e., without an implementation and have only method declaration.

☐ Example:

```
public abstract class  Graph {
    public abstract void draw();
    void getLocation() {

        ..


    }
}
```

☐ In Java, multi-inheritance with classes (extending from

multiple classes) including abstract classes is not allowed. Java supports only single inheritance for the classes.

☐ The implementation class must implement all of the abstract methods. Otherwise, the class must also be declared as abstract.

☐ Implementation class Example:

```
public class  GraphImpl extends Graph {
    void draw() {
        //statements

    }
}
```

272. **What are the differences between an interface and abstract classes?**

☐ In general, interfaces formulate a contractual agreement with clients, and abstract classes formulate hierarchical relationship.

☐ In the interfaces, by default all methods are public, fields are static and final whereas, in abstract classes, the fields can be non-static or nonfinal and can define public/protected/private methods.

☐ In interface classes, all methods are implicitly abstract and thereby not explicitly added the abstract modifier to the methods. Whereas abstract classes can have 1 or more abstract methods and must be declared as abstract methods.

☐ Interfaces are defined with interface keyword whereas abstract classes and methods are defined using abstract keyword.

☐ Also, the abstract class can implement interfaces, but it has to declare as abstract if any method is not implemented.

☐ Interfaces can support multiple inheritance (extend multiple interfaces) whereas abstract classes support only single inheritance (only one abstract class can be extended). That means a single class can implement multiple interfaces whereas only one abstract class can be extended.

☐ Both interfaces and abstract classes are similar where these can't be instantiated to create the concrete objects and instead either implemented or extended in creating the concrete objects.

273. When do you use interfaces and abstract classes?
☐ Interfaces can be used in some of the use cases like below.
  ☐ Need a specific contract per client without concerning on the implementation.
  ☐ Multiple inheritance data type is needed.
  ☐ Unrelated classes should be following some contract by implementing those interfaces to have different behaviors.
☐ Abstract classes can be used in some of the use cases like below.
  ☐ Sharing common code (common methods and members) across the closely related classes.
  ☐ Declare non-static and nonfinal fields.
  ☐ Need a hierarchy among the classes.

274. How do you write constructors?
☐ In OOP, constructors form the basis for creating the objects from the class blueprint.
☐ Java class constructors can be declared in similar to methods but as a special type of method with name same as the class name and no return type.
☐ A class can contain any number of constructors either with a different set of arguments or even without any arguments, which is called the default constructor.
☐ If no constructors defined in class, then Java automatically provides one default constructor. This default constructor calls super class's default constructor automatically. If the class doesn't have direct inheritance, then it will call the very top level Object class's default constructor, which is empty and does nothing.
☐ Note that if any constructor is defined in class, then the

compiler will not provide a default constructor and also it doesn't call superclass's default constructor automatically.

☐ Example constructors code snippet:

```
public class UserProfile {
    String userName;
    String name;
    String email;

    //No argument constructor
    public UserProfile() {
        this.userName="admin";
        this.name = "Administrator";
        this.email = "appadmin@gmail.com;
    }
    // Non default constructor
    public UserProfile(String userName, String name,
    String email) {
        this.userName = userName;
        this.name = name;
        this.email = email;
    }

    public static void main(String [] args) {
        UserProfile p = new UserProfile();
        UserProfile p1 = new UserPro-
    file("jdbabu","Jagadesh Munta,
    "jagadesh.munta@gmail.com");
    }
}
```

☐ The access modifiers can also be specified to the constructors and will have the effect on how other classes can access the class.

☐ For example, to define a Singleton class, you can define private access modifier to the default constructor so that no other class can construct the objects other than its class itself.

275. Can you use a default constructor without defining it in a class? Please explain why or why not?

☐ Yes. The default constructor is automatically provided by Java when there are no constructors defined. So, one can use the default constructor to create the objects. Also, the superclass's default constructor is called automatically and if no superclass, then top level Object class's default constructor is called.

276. In class, if you have defined a parametric constructor only, then can you construct the objects with default constructor? In this context, does java provides the default constructor?

☐ No. When the class declares any constructor, then Java will not provide the default constructor. Thereby one can't use it unless default constructor is defined within the current class in addition to the parametric constructor.

277. What is an inner class? What it represents in OOP? Describe more on nested classes?

☐ An inner class is a non-static nested class that is defined within a public class called outer class (enclosing class). That means an outer class can contain one or more inner classes.

☐ This kind of nested class represents the encapsulation in OOP(Object Oriented Programming).

☐ Typical use cases of nested classes are as below.

☐ Needs more closed logical grouping or having local custom type in the class

☐ Needs more encapsulation

☐ Needs more readable and maintainable code with logically related functionality together.

☐ Nested classes are 2 types:

☐ Static nested classes

• It is a static class member type in another class and should be referenced as a class member. It can only reference static members of the enclosing class.

☐ Non-static or Inner classes

- Inner classes belong to the objects/class instances.
- Further classified as 2 types
  - o Local classes
    - ■ These are inner named classes that are declared within a method.
  - o Anonymous classes
    - ■ These are inner unnamed (no name) classes declared within a method.
    - ■ These classes are declared and instantiated at the same time. Note that these classes only used once unlike local classes.

☐ The general syntax/example is as below:

```
public class MyOuterClass {
    // other members

    static class MyNestedClass {
    //statements
    }

    class MyInnerClass {
    //statements
    }

    private void testMethod1() {
        class MyLocalClass {
        // statements
        }

        // Anonymous class
        MyTest mt = new MyTest() {
            public void test1() {
            }
        }
```

}

> *public static void main(String [] args) {*
> *MyOuterClass.MyNestedClass nc = new My-*
> *OuterClass.MyNestedClass();*
>
> *MyOuterClass main = new MyOuterClass();*
> *MyInnerClass inner = main.new MyInner-*
> *Class();*
> *}*
> *}*

278. **How does the generated class look like for an inner class?**
   - ☐ The generated inner class name would be in the below form as <outer-class-name>$<inner-class-name>.class
   - ☐ Examples:
     - ☐ Main$UserProfile.class
     - ☐ MyOuterClass$MyInnerClass.class

279. **What is meant by access modifier? Where do you use? What are different access modifiers?**
   - ☐ The access modifiers, also called access controls are the keywords that determine whether other classes can access specific fields or methods or members of the current class.
   - ☐ These are used to achieve encapsulation (data/implementation hiding) in OOP programming for the protection of members.
   - ☐ List of access modifiers at class level:
     - ☐ public : this class can be accessed by any class.
     - ☐ package-friendly or no access modifier keyword: this class can be accessed only by the same package class.
   - ☐ List of access modifier at member level:
     - ☐ public : this member is
       - • accessible i) in the current class ii) in the same package classes iii) in sub-classes iv) any other

classes.

- ❑ protected: this member is
  - accessible i) in the current class ii) in the same package classes iii) in sub-classes
  - NOT accessible by other classes.
- ❑ package-friendly or no access modifier keyword: this member is
  - accessible i) in the current class ii) in the same package classes
  - NOT accessible i) in sub-classes ii) by other classes.
- ❑ Private: this member is accessible ONLY in the current class
- ❑ See the below summary as the table view for easy understanding.

Access Modifier type to a member	Accessible from its own class	Accessible from its Package	Accessible from its Subclass	Accessible from any other or World
public	Yes	Yes	Yes	Yes
protected	Yes	Yes	Yes	No
<no modifier> or package friendly (no keyword for this)	Yes	Yes	No	No
private	Yes	No	No	No

280. How do you provide access when you have private access members?
- [ ] For this case, provide the public methods so that external classes can use.
- [ ] In fact, this is the typical way to do the data encapsulation.
- [ ] The recommendation is to use private access modifiers for fields and provide public methods to interact with other classes.

281. Can you assign multiple access modifiers to a single member?
- [ ] No. Only one access modifier keyword is allowed.

282. What is final keyword significance? Where do you use?
- [ ] The "final" keyword is to indicate that the value of a variable is fixed and can't be modified. It can be used for variables, constants, methods and classes.
- [ ] If the "final" keyword is used for a method, then this method can't be overridden.
- [ ] If "final" keyword is used for a class, then this class can't be inherited by any class.
- [ ] Example: To define constants, use final as below -
  static final int MAX_COUNT=1000;

283. Can you define a private constructor? If yes, why do you do?
- [ ] Yes. One of the main use case to define a private constructor is create singleton class (design pattern) where only a single instance of a class exits in the JVM. The external access is provided through another public static method or static instance variable than directly creating the objects from constructors.

284. **What is a Java exception? Could you please brief on different types of exception?**

☐ The Java exception is an event that disrupts the normal flow of execution.

☐ In general, there are 2 types of events occur in Java.

i) Errors

- Errors are the abnormal conditions that can occur during runtime and user app can't catch to recover in the program.

- These are kind of uncheck exceptions where the app can throw the Error subclasses in the potential occurred code.

ii) Exceptions are 2 types

- Checked Exceptions
  - These are the exceptions that compiler can check for proper handling before runtime. There is an obligation in the code where raised exceptions should be handled or pass up to the stack. Otherwise, the compiler produces errors.

- Unchecked Exceptions/ Runtime Exceptions
  - There is no obligation in the code to handle this kind of exceptions. The compiler will not check for handling these exceptions and no errors produced otherwise.
  - Catch the exceptions using try-catch-finally block as below example.

☐ See the later questions on the differences between these exceptions.

☐ Example of exceptions handling.

try {
    // statements that can raise checked exception.
} catch (Exception e) { // catch with top level Exception class or specific subclass such as FileNotFoundException.
        e.printStackTrace(); //print the stack trace
        //other statements to handle the exception.
        Or re throw

// throw new Exception(e);
} finally {
    //statements get executed always, irrespec-
    tive of exception raised or not.

}

285. How is the Exception and Error classes tree?
- [ ] java.lang.Object
  - [ ] java.lang.Throwable
    - java.lang.Error
    - java.lang.Exception → Used (extend) for checked exceptions
      - o java.lang.RuntimeException → extend for unchecked exceptions

286. How to handle Java exceptions? Which exception to handle first when multiple exceptions to be caught?
- [ ] Use try-catch or try-catch-finally block code to handle the raised checked exceptions. The potential exception raising code must be surrounded by try block and then matching exception class must be in the catch block, which gets executed automatically when there is a matched catch block. Otherwise, the compiler can raise an exception if that exception is checked exception.
- [ ] (or) Use "throws <exception class>" in the method to pass in the method call stack when the current code is not able to handle the exception directly.
- [ ] In the catch arguments, beginning exception classes must be specific class names and later should be generic or super classes. Otherwise, the next Exception classes might not be caught as super classes can match the exception class before child classes.
- [ ] For example, FileNotFoundException and some other IO-Exception raised, then it should be like as below (FileNot-

FoundException must be before IOException or Exception classes).

```
try {
//..
} catch (FileNotFoundException fnf) { //...
} catch(IOException ioe) { //..
} catch(Exception e) { //..
}
```

☐ Below is the general syntax for handling exceptions. The finally block gets executed all the time irrespective of the catch blocks executed or not. To simply print the stack trace, use printStackTrace() method on that object.

```
try {
        //statements
} catch (<exception> <variable>) {
        // print stack trace or handle the event
        //<variable>.printStackTrace();
} catch (...) {
        // print stack trace or handle the event or re
throw using throw to raise another exception
}
.....
} catch (...) {
        // print stack trace or handle the event
} finally {
        // optional block and always get executed –
exception raised or not
        // close resources or so
}
```

☐ In Java 7 and later versions, multiple types of Java exceptions can be caught in the same catch block instead of duplicating catch block code as in prior versions. Example:

```
catch (Exception1 | Exception2 ex) {
        // print stack trace or handle the event
        ex.printStackTrace();

}
```

287. What are the differences between checked exceptions and unchecked/runtime exceptions?

☐ Both checked and unchecked exceptions indicate some event happened rather than the normal flow of the program. The following are the differences, and there has been a controversy where one side of programmers preferred checked, and other side preferred unchecked exceptions.

Checked Exceptions	Unchecked/Runtime Exceptions
User code must catch the exception or rethrow the exception. Otherwise, it is a compilation error.	No to need to catch the exception in the user application.
Custom application exception should extend from Exception class or other subclasses that are not extended from RuntimeException class.	Custom application exception should extend from RuntimeException class or its subclasses.
Use the checked exceptions when there is a reasonable way to recover by the client code.	When there is no way to handle the raised exception, then better to go with unchecked/runtime exceptions.
Example: FileNotFoundException raised when input file doesn't exist at the given path.	Example: NullPointerException raised when a null object is dereferenced.

288. **How to resolve when there is an exception stacktrace?**
- ☐ When there is an exception stack, then first see the stack trace and calls stack. Note the exception message and take the action.
- ☐ So, the stack trace/stack dump is really required when filing bugs or debugging the exception issues.

289. **How to raise exceptions?**
- ☐ Use the throws statement to pass or throw the exception to the called method instead of handling (try-catch) in the same method.
- ☐ Use throw statement to raise a new exception.
- ☐ Example:

    public static String search() throws NullPointerException
        return findEmployeeId(0);
    }
    public static String search2() throws Exception {
      // actual search for employee
      // if not found, then throw exception
      throw new EmployeeNotFoundException(); //user exception
    }

290. **How to create a new custom or user defined checked exception?**
- ☐ To create a new checked Exception
  - ☐ Inherit the class from Exception
- ☐ To create a new unchecked or Runtime
  - ☐ Inherit the class from RuntimeException
- ☐ Here is the sample checked exception class.

    public class EmployeeNotFoundException extends Exception{
      public EmployeeNotFoundException() {
      //super();
      super("Employee is not found");

```
}
public EmployeeNotFoundException(String mesg) {
super(mesg);
}
}
```

☐ In the application code, use the below statement to raise the exception.

```
throw new EmployeeNotFoundException("Employee
"+empId+" is not found");
```

291. **What is a conditional operator, "?:"?**
   ☐ A conditional operator is a short form of "if-else" conditional statement.
   ☐ General syntax:
      ☐ (condition)? val1: val2
      ☐ (first)? second: third
   ☐ The first argument should return a boolean value.
   ☐ Second and third arguments should never return void.
   ☐ Example:
      Short form:

```
max = (a>b)? a : b
```

      //The above is equivalent to the below if statement.

```
if (a > b) {
max = a;
}
else {
max = b;
}
```

292. **How and where to use "for-each" statement?**
   ☐ The "for-each" statement is a short form of "for" loop.
   ☐ It is used when a series (of values), each successive value is to be referenced.
   ☐ Typically, used in

i) methods of Arrays and Collections.

ii) Iterable (anything that implements Iterable<E>) class.

☐ The general syntax for for-each is as below.

for (type v : array) {

//body loop and v is going to have successive objects from the array.

}

293. **What is "enum" data type and how to use?**

☐ The "enum" data type a special data type where name and values are referenced from each other instead of using separate mapping (name=value mapping).

☐ For example, to use the sizes (Large, Medium, Small) or days (weekdays as below), then enum will help to represent as is instead of mapping as 1, 2, 3, etc.

☐ Usually, enum datatype specified as a separate class than a simple variable defined in the current class.

☐ Examples:

// enum type variables
enum WeekDay { MONDAY, TUESDAY, WEDNES-
DAY, THURSDAY, FRIDAY, SATURDAY, SUNDAY };
enum Size {SMALL, MEDIUM, LARGE};

// To reference the above enum variables
for (WeekDay d: EnumSet.range(WeekDay.THURS-
DAY, WeekDay.SUNDAY)) {
System.out.println(d); // prints THURSDAY, FRIDAY,
SATURDAY, SUNDAY
}

294. **How to write a recursion method? What is the core advantage if it? Where to pay attention?**

☐ Recursion is nothing but a method calling itself (self-calling).

☐ The advantage is that some of the problems are in recursion nature and easy to solve with recursion way than non-

recursion way.
☐ Below are the core steps to write a recursion method.
  ☐ First, form the "Base case"
  ☐ Next, process to get closure to the Base Case
  ☐ Last, make a recursive call to pass simple problem back
☐ Examples of recursion in nature
  ☐ Factorial of N
  ☐ Fibonacci numbers
☐ The major attention to pay in recursion is that avoid an infinite loop. The stackoverflow error can happen if the proper way of processing to get closure to the base is not done. So, the proper handling of exit condition is important.
☐ See the sample java code listings at the end of the book covering the recursion code.

295. **What are the different Java I/O classes?**
☐ The below are the list of basic I/O classes work with files/console/devices.
  ☐ Standard I/O (Input/Output)
    • System.in
    • System.out
    • System.err
  ☐ Byte Streams
    • FileInputStream
    • FileOutputStream
  ☐ Character Streams
    • FileReader
    • FileWriter
  ☐ Buffered Streams
    • BufferedReader
    • BufferedWriter
  ☐ Line I/O
    • BufferedReader
    • PrintWriter

☐   Data Streams
  ● DataInputStream
  ● DataOutputStream
☐   Object Streams
  ● ObjectInputStream
  ● ObjectOutputStream
☐ See the sample java code listings at the end of the book covering the Java I/O code.

296. **What are Java Collection and Java Collection frameworks?**

☐ In simple terms, Collection is a container.

☐ A collection is an object that groups multiple objects.

☐ In general, Collection represents a natural group of items.

☐ The collection has methods that stores, retrieves, manipulates and communicates aggregated data.

☐ In Collection, the objects are called Elements.

☐ Collections can be either Ordered or Unordered group of elements.

☐ The Java Collections Framework is a unification of Interfaces, Implementations and Algorithms that work on a group of objects.

297. **What are the advantages of Java Collections?**

☐ Some of the key advantages of Java Collections are as below.

  ☐ Reduces programming effort

  ☐ Increases program speed with quality implementations

  ☐ Re-usability

298. **What are the core interfaces in Collection framework?**

☐ The Collection interface is the top-level interface in the Collections framework.

☐ Java doesn't directly provide any implementation classes

at Collection interface and instead provide the implementations at the sub-interfaces such as List and Set.

☐ Collection interfaces are generics (type) for compile time check than runtime type check and it can reduce runtime errors.

  ☐ public interface Collection<E> extends Iterable<E>{ ...} where E is the type of object contained in the collection.

☐ Here is the hierarchy of java collection interfaces. Please note that the Map is not in the same class hierarchy as Collection.

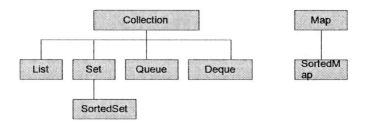

299. What are the common methods in the Collection (interface)?

☐ The Collection interface class contain methods ike size(), isEmpty(), contains(), add(), remove(), clear() etc., for for basic operations; bulk operations like containsAll(), addAll(), retainAll(); and toArray() operations.

public interface Collection<E> extends Iterable<E> {
  // Basic operations
  int size(); // to find the number of elements in the collection.
  boolean isEmpty(); // to check if the current collection is empty or not. Return true if it is empty.
  boolean contains(Object element);
  // optional
  boolean add(E element);
  // optional
  boolean remove(Object element);
  Iterator<E> iterator();

// Bulk operations (working with other collections)
boolean containsAll(Collection<?> c);
// optional
boolean addAll(Collection<? extends E> c);
// optional
boolean removeAll(Collection<?> c);
// optional
boolean retainAll(Collection<?> c);
// optional
void clear();

// Array Operations to convert the collection to an
array.
Object[] toArray();
<T> T[] toArray(T[] a);
}

300. **What is Set interface, and its implementation classes?**
   □ A Set is a collection that can't contain any duplicates.
   □ It is an abstraction of a mathematical set.
   □ The Set interface has the same methods/operations as the Collection except that it is constrained to remove duplicates.
   □ The Set is used in place of old Vector class (now it is a legacy class after collections framework).
   □ Set interface extends Collection.
      □ public interface Set<E> extends Collection<E> { ...}
   □ The following are some of the Set real world examples.
      □ Cards in Poker
      □ Courses in Student's schedule
      □ Processes running on a machine
   □ The list of Set implementation classes from Java Collections Framework is as below.
      □ HashSet (best performing): Elements are stored internally like a hashtable. There is no elements order guarantee in this implementation.
      □ TreeSet: Elements are stored using the red-black

tree and the elements are ordered based on values.
- ☐ LinkedHashSet: Elements are similar to HashSet except that it preserves the order in which the elements were added.
- ☐ Examples with bulk operations
  - ☐ Set<Type> union = new HashSet<Type>(s1);
    - union.addAll(s2);
  - ☐ Set<Type> intersection = new HashSet<Type>(s1);
    - intersection.retainAll(s2);
  - ☐ Set<Type> difference = new HashSet<Type>(s1);
    - difference.removeAll(s2);

301. **What is List interface, and its implementation classes?**
- ☐ A List is an ordered collection or sequence of elements container. The insertion order is preserved/maintained.
- ☐ The List interface adds more methods on top of Collection for the below functionality.
  - ☐ Positional access
  - ☐ Search
  - ☐ Iterator
  - ☐ Range view
- ☐ The below are the implementation classes
  - ☐ ArrayList (best performing)
  - ☐ LinkedList
- ☐ Two list objects are equal when same elements are in same order.
- ☐ ListIterator extends Iterator to provide forward or backward indexing of elements.
- ☐ Below is the List interface and methods include get(), set(), remove(), indexOf(), lastIndexOf() etc.,
  public interface List<E> extends Collection<E> {

  // Positional access
  E get(int index);
  // optional
  E set(int index, E element);

```
// optional
void add(int index, E element);
// optional
E remove(int index);

// Bulk (optional)
boolean addAll(int index, Collection<? extends E> c);

// Search
int indexOf(Object o);
int lastIndexOf(Object o);

// Iteration
ListIterator<E> listIterator();
ListIterator<E> listIterator(int index);

// Range-view
List<E> subList(int from, int to);

}
```

☐ Example code snippet:
```
// list3 = elements in list1 and list2
List<Type> list3 = new ArrayList<Type>(list1);
list3.addAll(list2);
```

302. **What are different algorithmic methods available in the List collection?**
     ☐ Below are the List algorithms.
        ☐ Sort (using merge sort/stable sort, and no re-order-ing of elements is required)
        ☐ Shuffle
        ☐ Reverse
        ☐ Rotates
        ☐ Swap
        ☐ ReplaceAll
        ☐ Fill
        ☐ Copy

☐ IndexOfSubList
☐ lastIndexOfSubList

303. **Could you explain the Map collection?**
☐ Map collection maps the keys to values. Mainly, it holds key-value pairs.
☐ The Map can't contain duplicate keys.
☐ The Map interface is not in the same Collection interface hierarchy.
☐ It is similar to the old HashTable class.
☐ The below are implementation classes for Map.
   ☐ HashMap
   ☐ TreeMap
   ☐ LinkedListMap
☐ Map interface operations are put(), get(), remove() etc. as below.

```
public interface Map<K,V> {
    // Basic operations
    V put(K key, V value);
    V get(Object key);
    V remove(Object key);
    boolean containsKey(Object key);
    boolean containsValue(Object value);
    int size();
    boolean isEmpty();

    // Bulk operations
    void putAll(Map<? extends K, ? extends V> m);
    void clear();

    // Collection Views
    public Set<K> keySet();
    public Collection<V> values();
    public Set<Map.Entry<K,V>> entrySet();

    // Interface for entrySet elements
    public interface Entry {
```

```
K getKey();
V getValue();
V setValue(V value);
    }
}
```

304. How should you write the classes (the rules to be followed) in order to use custom Java beans as elements in a collection?

☐ At a minimum, the Java bean (say Employee) should override the below two methods to work as expected otherwise unexpected behavior can happen. This mainly matches the stored objects in the collection.

    ☐ equals() : should have the logic to compare the objects.

    ☐ hashCode() : override this method whenever equals is overridden. A unique value to be returned. Also, note that don't change the return value once the object is stored in the collection. Example: don't use current timestamp method as the return value.

☐ Also, implement Comparable to do the automatic sorting like in TreeSet (or) use Comparator class if sorting algorithm is going to be used in that collection.

☐ See the below code snippet to show required methods to implement in collection element class.

```
/**
 * override equals() to say that two employees are equal
only when
 * employee names and ids are equal.
 */
public boolean equals(Object o) {
        if (o==null) { return false; }
        if (o==this) { return true; }
        if (! (o instanceof Employee)) {
                return false;
        }
        Employee e = (Employee)o;
```

```
        if ( (e.get-
        Name().equals(this.name))&&(e.getId()==this.i
        d)){
                return true;
        } else {
                return false;
        }
}

/**
* Required whenever equals overridden
* @see java.lang.Object#hashCode()
*/
public int hashCode() {
    return id;
}

/**
* Below method is required for ordering/sorting of ele-
ments.
*/
@Override
public int compareTo(Employee o) {
        int nameCompare = name.compareToIgnore-
        Case(o.getName());
        return (nameCompare!=0 ?nameCompare: new
        Integer(id).compareTo(o.getId())));
}
```

305. If there is a requirement where a million records should
     be read from DB and would like to make them unique and
     sorting. Which collection data structure is appropriate?
     ☐ TreeSet is more appropriate because Set will remove du-
     plicates and Tree will make sure sorting automatically.

306. If there is a requirement where some kind of paired objects to be stored, then which collection data structure is appropriate?
   □ HashMap more appropriate because it is efficient to store key-value pairs.

307. How to choose a specific Collection data structure? What are different performance characteristics (Big O-complexity)?
   □ The following summary table gives each collection and basic purpose. You can check the requirement and pick the appropriate data structure.

Inter-face	Collection Imple-mentation	Basic purpose	Performance
List	ArrayList	Duplicates + Indexing + Insertion order	O(1) for size, isEmpty, get, set, iterator operations. O(n) linear time for add and all other operations.
	LinkedList	Duplicates + Indexing + Iterator from both sides (doubly linked list implementation)	O(n) for get and remove. O(1) constant time for add and Iterator.remove.
Set	HashSet	No duplicates + No specific order	O(1) constant time for basic operations (add/remove/contains)+
	TreeSet	No duplicates + Sorted elements	O(log(n)) for basic operations (add/remove/contains)
	LinkedHashSet	No duplicates + Preserving the insertion order	O(1) constant time for basic operations (add/remove/contains)
Map	HashMap	Key-Value pair + No specific order for keys	O(1) constant time for basic operations (get and put)
	TreeMap	Key-Value pair + Sorted keys	O(log(n)) time for get, put, remove, contains operations
	LinkedHashMap	Key-Value pair + Preserving the keys insertion order	O(1) constant time for basic operations (add, contains, remove)

JDBC

308. **What is JDBC? Could you please explain about different JDBC driver types.**

☐ JDBC stands for Java DataBase Connectivity. It is the platform independent API used to work with different vendor databases from Java code.

☐ The current API spec version is 4.0 and is called JDBC4.0. The Java packages for JDBC API are java.sql and javax.sql. The API has been included in both Java SE and Java EE editions.

☐ To work with any database, there is a need to use vendor drivers implemented by installing client or adding to library path or putting the jar in the classpath.

☐ There are 4 types of JDBC drivers (Reference link)

    ☐ Type 1 driver: Drivers that have been implemented the JDBC API by mapping to another database access API such as Microsoft's ODBC (Open Data-Base Connectivity used for programming with MSAccess, SQLServer DB). This type of driver is also called JDBC-ODBC bridge. Portability is limited with this driver as this not written in pure Java code. Below is the execution path.

        ● Java →JDBC →ODBC →MS Access /SQLServer

    ☐ Type 2 driver: Also called Native drivers. Drivers that have been implemented partly in Java and partly in native code to interact with the native client(platform specific libraries) in order to connect to the DB. Portability is limited with this driver as it is not written in pure java.

    ☐ Type 3 driver: Also called Middleware Data Source (written in pure Java). Drivers that have been implemented the JDBC API with Java that communicates with Middleware (with the data source in application servers such as WebLogic/GlassFish) in order to connect to the database. Middleware maintains the data sources with DB connection pool and efficient reuse of expensive DB connections. The JDBC code will have logical data source name, and actual DB configuration will be mapped in the application server.

☐ Type 4 driver: Also called Thin drivers (written in pure Java). Drivers that implement the network protocol of specific data source. The client directly connects to the data client. These drivers are simple jar files to put in the classpath and no installation/setup needed.

• Example: Oracle thin driver ojdbc.jar library for Oracle DB.

309. Could you please explain end-to-end steps in a typical JDBC program?

☐ The following are the key steps along with code snippets in a typical JDBC program.

(1) Register/load the driver (similar to the code snippet as below).

DriverManager.registerDriver (new oracle.jdbc.OracleDriver());
(or)
Class.forName("oracle.jdbc.OracleDriver");

Alternatively, you can register the driver when launching the JavaVM (while execute your application), as follows:

java -Djdbc.drivers = oracle.jdbc.OracleDriver
<ClassName>;

(2) Get DB Connection

- There are 3 ways to perform DB connection.

  i) DriverManager approach like below code snippet.

  Connection conn=DriverManager.getConnection(connectstring_or_jdbcurl,uname,passwd);

  Example: Connection conn = DriverManager.getConnection(
  "jdbc:oracle:thin:@<host>:<port>:<sid>","<user>","
  <passwd>");

  ii) DataSource approach like below code snippet.
  OracleDataSource ods = new OracleDataSource();
  // set necessary properties (JDBC URL, etc)
  java.util.Properties prop = new java.util.Properties();
  ...
  prop.put(....)
  ods.setURL(url);

  // get the connection
  Connection conn = ods.getConnection();

  iii) JNDI approach like below code snippet.
  javax.sql.DataSource ds = (javax.sql.DataSource) ctx.lookup("java:comp/env/my-datasource");
  java.sql.Connection conn = ds.getConnection();

(3) Create Statement/PreparedStatement/CallableStatement

- To create Statement
  Statement statement = conn.createStatement();

- To create PreparedStatement
  PreparedStatement preparedStatement = conn.prepareStatement();
- To create CallableStatement
  CallableStatement cs = conn.prepareCall("{call <procedure>}");

(4) Execute Query/Update SQL
   ☐ There are 3 different statement execution methods
   i) executeQuery(String sqlstmt)
     ○ Typically used to run a SELECT SQL statement.
     ○ Returns ResultSet object.
     ○ Code snippet:
       ResultSet rs = stmt.executeQuery("SE-LECT empno, ename FROM emp");
   ii) executeUpdate(String sqlstmt)
     ○ The executeUpdate(String sql) method is invoked on the statement object for DML (INSERT/UPDATE/DELETE) and DDL (i.e., CREATE TABLE)
     ○ It returns an int value.
     ○ Code snippet:
       int rowcount = stmt.executeUpdate("CRE-ATE TABLE table1 (numcol NUM-BER(5,2), strcol VARCHAR2(30)");
       int rowcount = stmt.executeUpdate("DE-LETE FROM emp WHERE empno = 2354");
   iii) execute(String sqlstmt)
     ○ The execute(String) method can be invoked on the statement object for any SQL statement (i.e., query, DML, DDL)
     ○ It returns a boolean value.
     ○ Code snippet:
       boolean result = stmt.execute(SQLstate-ment);

```
if (result) {// was a query - process results
ResultSet r = stmt.getResultSet(); ...
} else { // was an update or DDL - process
result
    int count = stmt.getUpdateCount();
}
```

(5) Process Results
- ☐ The ResultSet is the object that is returned from executing the Statement and maintains a cursor pointing to the current row.
- ☐ The next() method in the ResultSet allows iterating through the rows that made the result set, and the getXXX() method is for retrieving the values of the columns where XXX indicate various data types or column types.
- ☐ Note that without first having rs.next(), the results can't be retrieved as the cursor doesn't point to the available row.
- ☐ Typical ResultSet process loop is as below.
    while (rs.next() { XXXX obj=rs.getXXXX(<column name>) }
  - Code snippet:
    ```
    while (rs.next()) {
        String ename = rs.getString("ENAME");
        int empno = rs.getInt("EMPNO");
        ...
    }
    ```

(6) Close resources
- ☐ Free up the resources with the below steps
    i) Close the resultset object
    ii) Close statement object
    iii) Close connection objects
    Use these statements the finally block (in try-catch-finally) so that always get executed even when there are partially allocated resources due to exceptions.
    rs.close();

stmt.close();
conn.close();

310. **What is JDBC URL or Connect string? Can you give examples?**
☐ JDBC url is a connection string that is used in the Type4 thin driver. The following is the syntax.
   ☐ jdbc:<subprotocol>:<subname>//<host>:<port>/[databasename][,user=xxx,password=zzz]

☐ Examples:
   ☐ Oracle
   • Driver: oracle.jdbc.OracleDriver
   • JDBC Url: jdbc:oracle:thin:@localhost:1521:xe
   ☐ MySQL
   • Driver: com.mysql.jdbc.Driver
   • Url: jdbc:mysql://localhost:3306/EmployeeDB
   ☐ SQLServer
   • jdbc:microsoft:sqlserver://127.0.0.1:1433;user=User;password=Password;databasename=DBName

311. **How to create a datasource in WebLogic?**
☐ In WebLogic, create DataSource using Admin Console by navigating to the below.
   ☐ Goto http://localhost:7001/console → Services->JDBC->DataSources->New
☐ Then add jdbc code in your program to do the DataSource lookup:
Properties props = new Properties();
props.put(Context.INITIAL_CONTEXT_FACTORY, "weblogic.jndi.WLInitialContextFactory");
props.put(Context.PROVIDER_URL, "t3://localhost:7001");
ctx = new InitialContext(props);
ds = (DataSource) ctx.lookup("jdbc/employeedb");

← End: Skill#9. Java & JDBC ←

Good!
Keep going and never give up!!
Please re-read again for more clarity and feel free to contact for help!!!

→ Start: Skill#10. ANT →

Skill#10. ANT

The ANT is a build framework. Once it was popular and still is being used as Java build framework for both product code and test code in most of bigger software organizations. Having an understanding and hands-on experience for both developers and QA is good.

312. What is Apache's ANT? What are the core elements?
- ☐ The Apache's Ant is a popular open source build process automation framework/tool used for Java based projects.
- ☐ The purpose of ANT is similar to make or gnumake utilities used for building software in early days and especially for C/C++ programs. Also, Maven is another build tool. ANT is written Java.
- ☐ ANT build scripts or projects are in XML (eXtended Markup Language) files. Typically called ant "build.xml" files.
- ☐ It is easy and extensible with Java.
- ☐ ANT is mainly a CLI (Command Line Interface) called "ant" tool, and there is no GUI.

313. Why and where do you use? Any alternatives?
- ☐ ANT is used to simplify by automating the repetitive build steps while developing or testing the Java projects.
- ☐ The build steps include clean, compile, package the bundle, run tests, etc.
- ☐ The other alternatives could be Maven, make, gnumake, etc.

314. How do you design your project workspace and how do you build the project? What do you write?
- ☐ The general test and dev project workspace start with a

high-level directory based on the project name.
- ☐ The subdirectories of project directory contain src, doc, build xml files, build properties, common build files and lib directory. Also bin directory, which is not in the source code repository but will get generated.
- ☐ The src folder contains the subdirectories with java package and there the actual .java source files.
- ☐ The bin folder is created automatically during the project build where compiled artifacts like .class files, .jar files or .ear files would be generated.
- ☐ The doc folder contains the generated Javadoc or written help files.
- ☐ The build.xml and build.properties contain the ANT project files for building the project.
- ☐ The common folder contains the commonly used ant files or tasks or any other utilities.
- ☐ The lib folder contains the dependent libraries like third-party .jar files.
- ☐ The snippet for the workspace structure is as below.

```
../projectdir
        /src/<pkg>/*.java
        /bin/<pkg>/*.class
        /doc/*.html
        /build.xml
        /build.properties
        /common/...
        /lib/...
```

315. **Is ANT cross platform? Can we run on all platforms?**
- ☐ Yes. ANT build files are XML files, and same xml file can be used. Also, the ANT tasks also cross platform framework as it is written Java, which makes the programs platforms independent. The ANT itself (binaries) should be download for each platform but no need to do any migration/porting of build.xml files and any other ANT tasks.

316. What is minimally required to run ANT build file?
   ☐ At minimum, we need
      ☐ Installation of Java and ANT
      ☐ ant file, build.xml

317. How to setup ANT?
   ☐ First, download binary distribution from Apache site. The latest zip from http://ant.apache.org
   ☐ Install is a simply unzip the downloaded .zip archive: apache-ant-1.9.0-bin.zip in C:\ and it will create C:\apache-ant-1.9.0-bin folder.
   ☐ Set system environment variables
      ☐ On Windows
         • set ANT_HOME=C:\apache-ant-1.9.0
         • set JAVA_HOME=C:\Java\jdk1.6.0_29
         • set PATH=%PATH%;%ANT_HOME%\bin
         • For double check, run "echo %ANT_HOME%"
      ☐ On Linux/Unix (sh/bash shell)
         • export ANT_HOME=/home/jmunta/apache-ant-1.9.0
         • export JAVA_HOME=/home/jmunta/jdk1.6.0_29
         • export PATH=$JAVA_HOME/bin:$ANT_HOME/bin:$PATH
         • For double check, run "echo $ANT_HOME"
   ☐ Run below command to check if setup is ok.
      ant -version

318. What is meant by ant target?
   ☐ ANT target is tag/element in the build file to define a build step or operation.
   ☐ ANT targets are composed of tasks as a container to do the desired build operation or state.

☐ One can think like an orchestration of various targets create build automation through the ant build file.

☐ ANT target contain name, properties, description attributes.

☐ ANT targets are referenced with the target name and are being called from ant tool to do the actual build process.

☐ Other ANT targets can be called inside a target or can have dependent targets.

319. How do you define a target in the build xml?

☐ The ANT target is defined with "<target>" xml tag name and should have a name attribute. Inside the target, call the tasks for desired logic.

☐ The snippet to compile build step is as below:

```
<target name="compile" description="Compile java code" depends="init">
    <javac classpathref="classpath" srcdir="${src.dir}" destdir="${build.dir}"/>
</target>
```

320. What is ant task?

☐ The ant task is the basic and core atomic action being performed in the ant. All the useful activities are coded as tasks. One can think these as the build API for ANT build files.

☐ These tasks were written in Java and also it is the way of extending the ant functionality.

☐ There are many in-built tasks for various actions are already available in the ant library and defined for build files.

☐ For example: java is a task to execute a java program. Simply call this task element in a target element of the build.xml.

☐ For any new functionality, write a new task and define it in the build.xml. If already ant tasks library is provided by third party tool to integrate into ant, then simply define

that task in the build.xml before calling it in the target.
- ☐ The tasks will be called in the target, which is the container of tasks to create the build step.
- ☐ Refer for more details on existing tasks
  http://ant.apache.org/manual/tasksoverview.html

321. **How do you write and define a task in the build xml?**
- ☐ First, create the task code in Java.
  - ☐ Simply write a java public class, which extends Task.
  - ☐ Override execute() in the task class.

  import org.apache.tools.ant.Project;

  ```
  public class MyNewTask {
  private Project project;
  public void setProject(Project proj) {
     project = proj;
  }
  public void execute() {
     String message = project.getProperty("ant.project.name");
     project.log("Here is my new project '" + message + "'.", Project.MSG_INFO);
  }
  }
  ```

- ☐ Next, define the task using <taskdef> tag in the ANT build file. It can be done at project scope or at target scope. See the below snippet:

  ```
  <taskdef name="mytask" classname="MyNewTask" classpath="${ant.project.name}.jar"/>

  <target name="use" description="My New Task" depends="jar">
       <mytask/>
  </target>
  ```

```
<target name="use2" description="My New Task2"
depends="jar">
    <taskdef name="mytask2" classname="MyN-
ewTask" classpath="${ant.project.name}.jar"/>
    <mytask2/>
</target>
```

☐ Refer the link on how to write a
new task -
http://ant.apache.org/manual/tuto-
rial-writing-tasks.html

322. **How do you load the parameters from a file? Also from Java system properties?**
   ☐ To load the properties from a file, one can use <loadprop-
   erties> task and then just refer using ${propertyname}.
   <loadproperties srcFile="file.properties"/>
   ☐ The default Java system properties can be referenced directly as those properties already available in build.xml.
      ☐ For example: ${java.version} for java version
      ${os.name} for operating system version etc.
   ☐ The new system properties can be supplied from ant using
   "-Dname=value", similar to Java program runtime and the
   property can be read directly as other property reference
   using ${propertyname}.
      ☐ -Dpropertyname=value
   ☐ Refer the link for available Java properties http://docs.or-
   acle.com/javase/7/docs/api/java/lang/Sys-
   tem.html#getProperties%28%29

323. **How do you reference properties? What are different in-
built properties?**
   ☐ The reference to the property can be done using ${prop-
   ertyname} in the project or target scope.
   ☐ Some of the in-built properties are: ${ant.version} to get

the version, ${ant.project.name} to get the current project name etc.
☐ Refer: http://ant.apache.org/manual/properties.html

324. How to group multiple targets to run from single target?
☐ Two ways:
☐ Using depends attribute of the target. In this case, target1 is called first when all target is executed, then target2, after that target2, then target3 and finally the code inside "all" target itself.

```
<target name="all" depends="target1,target2,target3" >
...
</target>
```

☐ Directly calling the targets using <antcall> task.

325. What is the depends attribute? What is description attribute?
☐ The "depends" attribute in the target is to call other dependent targets one by one before actually running the tasks inside that target.
☐ Example:In below target's "depends" case, target1 is called first when all target is executed, then target2, after that target2, then target3 and finally the code inside "all" target itself.

```
<target name="all" depends="target1,target2,target3" >
...
</target>
```

326. Do you need have all the time build.xml? Or any file is ok? What is the difference having the build.xml or another file name?
☐ No. The default filename for ant to recognize without supplying the file name is "build.xml". Any other name can be used for a project but while running ant targets, then

supply with -f <filename> like "ant -f mybuild.xml".

327. **What are the minimal things required in build.xml?**
    □ The build xml should be in XML format with <project>
    root tag and at least one <target> defined.

328. **How do you run a target from cmd or terminal? Can you run a task directly from ant command at the terminal?**
    □ To run a target at CLI, use "ant" command with target names as arguments as below.
        ant <target1> <target2> <target3> ...
    □ No. We can't run a task directly at ant command level and instead, wrap that task inside a target and then call that target as above command line.

329. **How to set a default target to be executed without specifying with ant command?**
    □ In the <project> tag of build.xml, use default attribute. default="<targetname>".

330. **Can you run any program from ANT? If yes, how?**
    □ Yes. Using <exec> task. It can execute any command/binary/script from that task. Use that in the target of build.xml.

331. **What do you need to run build.xml? Any downloads?**
    □ To run the ANT build.xml, one has to setup the ANT environment, which needs ant binaries to be downloaded. Also, JDK should be available and set JAVA_HOME environment variable.
    □ See 317 for more details on ANT setup.

332. **How do you set the classpath?**
    □ Two ways to set the directory/jar paths in the classpath

for <java> or <javac> or any other tasks accepting the classpath.

☐ Directly set the task's classpath attribute value to all the directories/jars to include in the classpath.

<javac classpath="${build.dir}" srcdir="${src.dir}"
destdir="${build.dir}"/>

☐ Define the path reference with all directories & jars and then use the classpathref attribute.

<path id="classpath">
<fileset dir="${build.dir}"/>
</path>

<javac classpathref="classpath" srcdir="${src.dir}"
destdir="${build.dir}"/>

333. What is classpathref in the ANT build and what is its significance?

☐ The classpathref attribute of some tasks is to accept the path reference id for the file set to use in the classpath. Usage: define the path reference with all directories & jars and then use the classpathref attribute.

<path id="classpath">
<fileset dir="${build.dir}"/>
</path>

<javac classpathref="classpath" srcdir="${src.dir}"
destdir="${build.dir}"/>

☐ The path reference is to create a common id for the set of files and then use wherever it can be referenced (using the name) instead of duplicating the paths everywhere needed.

334. What do you need to integrate any software?
- ☐ First is to see if the software/tool to be integrated is provided ant tasks/library.
  - ☐ If yes, then download that library (jar file) and define the task build.xml with the name according to their documentation or other name.
  - ☐ If no, then write a new task and define the task in the build.xml. This might be complex to write the code, then follow below #b option.
- ☐ If no ANT task library is provided, then simple way is to execute using <exec> task as long as CLI (command line) execution provided by that software.

335. How do you integrate Java compilation and execution (snippet) process in the ant build file?
- ☐ For compilation, use <javac> ant task and use <java> ant task for running java program. Below is the snippet from build.xml.

  <!-- Compile -->
  <target name="compile" description="Compile java code" depends="init">
  *   <javac classpathref="classpath" srcdir="${src.dir}" destdir="${build.dir}"/>*
  </target>

  <!-- Run -->
  <target name="run" description="Run the main program">
  *   <java classname="com.everydayon.javacollections.main.SampleCollections" classpath="${project.jar}"/>*
  </target>

336. How do you create a jar in ant framework (snippet)?
- ☐ Use <jar> ant task to create the jar. Below is the snippet from build.xml.

```
<!-- Build -->
<target name="build" description="Build jar" de-
pends="compile">
    <jar basedir="${build.dir}" jarfile="${pro-
ject.jar}">
        <fileset dir="${build.dir}" in-
cludes="*.class"/>
    </jar>
</target>
```

337. **How do you integrate JUnit runtime in ant framework (snippet)?**
   □ Use <junit> ant task to integrate junit tests.
   □ Snippet is as below:
   ```
   <?xml version="1.0" ?>
   <project name="testexamples" default="run">
     <target name="run" description="Running junit
   tests">
       <junit printSummary="true">
       <classpath>
         <pathelement location="${basedir}"/>
         <pathelement location="C:\\Users\\work-
   space\\bin"/>
       </classpath>
       <formatter type="xml"/>
       <test name="JUnitTestExample1"/>
       <test name="com.everydayon.misc.test.JUn-
   itCheck"/>
       </junit>
     </target>
   </project>
   ```

338. **How do you integrate TestNG runtime in ant framework (snippet)?**
   □ Define the testng task using the testng jar provided by TestNG and use that task in the targets.

☐ See the below snippet:

```
<project name="TestNGExamples" default="run">
  <property name="testclasses.dir" value="C:\\Us-
ers\\Jagadesh Babu Munta\\workspace\\Java-
Feb2013\\bin"/>
  <path id="cpath">
   <pathelement location="C:\\testng-6.8\\testng-
6.8.jar"/>
   <pathelement location="${basedir}"/>
   <pathelement location="C:\\Users\\Jagadesh Babu
Munta\\workspace\\bin"/>
  </path>
  <taskdef name="testng" classpathref="cpath"
       classname="org.testng.TestNGAntTask" />
  <target name="run-group1" description="Running
group1 tests">
   <testng classpathref="cpath" groups="group1">
   <classfileset dir="${testclasses.dir}" in-
cludes="**/testng/*.class"/>
   </testng>
  </target>
  <target name="run-group2">
   <testng classpathref="cpath" groups="group2">
   <classfileset dir="${testclasses.dir}" in-
cludes="**/testng/*.class"/>
   </testng>
  </target>
  <target name="run-all">
   <testng classpathref="cpath">
   <classfileset dir="${testclasses.dir}" in-
cludes="**/testng/*.class"/>
   </testng>
  </target>

  <target name="run" depends="run-group1"/>
</project>
```

339. Can you include one build.xml in another build.xml?
- ☐ Use <include> task to include another build.xml to current build.xml file.

```
<!-- This project included common build file where it
might have contained all common targets used by the pro-
jects -->
<project name="project1" basedir="." default="usage">
    <include file="common/common.xml"/>
</project>
```

340. How can you call another target from same build file?
- ☐ The <antcall> task can be used to call another target in the same build file.

```
<antcall target="name"/>
```

341. How can you call a target from one build.xml in another build.xml?
- ☐ The <ant> task can be used to call a target from another build.xml

```
<ant antfile="dir/build.xml" target="name"/>
```

342. How do you print messages on the console? How do know supported ant tasks?
- ☐ Using <echo> task with message attribute or as an element.
- ☐ For the supported ant tasks, one has to refer the ANT user manual for tasks. See at http://ant.apache.org/manual/tasklist.html
- ☐ Find the related code snippet from the build.xml

```
<echo message="Building the project"/>  (or)
<echo>
    ant  compile : compiles java code
            ant build: creates jar
</echo>
```

343. How do you know supported ant targets from a ant build.xml?
    □ To see the list of targets and description, one has to set the description attribute in the target. <target name="x" description="message">
    □ Then run "ant -p" to get get the list of supported targets. If targets don't have the description attribute, then those will not be listed.

344. What is fileset? Where do you use?
    □ The <fileset> element is being used for many tasks such as jar etc. while processing the set of files.
    □ For example jar task to jar file files, then as <fileset> is the way to use for including (includes attribute) and also excluding (excludes attribute). Below is the usage:
        <fileset dir="${build.dir}" includes=".class"/>*

345. What is the end-to-end flow (in build.xml) to build and run a Java application?
    □ First, define the workspace structure for the test or dev project. Most of the time, replicate with already working workspace structure.
    □ Next is to create the ant build file and or properties files for the project.
    □ For this, create a single ant xml called build.xml per project.
    □ Define the <project> root tag in the build.xml as below.
        <project name="projectname" default="target" basedir=".">
    □ Then, start adding the targets depending on the build steps. For each build step, create a target (<target>) with unique name as appropriate with build step name. You can define more targets for certain common things and call those targets appropriately in the build step targets. Form the dependency (depends attribute) and calling order on those targets.

☐ Example: Define clean, compile, build, run, usage, all, etc. targets in the build.xml and all can depend on "clean, compile, build, run".

☐ The target itself would have tasks based on the build step. Check the ANT documentation for ant task definition on finding the appropriate one and usage.

☐ We can define the common properties in a separate file and load those files or within the build.xml.

☐ Set the description at project and targets so that documentation of the about the build process can be achieved.

☐ Add comments as needed with standard xml way : <!-- like xml -->

☐ Below is the sample build.xml to understand all the parts. Using this build file, one can run as "ant all" to execute all the build steps.

```xml
<?xml version="1.0" encoding="UTF-8" ?>
<!--
    project1 build file
-->
<project name="project1" default="usage"
basedir=".">
    <description>
            Build system for project1
    </description>
    <property name="project.dir" value="."/>
    <property name="src.dir" value="${pro-
ject.dir}/src"/>
    <property name="build.dir" value="${pro-
ject.dir}/bin"/>
    <property name="doc.dir" value="${pro-
ject.dir}/doc"/>
    <property name="project.jar" value="${ant.pro-
ject.name}.jar"/>

    <target name="usage" description="usage">
        <echo>
                ant  compile : compiles java code
```

```
                ant build: creates jar
            </echo>
    </target>


    <path id="classpath">
            <fileset dir="${build.dir}"/>
    </path>


    <!-- Clean -->
    <target name="clean" description="Clean the build
directory and doc directory">
            <delete dir="${build.dir}"
failonerror="false"/>
            <delete dir="${build.dir}"
failonerror="false"/>
    </target>
<!-- Init -->
    <target name="init" description="Initialize the pro-
ject build locations">
            <mkdir dir="${build.dir}"/>
            <mkdir dir="${build.dir}"/>
    </target>


    <!-- Compile -->
    <target name="compile" description="Compile java
code" depends="init">
            <javac classpathref="classpath"
srcdir="${src.dir}" destdir="${build.dir}"/>
    </target>


    <!-- Build -->
    <target name="build" description="Build jar" de-
pends="compile">
            <jar basedir="${build.dir}" jarfile="${pro-
ject.jar}" >
                    <fileset dir="${build.dir}" in-
cludes="*.class"/>
            </jar>
```

```
        </target>

        <!-- Run -->
        <target name="run" description="Run the main pro-
gram">
                <java classname="com.everydayon.javacol-
lections.main.SampleCollections" classpath="${pro-
ject.jar}"/>
        </target>

        <!-- All -->
        <target name="all" description="Run all steps" de-
pends="clean, build, run">
                <!--
                <antcall target="clean"/>
                <antcall target="build"/>
                <antcall target="run"/>
                -->
        </target>

</project>
```

← End: Skill#10. ANT ←

Good!
Keep going and never give up!!
Please re-read again for more clarity and feel free to contact for help!!!

→ Start: Skill#11. Maven →

Skill#11. Maven

The Maven is a build framework used everywhere in the recent Java projects. It addresses some of the dependency resolution problems with Java project build process that was a burden with ANT. Maven makes the build process simple by using conventions. Thereby Maven is a significant survival skill for both developers and QA automation engineers.

346. What is Maven? Why and how do you use? What are other alternatives?
   □ Maven is a modern build framework/tool to automate the build process for Java based projects.
   □ At high level, Maven is a software project management and comprehension tool used for project
      □ Creating builds
      □ Generating site/documentation
      □ Resolving dependencies
      □ Source code management integration
      □ Maintain different releases
      □ Distribution of releases to the repositories.
   □ Maven is based on Project Object Model (POM), which is the model for the project and is an XML file.
   □ Maven follows the convention over configuration theme.
   □ Maven defines the standard directory structure.
   □ Also note that it is not ANT extension (there is no specific relation)
   □ The alternatives include ANT, make, gnumake, gmake, etc.

347. What are key objectives and features of Maven?
   □ Maven key features include
      □ Creating builds
      □ Generating site/documentation

☐   Resolving dependencies
☐   Source code management integration
☐   Maintain different releases
☐   Distribution of releases to the repositories.

☐ Maven objectives include
  ☐   Comprehensive process for developer
  ☐   Making the build process easy
  ☐   Providing a uniform build system
  ☐   Providing quality project information
  ☐   Providing guidelines for best practices development
  ☐   Allowing transparent migration to new features

348. How does Maven use Convention over Configuration?

☐ Maven uses the convention on the workspace on the sources, where to keep the classes, and distribution files and test results, etc.
☐ Thereby Maven is much simpler and reduces a lot of boilerplate script.

349. How to install and setup Maven - steps?

☐ Install mvn
  ☐   Download and unzip - http://maven.apache.org/download.cgi
☐ Set environment
  ☐   M2_HOME=<installed-path>
  ☐   JAVA_HOME=<jdk-loc>
  ☐   PATH=%PATH%;%M2_HOME%\bin
☐ To check the setup, find the version by running the command -
    mvn –version
☐ The general maven command usage is
    mvn [options] [<goal(s)>] [<phase(s)>]

350. What is the latest Maven version?

☐ The latest Maven (mvn) version is 3.03 and other versions

are 2.2.1, 2.0.11, 1.x.

351. How do you create a new project workspace using archetype or project template?

☐ To create a new project from scratch, one can use the below command:

mvn archetype:generate
-DgroupId=com.everydayon -DartifactId=myapp
-DarchetypeArtifactId=maven-archetype-quickstart
-DinteractiveMode=false

352. Describe the default workspace structure created by Maven?

☐ The default workspace structure created by
mvn archetype:generate is
(select defaults and groupId as pkg name and artifactId as appname myapp)

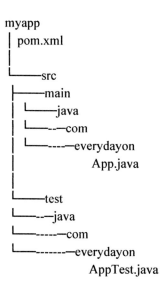

```
myapp
| pom.xml
|
└──────src
   ├──────main
   |  └──────java
   |  └──----com
   |  └──-----everydayon
   |              App.java
   |
   └──────test
   └──---java
   └──------com
   └──-------everydayon
               AppTest.java
```

353. What is POM? What is its core value?

- ☐ POM stands for Project Object Model.
- ☐ The pom.xml is the default POM file for maven build script file.
- ☐ The pom.xml is everything you need for a project and it might be a big file
- ☐ POM follows the Object Oriented principles like Inheritance (parent/child relation), Aggregation with multiple modules.
- ☐ In summary, POM xml contains the project information, properties, build information, profiles, dependencies, authors, scm, etc.
- ☐ The sample pom.xml is as below:

```
<project xmlns="http://maven.apache.org/POM/4.0.0"
xmlns:xsi="http://www.w3.org/2001/XMLSchema-instance"
 xsi:schemaLocation="http://maven.apache.org/POM/4.0.0
http://maven.apache.org/xsd/maven-4.0.0.xsd">
  <modelVersion>4.0.0</modelVersion>
  <groupId>com.everydayon</groupId>
  <artifactId>myapp</artifactId>
  <version>1.0-SNAPSHOT</version>
  <packaging>jar</packaging>
  <name>myapp</name>
  <url>http://maven.apache.org</url>
  <properties>
    <project.build.sourceEncoding>UTF-8</project.build.sourceEncoding>
  </properties>
  <dependencies>
    <dependency>
        <groupId>junit</groupId>
        <artifactId>junit</artifactId>
        <version>3.8.1</version>
        <scope>test</scope>
    </dependency>
  </dependencies>
```

</project>

354. Describe briefly the skeleton of POM file.

☐ The pom.xml (called POM xml) contains the following elements/sections describing the project so that maven can do the desired actions.

☐ At high level, POM xml contains -

    ☐ Basic project artifact details such as groupid, artifactid, version, packaging, etc.

    ☐ Dependencies, modules, properties

    ☐ Build settings <build>, <reporting>

    ☐ More project information such as name, description, developers, contributors, licenses, etc.

    ☐ More on environment settings such as Issue management, SCM, Repositories, SCM, Plugin repositories, Distribution Management, Profiles, etc.

☐ POM xml skeleton is as below:

<project xmlns="http://maven.apache.org/POM/4.0.0"
xmlns:xsi="http://www.w3.org/2001/XMLSchema-instance"
xsi:schemaLocation="http://maven.apache.org/POM/4.0.0
    http://maven.apache.org/xsd/maven-4.0.0.xsd">
  <modelVersion>4.0.0</modelVersion>

  <!-- The Basics -->
  <groupId>...</groupId>
  <artifactId>...</artifactId>
  <version>...</version>
  <packaging>...</packaging>
  <dependencies>...</dependencies>
  <parent>...</parent>
  <dependencyManagement>...</dependencyManagement>
  <modules>...</modules>

```
<properties>...</properties>

<!-- Build Settings -->
<build>...</build>
<reporting>...</reporting>

<!-- More Project Information -->
<name>...</name>
<description>...</description>
<url>...</url>
<inceptionYear>...</inceptionYear>
<licenses>...</licenses>
<organization>...</organization>
<developers>...</developers>
<contributors>...</contributors>

<!-- Environment Settings -->
<issueManagement>...</issueManagement>
<ciManagement>...</ciManagement>
<mailingLists>...</mailingLists>
<scm>...</scm>
<prerequisites>...</prerequisites>
<repositories>...</repositories>
<pluginRepositories>...</pluginRepositories>
<distributionManagement>...</distributionManage-
ment>
<profiles>...</profiles>
</project>
```

355. What is groupId? What is artifactId? What is version?
   □ Maven's groupId is the company's reverse domain or Java package name style.
   □ Maven's artifactId is the project codename/short name.
   □ POM's version is the current major.minor version

356. **What is the jar name look like based on the above?**
   ☐ The packaged jar name is going to be <artifactId>-<version>.jar

357. **What is Maven repository? Describe both local and central repositories?**
   ☐ Maven stores all the dependent libraries in the local disk while resolving the project dependencies resolution during the build process.
   ☐ Local repository is on the local file system, and default is ~/.m2 (note that it can be changed from the Maven's config/settings.xml or user's settings.xml or given settings.xml path to –s option in the maven command).
   ☐ Central or Remote repository is the common website storing all the dependent projects (jar and pom xml files) so that maven can download automatically to the local repository if local doesn't have those jar files.
   ☐ Both of the above repositories can be configured at the project level or globally or at user settings.xml file.

358. **What is the default local repository path?**
   ☐ The default directory is .m2 under user's home directory. (~/.m2/repositories)

359. **Where do you set the dependency information?**
   ☐ The dependencies should be in the project's pom.xml under <dependencies></dependencies>.
   ☐ Typically, you can search at the http://search.maven.org site for the third party software dependency or directly look at the documentation provided by third-party for the actual groupId, artifactId, and version.
   ☐ The scope for the dependency is up to the current project to indicate when to include at appropriate stage of the build (such as such as compile or runtime or test or system etc.). Example scope for junit dependency is only to in-

clude in test stage but not for maincode compile. The default scope is compile.

☐ See the below pom.xml snippet for junit dependency.

```
<dependencies>
    <dependency>
        <groupId>junit</groupId>
        <artifactId>junit</artifactId>
        <version>3.8.1</version>
        <scope>test</scope>
    </dependency>
</dependencies>
```

360. How to set the dependency to download testng 6.9.6 version? And also selenium java 2.46.0 jar?

☐ The below pom.xml snippet is the dependency for testng and selenium.

```
<dependencies>
    <dependency>
        <groupId>org.testng</groupId>
        <artifactId>testng</artifactId>
        <version>6.9.6</version>
        <scope>test</scope>
    </dependency>
    <dependency>
        <groupId>org.seleniumhq.selenium</groupId>
        <artifactId>selenium-java</artifactId>
        <version>2.46.0</version>
    </dependency>
</dependencies>
```

361. What are the commands to compile sources, build jar, and run tests?

☐ mvn compile : to compile main sources

☐ mvn test : to run tests (which includes main compile, test compile)

☐ mvn package : to get the jar (note: <packaging>jar</packaging> mentioned in pom.xml) (also this phase include all tasks as in mvn test)

362. What is the main sources directory path? What is the test sources directory path?
- □ The main source code should be at <project>/src/main/java/<pkg>/*.java and resources should be at <project>/src/main/resources/*.properties etc.
- □ The test source code should be at <project>/src/test/java/<pkg>/*.java and resources should be at <project>/src/test/resources/<pkg>/*.properties, etc.

363. Where are the classes get generated for both product and tests?
- □ Main classes will be under <project>/target/classes/<pkg>/*.class [Note: <project> is the project directory path and <pkg> is the java package.]
- □ Test classes will be under <project>/target/test-classes/<pkg>/*.class [Note: <project> is the project directory path and <pkg> is the java package.]

364. Do you need to download the dependent jars all the time from the internet (central repository)? How to force the update?
- □ No. Only first time need the internet connection if the dependent jars are not in the local repository and note that the downloaded jars would be saved in local maven repository (~/.m2/repository/..) and later used automatically.
- □ mvn -U option is to force the updating of packages.

365. What is the command 'mvn install' does?
- □ "mvn install" command would copy the project artifact (packaged jar as <projectname>-version.jar to the local maven repository.

366. **How to publish the artifacts to central repository?**

☐ "mvn deploy" command would publish the project's artifact to the central repository configured in the settings.xml or project's pom.xml. The default Maven repository at http://repo.maven.apache.org/maven2/ .

367. **Where do you check if any third party dependent jar is needed?**

☐ In general, we can check in the maven central repository (http://search.maven.org) and look for the artifact or group id.

368. **How to generate the product documentation? Where does it generate the files (index.html etc.)?**

☐ Run "mvn site" command to generate the project website from information in pom.xml.

369. **What is a maven plugin? What is main functionality?**

☐ Maven is a collection framework of various plugins. These plugins will have all the code that is required to perform the build action. These plugins are the heart of the maven build lifecycle phases. The plugins will have the goals and should be coded.

370. **What is a maven goal? Where is it used?**

☐ Maven goal is the part of the plugin to perform some action. During the build lifecycle operations, goals will be used along with plugin name or call the default goal.

☐ Usage is "mvn <plugin-name>:<goal>".

☐ To get the list of goals, one can use the command - "mvn help:describe -Dplugin=<pluginname>"

☐ To get more details about a particular goal of a plugin, then use the command like surefire plugin's test goal - "mvn help:describe -Dplugin=surefire -Ddetail=true -Dgoal=test".

371. What is a build phase? How do phases relate to plugins?

☐ The build lifecycle operations are divided into phases and can be used directly with mvn <phase> command without having "plugin:goal". Those plugin goals are tied with regular build operations or phases.

372. What are default phases in the maven build lifecycle?

☐ The following are the default phases in the maven build lifecycle of projects and all the prior phases will be included automatically by next phase.

☐ These can be invoked as "mvn <phase>". Example: mvn test

    ☐ validate: validates if the project is correct and all necessary information is available in pom.xml.

    ☐ compile: compiles the main source code of the project.

    ☐ test: tests the compiled source code after compiling test code and using a suitable unit testing framework. These tests should are not required the code be packaged or deployed.

    ☐ package: take the compiled code and package it in its distributable format, such as a jar.

    ☐ integration-test: process and deploy the package if required into the environment where integration tests can be executed.

    ☐ verify: run any checks to verify that the package is valid and meeting the quality criteria.

    ☐ install: install the generated package into the local repository for use as a dependency in other projects locally.

    ☐ deploy: used in an integration or release environment and copies the final package to the remote repository for sharing with some other developers and projects.

    ☐ site: generates the website pages for the project from the information in pom.xml.

373. **How do you clean up the build?**
- Run "mvn clean" in the project directory and it removes target folder.

374. **What is meant by maven local settings and global settings? And where do they located?**
- The maven behavior depends on the maven settings. There are 3 different places for settings and maven checks in the same order as below for any settings (means it checks the next only if not found in the prior settings).
  - pom.xml file - some configuration details. It is included in the project distribution.
  - Local or user level settings: <user-home>/.m2/settings.xml file and any other file, use with mvn -s option.
  - global settings file - <maven-install>/config/settings.xml
- Note that all settings are not tied to the particular project and instead used across multiple projects. Also, some settings are not to be bundled in the project's package. In these cases, use the user's/local or global settings.
- Use the local/user's settings when the same user is working on multiple projects, which need different settings.
- Use the global settings common across the projects such as proxy settings, dependency maven repositories etc.
- See more details at http://maven.apache.org/settings.html

375. **What do you need while publishing an artifact to a repository?**
- The following 3 things at minimum required:
  - Successful artifact (package jar) generation.
  - Access to the central repository to publish the artifact and should be configured in the settings.xml
  - Internet connection and proxy settings if any needed to be in the settings.xml file.

☐ Run "mvn deploy" command to publish the artifact.

376. How to generate eclipse project files?
☐ To add local repository to Eclipse IDE use command like
mvn -Declipse.workspace="<eclipse-workspace>"
eclipse:add-maven-repo
☐ To convert existing maven project to eclipse project, use
"mvn eclipse:eclipse" command. This process will gener-
ate all the settings required to recognize as eclipse project.
Then simply open this project in the eclipse IDE.
☐ To get help on eclipse plugin use " mvn help:describe -
Dplugin=eclipse" command.

377. How do you generate ANT build files automatically from
existing Maven project?
☐ To generate ant build files, use "mvn ant:ant" command.
After that you can simply do "ant <phase-as-target-
name>" to use with ant.

378. What project files do you check into source code repository?
☐ All the project sources under <project>/src/.., pom.xml
and other related non-binary files would be checked-in.
But not the files in target directory, which contains all dynamically generated files from maven.

379. Do you generate pom.xml and other files again if you accidentally deleted the files?
☐ No, unless it is a new project and not yet checked into
source code repository.
☐ Usually, do the checkout from source code repository.

380. What happens if you accidentally deleted target folder?

☐ The target folder is automatically generated when a maven build phase is executed to keep the classes, packaged jar, test results/reports, site files.

☐ So, simply run "mvn test" or "mvn package" again to get the target folder with required build artifacts.

381. How do you compare Maven with ANT?

☐ Maven and ANT are in similar as build tool/frameworks. Maven and ANT both are extensible through Java programming.

☐ Maven and ANT are different build files and handling of the build lifecycle. Maven uses pom.xml whereas ANT uses build.xml.

☐ Maven follows the convention over the configuration methodology; whereas ANT goes with configuration. Maven project's workspace is simple and same for all projects and whereas ANT projects could be different and need to be designed every time.

☐ Maven's main power is in automatic dependencies and transient dependencies resolution of the project. In ANT, one has to copy and take care of the build files.

☐ Maven's build phases are fixed and automatic whereas in ANT one has to -recreate or duplicate those targets in build files.

☐ Distribution/sharing of maven artifacts is easy and well organized. In ANT, it has to be taken care by build file every time.

☐ Maven has built-in site phase to generate the website automatically whereas ANT doesn't have any and one has to take care in the build file.

☐ The latest projects do prefer Maven than ANT. Also, both can exist and one can call from another build tool.

← End: Skill#11. Maven ←

Good!
Keep going and never give up!!
Please re-read again for more clarity and feel free to contact for help!!!

→ Start: Skill#12. JUnit →

Skill#12. JUnit

The unit testing should be one of core tasks for any Software developer. The JUnit is an old but simple and popular framework for Java projects. This test framework is still being used in many organizations and lot of IDEs support the automatic test code generation and execution. Having JUnit experience is an essential skill for developers.

382. What is JUnit?
- ☐ JUnit is a Unit Testing framework for Java based projects.
- ☐ The framework was developed by Eric Gamma and Kent Beck (Authors in GoF Design Patterns).
- ☐ This framework is a basis for Test Driven Development (TDD) process with xUnit family (like NUnit).
- ☐ It is a very popular framework, which is free and Open Source.
- ☐ It is easy and simple to use and takes less time in writing tests.
- ☐ Most of the IDEs can generate the JUnit tests automatically.
- ☐ The JUnit framework itself is written in Java, and it is a cross platform.

383. What kind of testing framework is it? Who uses it - Developers or QA/QE?
- ☐ JUnit is mainly meant for unit testing and most of the time, it is not used for functional testing.
- ☐ Developers use JUnit framework. The QA automation might not be using this framework as it lacks some of the core integration required features.

384. **Where do you use JUnit?**
☐ JUnit framework is used for developing test cases, tests and test suites for individual modules or classes in a project.
   ☐ Leverage the Java annotations with latest JUnit versions.
   ☐ Used to create assertions for expected result check.
☐ JUnit can be used to running or drive the tests execution as it provides a TestRunner.
☐ JUnit can be used to generate test reports in XML as well as plain text.
☐ JUnit can be worked directly with IDEs (Netbeans, Eclipse, IntelliJ, etc.) and build frameworks such as ANT and Maven.

385. **What are all major versions in JUnit? Which version have you used? Differences between JUnit 4 or 4.x vs. JUnit 3 or 3.x?**
☐ Two major versions - JUnit 4 as the latest and JUnit 3 are available.
☐ JUnit 4 vs. JUnit 3
   ☐ JUnit 4 tests don't need to extend any base class (as it uses Java 5 annotations) whereas JUnit 3 tests should extend Test class.
   ☐ JUnit 4 uses @Before and @After annotations for any method name whereas JUnit 3 test classes should have setUp() and tearDown() methods for any setup or cleanup to be done before running the tests/test methods.
   ☐ JUnit 4 uses @Test annotation to mark any named test methods whereas JUnit 3 test methods should have the naming convention start with a test like testXYZ().
   ☐ JUnit 4 uses @BeforeClass and @AfterClass annotations to mark methods that can be executed only once per class before or after any test methods execution whereas JUnit 3 don't have any equivalent

support.

☐ In JUnit 4, the expected exceptions handling can be done using annotation @Test(expected == Exception.class) whereas in JUnit 3 should be done using regular java try/catch block.

```
try {
    ...
    fail();
} catch (Exception e) { assertTrue(true); }
```

☐ In JUnit 4, the tests timeout period can be set using the timeout attribute of @Test annotation, @Test(timeout = 1000) whereas in JUnit 3, the custom implementation should be done for long running methods and timeouts.

☐ In JUnit 4, tests can be ignored using @Ignore annotation whereas in JUnit 3, custom implementation with TestSuite.

☐ JUnit 4 is the latest and widely used compared to old JUnit 3.

386. **What do you need to start working with JUnit?**

☐ To use JUnit framework, at minimum :have the following

    ☐ Java SE 5 (1.5) or later versions for JUnit4.x

    ☐ junit.jar (pick the latest version) from http://www.junit.org/

☐ To Increase Productivity use the following additional software:

    ☐ Build tools like Ant, Maven, etc.

    ☐ IDEs like Eclipse, Netbeans, IntelliJ, etc.

☐ JUnit API doc from http://junit.sourceforge.net/javadoc/

387. **How to write, compile and execute a simple JUnit test program?**

☐ Create JUnit test class. Here is a sample code, which uses the @Parameterized.Parameters and Junit will automatically initialize the values before invoking the test methods (testSum1() will be executed with collection data returned by testData()).

```java
/**
 * JUnitCheck.java
 *
 */
package com.jd.module1.test;

import static org.junit.Assert.*;

import java.util.Arrays;
import java.util.Collection;

import junit.framework.Assert;
import junit.textui.TestRunner;

import org.junit.After;
import org.junit.AfterClass;
import org.junit.Before;
import org.junit.BeforeClass;
import org.junit.Test;
import org.junit.runner.JUnitCore;
import org.junit.runner.Result;
import org.junit.runner.RunWith;
import org.junit.runner.notification.Failure;
import org.junit.runners.Parameterized;

/**
 * @author Jagadesh Babu Munta
 *
 */
@RunWith (value=Parameterized.class)
public class JUnitCheck {
    int v1, v2 = 0;
    long expected = 0;
```

```
public JUnitCheck(int a, int b, long expected) {
        this.v1 = a;
        this.v2 = b;
        this.expected = expected;
}
/*
 * Fixers
 */
@BeforeClass
public static void completeSetup() {
        System.out.println("Setup for entire test
case...");
}

@Before
public void testSetup() {
        System.out.println("Setup before each test
run...");
}

@AfterClass
public static void completeTearDown() {
        System.out.println("Unsetup for entire test
case...");
}

@After
public void testearDown() {
        System.out.println("Unsetup before each test
run...");
}

@Test
public void testJ() {

}

@Test
```

```java
public void testJ1() {
        String s = "Test JUnit";
        assertEquals(s, "Test JUnit");
        //assertEquals(s, "Test JUni");
}

@Test
public void testJ2() {
        System.out.println("Running testJ2");
        String s = "Test JUnit";
        assertEquals(s, "Test JUn");
}

@Test(timeout=1000)
public void testJLongTime() {
        System.out.println("Running testJLongTime
with long duration");
        while (true);
}

@Test(expected=NullPointerException.class)
public void testJSample() {
        System.out.println("Running testJSample
with NPE");
        String s = null;
        s.toString();
}

@Parameterized.Parameters
    public static Collection testData() {
    return Arrays.asList(new Object[][] {
        { 10, 20, 30 },
        { 0, 0, 0 },
        { -100, 10, -90},
        { Integer.MAX_VALUE, 10, 2147483657L },
        { Integer.MAX_VALUE, Integer.MAX_VALUE,
2*Integer.MAX_VALUE },
        { Integer.MIN_VALUE, Integer.MIN_VALUE,
```

```
        2*Integer.MIN_VALUE }
            });
        }


    @Test
    public void testSum1() {
            System.out.println("Checking
"+v1+"+"+v2+"="+expected+"?");
            long s = v1+v2;
            long s1 = sum(v1,v2);
            System.out.println("Sum is "+s);
            assertEquals(expected, s1);
    }


    @Test
    public void testForOdd() {

    }



    /*
     * API sum method
     */
    public long sum(int a, int b) {
            return a+b;
    }

    /**
     * API method to test given number for odd.
     * @param n
     * @return boolean
     */
    public boolean isOdd(int n) {
            if (n%2 == 0) {
                    return false;
            } else {
                    return true;
            }
```

}

}

☐ Compile:
  javac -d . -cp .;C:\JUnitExamples\junit-
  4.11.jar;C:\JUnitExamples\hamcrest-core-1.3.jar
  JUnitCheck.java

☐ Execute using default runner JunitCore main class:
  java -cp .;C:\Junit\junit-4.11.jar;C:\Junit\hamcrest-
  core-1.3.jar org.junit.runner.JUnitCore com.jd.mod-
  ule1.test.JUnitCheck

388. What are different ways that you can run a JUnit test program?
  ☐ There are 5 ways to execute JUnit tests.
    ☐ JUnitCore default main class - *org.junit.run-*
      ner.JUnitCore
      java -cp .;C:\Junit\junit-
      4.11.jar;C:\Junit\hamcrest-core-1.3.jar
      org.junit.runner.JUnitCore TestClassFullName
    ☐ JUnitCore API in main() method of a test class.
      ☐ See the sample code.
  public static void main(String[] args) {
              Result res = JUnitCore.run-
  Classes(JUnitCheck.class);
              System.out.println("Run
  count:"+res.getRunCount());
              System.out.println("Fail
  count:"+res.getFailureCount());
              System.out.println("Ignore
  count:"+res.getIgnoreCount());
              *System.out.println("*** Failures*
  ***");
              for (Failure f: res.getFailures()) {
              System.out.println(f);

```
        }
            System.out.println("Is Test case
successful?" + res.wasSuccessful());
        }
```

- ☐ ANT
  - Sample build.xml snippet
    ```xml
    <?xml version="1.0" ?>
    <project name="testexamples" default="run">
        <target name="run" description="Running
    junit tests">
            <junit printSummary="true">
            <classpath>
                <pathelement location="${basedir}"/>
                <pathelement location="C:\\Us-
    ers\\Jagadesh Babu
    Munta\\workspace\\bin"/>
            </classpath>
            <formatter type="xml"/>
            <test name="JUnitTestExample1"/>
            <test name="com.jd.module1.test.Jun-
    itCheck"/>
            </junit>
        </target>
    </project>
    ```

- ☐ Maven
  - mvn test
- ☐ IDE (example: Eclipse)
  - Add Junit Library to the project
  - RunAs → Junit Test
  - See the Junit result window and console

389. **How do you run Junit tests from the command line? What do you put in the classpath?**
  - ☐ The command to execute the junit test is as below.

Java –cp junit.jar;hamcrest.jar org.junit.runner.Juni-tCore <testclassname>

☐ Add junit .jar and hamcrest.jar full paths in the java classpath.

390. Does Junit support annotations? Which version?

☐ Yes. Junit4.x supports annotations.

391. Describe the key annotations supported in Junit4?

☐ @Before

     ☐ This annotated method gets executed every time before running any test method. This is like a per method setup. Also executed the super class's @Before method before running in the current class.

☐ @BeforeClass

     ☐ This annotated method get executed once before running any test method. This is like a setup method to create some resources before running the test. Also executed the super class's @BeforeClass method before running in the current class.

☐ @After

     ☐ This annotated method get executed after running each test method. This is like a cleanup method per test. Also executed the super class's @After method after running in the current class.

☐ @AfterClass

     ☐ This annotated method get executed once after running all test methods. This is like a cleanup method to clean earlie resources after running all tests. Also executed the super class's @AfterClass method after running in the current class.

☐ @Test

     ☐ This annotated method indicates it as a test case, and Junit will create an instance of the class and execute this method. Any exceptions thrown from the method will be treated as a failure and if no exceptions, then test is treated as passed.

☐ @Ignore

   ☐ This annotated method indicates that the test should be ignored and disabled from the execution.

392. **What are the differences between Junit3.x and Junit4.x?**

   ☐ See the below table for key differences.

JUnit 3.x	JUnit 4.x
Use test class's base class as *Test-Case*	(no longer necessary)
Use method name as "*setUp*" for setup actions.	Use annotation *@Before* to setup method.
Use method name as "*tearDown*" for cleanup actions.	Use annotation *@After* to cleanup method.
Use test method name starting with test, something like "testXYZ"	Use annotation *@Test* to test methods.
(no equivalent existing)	Use annotation *@BeforeClass* (Once-and-only setUp) to run only once before running any test in the class.
(no equivalent existing)	Use annotation *@AfterClass* (Once-and-only tearDown) to run only once after running all tests.
Expected exceptions testing can be performed as below: try { ... fail() } catch (Exception e) { assertTrue(true) }	Use annotation *@Test(expected == Exception.class)* to check expected exceptions.
Use custom implementation to	Use annotation *@Test(timeout*

handle timeouts for long running methods.	= 1000) for time-out setting to the test method. Timeout is in milliseconds.
Use the custom implementation to ignore test using *TestSuite*	Annotation *@Ignore*

393. Why do you import JUnit assert methods as static? What is its advantage?

☐ Junit provides overloaded assertion methods for all primitives, object types and arrays. The method parameters order is expected value followed by the actual value.

☐ In the test class, do the following static import of Assert class methods so that the assertion method can be directly invoked without the class name reference (i.e., assertEquals() than Assert.assertEquals()).

import static org.junit.Assert.*;

☐ This style helps in avoiding the duplicate code of class name while referencing frequent assertion method names.

394. What is "no runnable methods" exception message? When do you get this?

☐ This exception message raised when no tests found or none of the methods were not marked with @Test in the current JUnit test class.

395. How do you generate a single HTML report from multiple JUnit results xml files?

☐ Using ANT JUnitTask, one can generate the test result xml files.

☐ After that, the ANT JUnitReportTask can be used to merge multiple test results xml files and generate a single html report.

☐ Example:
```
<junitreport todir="./summary">
  <fileset dir="./results">
```

```
<include name="TEST-*.xml"/>
</fileset>
<report format="frames" todir="./summary/html"/>
</junitreport>
```

396. **What happens when a test method or code inside it throws an exception?**
- ☐ The test is marked as a failure whenever an exception threw in the method.

397. **Can a test method contain multiple assertions? What happens if any assertion failed?**
- ☐ Yes. Each test method can contain multiple assertions.
- ☐ If any assertion failed then, the test will be marked as a failure and will not execute statements after that.

398. **What is your strategy to have assertions as one assertion per method or multiple assertions in a test method? Are there any advantages and disadvantages? What is the recommendation?**
- ☐ Writing one assertion per method would cause many simple test cases.
- ☐ Also having too many assertions per method would cause maintenance problems and hard to debug (going through all assertions) if there are any failures.
- ☐ The recommendation is to find the appropriate assertions based on the use case or test scenario under test. Typically, the use case might contain few assertions (maybe 3 or 4 assertions maximum than more than 10), and if there is a large use case, then it can be divided into multiple parts.

399. **How do you create test suites?**
- ☐ In JUnit 4, use the @RunWith and @Suite annotations to create the suite of individual tests.

□ Example: In the below code snippet, LoginTest, UserPro-
fileTest and LogoutTest are the individual test classes and
ProfileTestSuite is the test suite class.

import org.junit.runner.RunWith;
import org.junit.runners.Suite;

@RunWith(Suite.class)
@Suite.SuiteClasses({
  LoginTest.class,
  UserProfileTest.class,
  LogoutTest.class,
})

public class ProfileTestSuite {
  // the class can remain as empty and used only as a
  holder for the above annotations.
}

400. Can you group the JUnit tests like in TestNG?
  □ It is not possible grouping the way in similar to TestNG.
  But one can create different Suites as a group but tedious
  if same Test is there in different groups.
  □ Example snippet as below:
    @RunWith(Suite.class)
    @Suite.SuiteClasses({
      LoginTest.class,
      UserProfileTest.class,
      LogoutTest.class,
    })

401. How do you enable and disable test methods?
  □ Use @Ignore annotation to the test methods that need to
  be ignored.

402. **How do you distinguish a regular Java method vs. a JUnit test method? What are the rules to be followed for a test method?**

☐ The main difference of a JUnit 4 test method with a regular Java method is that JUnit test method has the @Test annotation.

☐ The JUnit test methods should be following the below rules.

   ☐ public java method

   ☐ returning void

   ☐ annotate with @Test in JUnit 4.

403. **Is JUnit a Data Driven framework? How do you write data driven test?**

☐ Yes. JUnit test framework is a data driven framework.

☐ For data-driven, use the @Parameterized.Parameters annotation with a method that returns the Collection object. Also have the parameterized constructor which take the same parameters as in the Parameterized method and initialize with instance variables. JUnit would construct the object and initialize the values. The individual test methods should utilize the instance variables for actual data to be used for the test. The JUnit 4 test class should be annotated with @RunWith(Parameterized.class).

☐ Example:

```
/**
 * ParameterizedTest.java
 *
 */
package com.jd.misc.test;

import static org.junit.Assert.assertEquals;

import java.util.Arrays;
import java.util.Collection;

import org.junit.Test;
```

```java
import org.junit.runner.RunWith;
import org.junit.runners.Parameterized;

/**
 * @author Jagadesh Babu Munta
 *
 */
@RunWith(Parameterized.class)
public class ParameterizedTest {
    int value = 0;
    boolean expectedValue = false;

    public ParameterizedTest(int value, boolean ex-
pectedValue) {
            this.value = value;
            this.expectedValue = expectedValue;

    }

    /*
     * Write a test method
     */
    @Test
    public void testForOdd() {
            boolean actual = isOdd(value);
            assertEquals(value+" is not odd ",ex-
pectedValue, actual);
    }

    @Parameterized.Parameters
    public static Collection data() {
            return Arrays.asList(new Object[][] { {2,
false}, {5, true},
                            {-10, false}, {100, false},
{50,true}});
    }

    /**
```

```
* API method to test given number for odd.
* @param n
* @return boolean
*/
public boolean isOdd(int n) {
    if (n%2 == 0) {
        return false;
    } else {
        return true;
    }
}
}
```

404. Do we need to follow naming rules for test methods in JUnit 4?
   □ No. Method name can be anything as long as it is public void and annotated with @Test.

405. Do you write a test class per a dev class? What is your strategy?
   □ The recommendation is to write a single JUnit test class per product or dev class. It can be executed whenever the prod/dev class changes and also the JUnit test class skeleton can be created automatically with IDEs.

406. What happens if a test method is declared as "private" and also it returns a value rather than void?
   □ The JUnit framework can't recognize and access to execute this test method when the test method is private or returns value.

407. Do you need the main() method in the JUnit test class? Why or why not?
   □ The main() in JUnit test class is not required because JUnit framework's default JUnitCore class will execute

the user JUnit tests.

408. **What is a JUnit Test Fixture? When do you use?**
   ☐ JUnit test fixture is a fixed state of a set of objects to base-line the running tests.
   ☐ These are used for preparing the environment to produce the consistent results.
   ☐ JUnit provided 4 fixture annotations - @Before, @Be-foreClass, @After, @AfterClass

409. **What is the Java package for JUnit? What is the main test runner program class?**
   ☐ The JUnit page is org.junit. And the main runner class is *org.junit.runner.JUnitCore.*

410. **How do you run JUnit tests as a batch without creating explicit suite class creation?**
   ☐ To execute the tests as batch use ANT's <batchtest> task, which defines the tests based on the pattern matching.
   ☐ Example:
   <junit printsummary="yes" haltonfailure="yes">

   ...

   <batchtest fork="yes" todir="${reports.tests}">
   <fileset dir="${src.tests}">
   *<include name="**/*Test*.java"/>*
   *<exclude name="**/AllTests.java"/>*
   </fileset>
   </batchtest>
   </junit>

411. **What are other frameworks in similar to JUnit?**
   ☐ TestNG framework is one of the similar frameworks for Java unit testing. TestNG can also be used for functional and integration testing.

412. **How do you develop the JUnit Tests? Can you explain end to end process for automating these tests?**

☐ The automation process of developing Java-based unit tests using the JUnit 4 framework is as follows.

    ☐ First, start writing a new Java public class with the test scenario name. Let us say, LoginTest for login validation.

        Example:
```
public class LoginTest {


}
```

    ☐ Typically, for a use case, there will be some setup or initialization of resources should be done once before all the tests or test steps automation. For example, Selenium driver object creation for browser automation and setting time waits, etc. For this, I would create a method and will be annotated with @Before.

        Example:
```
@Before
public void setup() {

    driver = new FirefoxDriver();

    ...

}
```

    ☐ Now, let us create the tests. For each test scenario, a separate test method should be created and within the method, all related test steps should be automated. The method should be annotated with @Test.

Example:
> *@Test*
> *public void loginTest() {*
>
>   ....
>
> *}*

☐ Repeat#4 for all test scenarios listed in Test Design Spec.

☐ Later, for unsetup of any resources such as browser close, I would create a method and annotate with @After, which will be executed once after all the test methods executed. For example, Selenium web driver quit.

Example:
> *@After*
> *public void unSetup() {*
>
>   *driver.quit();*
>
>   ...
>
> *}*

☐ The above test class method can be compiled after setting the classpath with JUnit jar files (independently or either through ANT or Maven). Run it using command line or from ANT or Maven.

☐ Once tests are running as expected, make the tests as parameterized to support the Data Driven approach.

☐ For this, use the @Parameterized annotation. Parameters with a method that return the Collection. Also have the parameterized constructor which take the same parameters as in the Parameterized method and initialize with instance variables. JUnit would construct the object and initialize the values. The individual test methods should utilize the instance variables for actual data to be used for the test.

☐ The parameterized method can read the data from

XLS sheet, DB, CSV file, Properties, etc., and supply the data as needed. See the code snippet example at question - "392. How do you write data driven test?"

☐ After executing the tests with JUnit main class, the test results produced and are in summary text or xml format based on the command options.

☐ Once the test run produces expected results, check-in the source code .java and .properties or .xml files or other related files into SCM and then integrated into the Hudson/Jenkins CI.

☐ Finally, schedule the runs on the daily or weekly basis on Jenkins/Hudson CI and get the emails with results. Please monitor and analyze the failures.

← End: Skill#12. JUnit ←

Good!
Keep going and never give up!!
Please re-read again for more clarity and feel free to contact for help!!!

→ Start: Skill#13. TestNG →

Skill#13. TestNG

The TestNG is one of the common framework used across the unit testing, functional testing, and integration (end-to-end) testing. TestNG is being used in most of the recent projects and specifically in Selenium based test projects. Having hands-on with this skill is essential for both developers and QA automation professionals.

413. **What is TestNG framework? what are the key goals with TestNG?**

   □ TestNG stands for Test Next Generation, and it is a popular, free and open-source unit testing framework for Java but aimed at Unit/Functional/Integration level.

   □ It is one of the base frameworks for Test Driven Development and is mainly inspired by JUnit, N-Unit family frameworks.

   □ TestNG introduced Java SE annotations first and more features in the framework compared to JUnit.

   □ TestNG is easy to use and platform independent as it is written in Java.

414. **What are key features of TestNG?**

   □ The below are the key features of TestNG framework.

        □ Supporting Java 5 annotations.

        □ Grouping of multiple tests (say - into different categories like smoke, short, large, etc.).

        □ Dependency among tests or group of tests.

        □ Data Provider to support data driven architecture at the method level.

        □ Flexibility in generating results/reports and invoking the tests.

        □ Nice HTML reporting for results.

        □ Integrated with most of the Java IDEs and also many ways to execute including Maven.

415. What are all required software and libraries to work with TestNG?

- ☐ Below are the minimum required software.
  - ☐ Java 5 (1.5) download JDK or IDE including Java.
  - ☐ TestNG (latest version) – http://testng.org/testng-6.8.zip
- ☐ To Increase Productivity use the following additional software:
  - ☐ Ant
  - ☐ Maven
  - ☐ IDEs
  - ☐ Install Eclipse plugin (Search TestNG in the market-place)

416. What are all different annotations supported by TestNG?

- ☐ The below are the various critical annotations in TestNG.
  - ☐ @BeforeSuite: this annotated method will be run before all tests in this suite.
  - ☐ @AfterSuite: this annotated method will be run after all tests in this suite.
  - ☐ @BeforeTest: this annotated method will be run before any test method belonging to the classes inside the <test> tag is run.
  - ☐ @AfterTest: this annotated method will be run after all the test methods belonging to the classes inside the <test> tag have run.
  - ☐ @BeforeGroups: this configured method will be executed before any test method in the list of groups.
  - ☐ @AfterGroups: this configured method will be executed after all methods in the list of groups.
  - ☐ @BeforeClass: this annotated method will be run before any test method in the current class is invoked.
  - ☐ @AfterClass: this annotated method will be run after all the test methods in the current class
  - ☐ @BeforeMethod: this annotated method will be run before starting (for each) a test (@Test) method.

☐ @AfterMethod: this annotated method will be run after completing (for each) a test method.

☐ @Test: Marks a class or a method as a test.

☐ @DataProvider: Marks a method as supplying data for a test method. The annotated method must return an Object[][].

☐ @Factory: Marks a method as a factory that returns objects that will be used by TestNG as Test.

417. What version of TestNG have you used? What kind of plugins have you used?

☐ TestNG used versions are 6.8.x and 6.9.x.

☐ Maven plugin to run the tests.

☐ IDEs - Eclipse, Netbeans environment.

418. What are the typical TestNG test development steps?

☐ The recommendation is to use Java IDE for making productive Java code development. First, get the installation of the Eclipse and Eclipse plugin (Search TestNG in Eclipse marketplace).

☐ Create a Java project as usual and Create package.

☐ Add the testng.jar (downloaded from testng.org) to the libraries.

☐ Create a new TestNG class in the project src directory (Right click on src, click New, Select Other, Select TestNG class).

☐ Select all annotations to generate the skeleton (At this point you should see the test class). NOTE: refactoring of package directory might be needed due to a bug in the plugin (this was messing up the package name with repeated value).

☐ Complete the test logic (invoke the APIs) and create DataProvider with test data.

☐ Add more assertions based on the test steps in a single test scenario.

☐ Add more test methods (i.e., add more test scenarios)

based on API under test.
☐ Add dependency and grouping of tests as needed.
☐ Now, it is ready to run the tests and can be done using the below steps.
   ☐ Run As -> TestNG test using Eclipse.
   ☐ Make sure expected test result is generated.
☐ Later, manually run using "java org.testng.TestNG" and testng.xml (which has been generated by eclipse).
☐ Repeat the above steps for refactoring and adding more TestNG tests.

419. **How does the report formats look like? Does this generate XML report?**
☐ The default TestNG report is html format, and the xml report is also generated.

420. **How do you execute TestNG tests?**
☐ There are four ways to execute the TestNG tests.
   ☐ IDE: using Eclipse plugin (during the development of tests). See details at
    http://testng.org/doc/eclipse.html
   ☐ Java Command Line: Use the java class, org.testng.TestNG and testng xml (multiple platforms and also integrate into some other program or tools).
    Using TestNG main class example:
    >java -cp ".;C:\testng-6.8\testng-6.8.jar;C:\Users\Jagadesh
    Babu Munta\workspace\bin" org.testng.TestNG
    testng.xml testng1.xml
    NOTE: You can add the above command to batch/shell script
    (say run.bat on windows and execute "run").
   ☐ Programmatically using its main() method using API from TestNG. Useful to create self-contained test execution or a driver.

☐ Using TestNG API

```
/**
 * Main method to run the tests
 * @param args
 */
public static void main(String [] args) {
        TestNG testng = new TestNG();
        testng.setTestClasses(new Class[] {
        TestNGCheck.class,
        MyFirstTestNG.class });
        testng.run();
}
```

☐ Integration with ANT: Use this way to do the regression testing automation.

421. **How do you integrate with ANT?**
   ☐ Define the testng task using TestNGAntTask class in the ANT build.xml.
   ☐ See the below build.xml snapshot.

```
<project name="TestNGExamples" default="run">
    <property name="testclasses.dir" value="C:\\Us-
    ers\\Jagadesh Babu Munta\\workspace\\bin"/>
    <path id="cpath">
            <pathelement location="C:\\testng-
            6.8\\testng-6.8.jar"/>
            <pathelement location="${basedir}"/>
            <pathelement location="C:\\Us-
            ers\\Jagadesh Babu Munta\\work-
            space\\bin"/>
    </path>
    <taskdef name="testng" classpathref="cpath"
    classname="org.testng.TestNGAntTask" />

    <target name="run-group1" description="Running
    group1 tests">
            <testng classpathref="cpath"
```

```
            groups="group1">
            <classfileset dir="${testclasses.dir}" in-
            cludes="**/testng/*.class"/>
            </testng>
    </target>
    <target name="run-group2">
            <testng classpathref="cpath"
            groups="group2">
            <classfileset dir="${testclasses.dir}" in-
            cludes="**/testng/*.class"/>
            </testng>
    </target>
    <target name="run-all">
            <testng classpathref="cpath">
            <classfileset dir="${testclasses.dir}" in-
            cludes="**/testng/*.class"/>
            </testng>
    </target>
    <target name="run" depends="run-group1"/>
</project>
```

422. **What are the steps in writing a data-driven test class with TestNG?**

   □ Data driven test approach is a two-step process as below:
   Step 1) Create a data provider method

   • Return value should be Object[][].

   • Rows indicate number records to use/pass as data to the test method.

   • Columns indicate the number of parameters matching the types of actual test method.

   • The data provider method can be in the same or different class.

   • The data can be read from different test data stores such as CSV, Excel sheet, DB, etc.

   • Syntax
   @DataProvider(name="profiledata")
   public Object [][] getSampleProfiles(){

> *Return new Object [][] {*
>   *{ "UserName1", "user1@com-*
> *pany1.com", "pwd1"},*
>   *{ "UserName2", "user2@com-*
> *pany2.com","pwd2"},*
>   *{ "UserName3", "user3@com-*
> *pany3.com","pwd3"}*
>   *}*
> *}*

- If it is in different class, then the method should be static.

> *public class TestDataProvider {*
> *@DataProvider(name="profiledata")*
> *public static Object [][] getSamplePro-*
> *files(){*
> > *Return new Object [][] {*
> >   *{ "UserName1", "user1@com-*
> > *pany1.com", "pwd1"},*
> >   *{ "UserName2", "user2@com-*
> > *pany2.com","pwd2"},*
> >   *{ "UserName3", "user3@com-*
> > *pany3.com","pwd3"}*
> >   *}*
> *}*
> *}*

Step 2) Use the data provider in the @Test

- Use dataProvider option in the @Test matching the name as data provider method. If it is in different class, then also specify additional dataProvider-Class=<classname.class> option.
- Syntax sample:

> *@Test(dataProvider="profiledata")*
> *public void loginTest(String userName, String*
> *emailId, String pwd){*
> > *//login test*
> *System.out.println("UserName="+userName);*

```
}
```

// If the data provider method is in different class. Note that data provider method should be static if it is in different class.
@Test(dataProvider="profiledata", dataProviderClass=TestDataProvider.class)
public void loginTest(String userName, String emailId, String pwd){
//login test
System.out.println("UserName="+userName);
}

- The above test will run for 3 times as there are 3 records provided by the data provider method.

423. **How do you group the tests?**
   □ There are 3 ways to do the grouping of tests in TestNG.
   □ Through <groups> tag under <suite> or <test> in testng.xml.

   <!DOCTYPE suite SYSTEM "http://testng.org/testng-1.0.dtd" >
   <suite name="TestSuite1" verbose="1">
   <test name="SmokeTests">
   <groups>
   <define name="sanity">
   <include name="functional.sanity"/>
   <include name="system.sanity"/>
   </define>

   <define name="functional.sanity">
   <include name="functional.mod1"/>
   </define>

   <define name="functional">
   <include name="functional.mod1"/>
   <include name="functional.mod2"/>

```
<include name="functional.mod3"/>
</define>

<define name="all">
<include name="sanity"/>
<include name="functional"/>
</define>

<run>
<include name="all"/>
</run>
</groups>

<classes>
<class name="com.jd.TestClass1"/>
</classes>
</test>
</suite>
```

☐ Through groups={} array as @Test parameter in test methods of test class.

    ☐ @Test(groups={"group1","group2","group3",..}) at class level or test method level.

    ☐ This annotated method is going to be in all those groups in the array.

    ☐ A single method can be in different groups.

☐ Groups can be used in the dependency or to execute them directly while running the tests.

424. **How do you set the dependency of test method on groups or other test methods?**

☐ The dependency can be achieved through the below @Test parameters - dependsOnMethods or dependsOnGroups or having both for a test method. Then this method depends on those groups and get executed after running those dependent test methods or test methods in those groups.

- ☐ If dependent methods have failures, then the current method would be marked as SKIP.
- ☐ Examples:
  - ☐ *@Test(dependsOnMethods={"testmethod2", "test-method3"})*
  - ☐ *@Test(dependsOnGroups={"group1","group2"})*
  - ☐ *@Test(dependsOnMethods={..}, @Test(dependsOnGroups={..})*

425. **How do you enable and disable the tests?**
- ☐ To enable, set the enabled parameter in @Test to true to set all methods in the class or at test method.

  @Test(enabled=true)
- ☐ To disable, set the enabled parameter in @Test to false to set all methods in the class or at test method.

  @Test(enabled=false)

426. **What is testng xml? How do you set the test suites and test classes?**
- ☐ The testng.xml is the configuration file for TestNG test/testsuite and is required for running TestNG tests.
- ☐ The test classes and groups and dependencies to be added in the testng.xml
- ☐ Example:

  <!DOCTYPE suite SYSTEM "http://testng.org/testng-1.0.dtd">

  <suite name="MyTestSuite1" verbose="1">
  <test name="MyTest1">
  <classes>
  <class name="Testclass1" />
  <class name="Testclass2" />
  <class name="Testclass3" />
  </classes>
  </test>

```
<test name="MyTest2">
 <classes>
  <class name="org.jd.mod1.TestClass1"/>
  <class name="org.jd.mod1.TestClass2"/>
  <class name="org.jd.mod2.TestClass2"/>
 </classes>
</test>
</suite>
```

427. **Can you run multiple testng xml files at a time? How?**
   - ☐ Yes. Supply the testng.xml files as arguments to the TestNG class.
   - ☐ Example to execute tests in testng.xml, testng1.xml and testng2.xml files.
   java -cp ".;C:\testng-6.8\testng-6.8.jar;C:\Users\JagadeshBabu Munta\workspace\bin"
   org.testng.TestNG testng.xml testng1.xml testng2.xml

428. **What is the default report directory? What is default report format?**
   - ☐ The default report directory is test-output and can be changed with -d <reportdirectory> of the command line of testng tests execution using java TestNG class.
   - ☐ The default reports include xml and html formats.

429. **What is the TestNG API java package?**
   - ☐ The Java package for TestNG API is org.testng.

430. **What are different assertions supported by TestNG Assert?**
   - ☐ The org.testng.Assert class defined various assertion methods with primitive data types and objects.
     - ☐ assertEquals(<primitive-type> actual,<primitive-type> expected); // asserts that actual and expected primitive values are equal.
     - ☐ assertEquals(<primitive-type> actual,<primitive-

type> expected, String message); // asserts that actual and expected primitive values are equal and display message.

☐ assertEquals(Object actual, Object expected); // asserts that given actual and expected objects are equal.

☐ assertEquals(Object actual, Object expected, String message);

☐ assertNotEquals(<primitive-type> actual,<primitive-type> expected); // asserts that given actual and expected primitive values are not equal

☐ assertNotEquals(<primitive-type> actual,<primitive-type> expected, String message); // asserts that actual and expected are not equal and display message.

☐ assertNotEquals(Object actual, Object expected); // asserts that given actual and expected objects are not equal.

☐ assertNotEquals(Object actual, Object expected, String message);

☐ assertNull(Object actual); // assert that actual object is null.

☐ assertNotNull(Object actual); // assert that actual object is not null.

☐ assertTrue(boolean actual); // assert that actual condition is true

☐ assertFalse(boolean actual); // assert that actual condition is false

☐ assertSame(Object actual, Object expected, String message);

431. How do you import methods than classes in TestNG class (as an example for assertEquals())?
   ☐ Use the static import in the TestNG test class like below.
   import static org.testng.Assert.*;

432. What are the similarities between TestNG and JUnit 4?

☐ Both supports Java-based unit testing and have test suites hierarchy.

☐ Both supports annotations.

☐ Both supports data-driven approach.

☐ Both supports tests reporting

☐ Both can be executed using IDE, Main program, Programmatic, ANT, Maven.

☐ Both are popular and open-source frameworks.

433. What are the differences between JUnit4 and TestNG? Which one do you use? Why?

☐ Comparing TestNG with JUnit, TestNG has more features and suitable for functional and integration testing in addition to unit testing. Thereby TestNG is preferred to use for QA automation.

☐ The below table summarizes the major differences.

JUnit4	TestNG
Mainly aimed at Unit Testing	Mainly aimed at Unit, Functional and Integration
No direct grouping of tests supported.	Grouping of tests supported.
No dependency between the tests.	Dependency between tests can be done.
Data driven is achieved with Parameterization at class level only.	Data driven is achieved with DataProvider at method also.
Output can be plain and xml	Output is html and xml by default.
Default reporting is plain text.	Default reporting is html web page (pretty).
Minimal annotations are available.	More annotations and flexibility
Package: org.junit.*	Package: org.testng.*
No need to have a separate xml for test suites configuration.	TestNG should have the testng xml file.

← End: Skill#13. TestNG ←

Good!
Keep going and never give up!!
Please re-read again for more clarity and feel free to contact for help!!!

→ Start: Skill#14. Hudson/Jenkins →

Skill#14. Hudson/Jenkins

In the Continuous Integration (CI) category, Jenkins/Hudson play a vital role with automated jobs for creating the product builds/bundles and also end-to-end regression test cycles. The Hudon/Jenkins functionality is extendable with plugins, and many of the plugins are already available. It is a widely used tool. Thereby having this skill by both developers and QA engineers gives a real strength.

434. What is meant by continuous integration (CI)? What are the key benefits of CI?
- ☐ CI is the software for automating the process of code integration.
- ☐ CI is continuous – 24x7
- ☐ CI is a way to streamline the development process.
- ☐ CI takes from Dev code to Testing to Production.
- ☐ CI dashboards will show the presence of process and act as a communication tool.
- ☐ CI monitors the version control system for changes.
- ☐ CI is required to maintain the code health.
- ☐ CI provides quick feedback on the product development.
- ☐ CI is a collaboration tool.
- ☐ CI allows 1-click trigger and rapid cycles.
- ☐ CI is used by development, release, and testing team to do processes automation completely.

435. What are different CI tools/software?
- ☐ Some of the free and open source CI tools are as below.
  - ☐ Hudson CI
  - ☐ Jenkins CI
  - ☐ Buildbot CI
  - ☐ Strider CD
  - ☐ Travis CI

☐ CruiseControl
☐ Go CD
☐ Tinderbox
☐ Gump
☐ Commercial tools
☐ Bamboo
☐ TeamCity

436. **Describe Hudson and Jenkins software?**

☐ Hudson is an open Source software from Oracle (originally from Sun Microsystems). It has been started as a hobby project by a Sun engineer (Kohsuke) in 2004 and full time in 2008 released as Open source project (under java.net). By 2010 it got a market share of ~70%. The source code has been hosted at https://github.com/hudson.

☐ Jenkins is open source CI, forked from Hudson (early 2011) by the community. Source is hosted at https://github.com/jenkinsci/jenkins/

☐ Both Jenkins and Hudson are Written in Java

☐ Typically used for java projects but can be used for other environments such as ruby/groovy/grails.NET

☐ Key advantages

• Easy to learn
• Extensive plugins support
• Larger Community

437. **What is the difference between Hudson and Jenkins? How to choose which one?**

☐ Hudson and Jenkins both are open source CI tools with the same original architecture and similar code base.

☐ Jenkins is having a number of plugins and very active community compared to Hudson now.

☐ If old projects already in Hudson, then better to continue.

☐ Else starting with Jenkins itself is fine as an active forum with a lot of plugins.

☐ In future, plugins standard might be coming with JSR330.

☐ Familiar with one tool means, both of them mostly know to you. Mostly, the plugins might differ in future.

438. How do you setup Jenkins?

☐ For Jenkins, multiple binary packages are available at http://jenkins-ci.org and download the appropriate binary file and follow instructions.

☐ One simple package is war, jenkins.war file and can be executed on any platform. The jenkins.war file contains the self-contained http (bundled jetty server) for Jenkins CI server. It can be executed independently or deploy on any web application server.

☐ To start the jenkins, just do the below step.

    ☐ java -jar jenkins.war

NOTE:

The default extraction directory is ~/.jenkins. If a different directory is required, then set JENKINS_HOME=<dir> before running above step.

For running background run as below so that process can run without closing when terminal window is terminated.

nohup java -jar jenkins.war &

☐ Verify the installation by browsing to the jenkins master URL - http://localhost:8080/

439. How do you change the default http 8080 port while starting the Jenkins?

☐ Use --port portnumber option in the Jenkins startup command to change the default port to the given portnumber.

440. What is a jenkins job? How do you create jobs in Jenkins? Who creates the Jenkins job?

☐ Jenkins job is the build process automation activity on the Jenkins master dashboard created by the user. It is customizable based on the desired way to execute the steps.

Jenkins master is going to execute or delegate the job execution to the slaves. It is only to way to get the CI process through Jenkins/Hudson.

☐ A typical jenkins job will have the basic build steps flow using the dashboard UI.

    ☐ Specify build name and description.

    ☐ Parameterize the build to accept input parameters.

    ☐ Checkout workspace from SCM

    ☐ Execute ant targets or maven goals or shell script

    ☐ Copy/archive the build artifacts like .war or some reports.

    ☐ Automatic execution at period times by schedule job like daily @7am, Sunday @6am

    ☐ Attach the job to a pool of slaves.

    ☐ Configure the email with status or summary results as build artifacts.

☐ To create the Jenkins jobs, one has to connect to the Jenkins master dashboard using the credentials if the Jenkins is secured and then follow similar to the below steps.

    ☐ Click on New Item

    ☐ Enter the job name and select one of the type of jobs. Preferred is the Freestyle project where one can use shell script or command like for build step.

    ☐ Fill the job configuration form and save it. Click on ? for help that particular field in the form. Click again ? to make it disappear.

        • Description and other parameters or concurrent builds or restricting to slave labels.

        • Advanced Project options

        • Source Code Management

        • Build Triggers

        • Build step -- add one or more of the below.

            o Execute Shell : preferred or easy way to handle

            o (or) Invoke ANT

            o (or) Invoke top level maven goals

            o (or) Execute windows batch command

- Post-build actions step - add
  - Archive artifacts : to save the required summary files or logs or any build artifacts like .zip/.tar/.war files.
  - E-mail notification : to send the build status in email.
  - NOTE: Install Email Extension plugin, which has more flexibility to do custom email with attachments/body/html content.
- ☐ Edit the configuration if changes needed later.
- ☐ Also select the options based on the required installed plugins.
- ☐ All Dev, RM, and QA/QE engineers would create and run the jobs on separate Jenkins or a common Jenkins master.

441. How long does it take to create a simple job for running your tests?

- ☐ Typically, the Jenkins job creation is done through master dashboard web UI wizard filling, and it will be less than 15mins if the build steps are already available to execute as CLI/shell script.

442. How do you schedule and/or run the builds?

- ☐ The execution of the jobs can be performed mainly two ways.
  - ☐ Build on-demand (whenever needed): Just click the build button and file the input parameter values and submit.
  - ☐ Build periodically: Based on the job scheduled time, the build automatically triggered with default parameter values.

443. **How do you schedule the build periodically? What field values set to schedule at 11pm on every day?**

☐ For periodic scheduling of jobs, select "Build periodically" option in the job configuration and enter the unix cron job format of scheduled time in the "Schedule text area".

☐ The format is having 5 fields: minutes hour day month day-of-week

- minutes : 0 to 59
- hour : 0 to 23
- day of the month : 1-31
- month : 0-11
- day-of-week : 0-7 (0 and 7 are Sundays)

☐ Please note on the below wild or ranges for any fields as below.

- * means any value matched.
- range : m-n
- m-n/x or */x : intervals of x
- multiple values: comma (,) separated

☐ To run a job @11pm every day, enter below in the time text.

0 23 * * *

444. **How to clean up old builds and workspace?**

☐ The builds use a lot of disk space as the jobs executed continuously. To save the space, it is required to limit or delete the builds.

☐ To delete old builds automatically, edit the job configuration, select option "Discard Old Builds". One can limit this by setting the number of builds or number of days.

☐ To delete the workspace, click on the Workspace link and then click Wipe Out Current Workspace.

445. **How do you configure the SCM (SVN) in a job?**

☐ The source code repository configuration is one of the key configuration for the build process. In the job configuration (to get to this, click on "Configure" link of the job), then go to Source Code Management section. Next, Select repository type (say "Subversion") and enter the Repository URL. If Git or new SCM is required, then install the appropriate Jenkins plugin.

☐ Please note that clicking on "?" (right side of the fields), would display the help on that field.

446. **How to install a Jenkins plugin?**
☐ From the Jenkins master dashboard UI, perform the below steps.
  ☐ Go to Manage Jenkins → Manage Plugins → Available tab → In Filter text, enter the name and you can see the plugin.
  ☐ Click and choose the appropriate button to install only or install and restart at the same time.
☐ Please note that most of the plugins will be effective only after Jenkins server restart. So, perform the restarting of Jenkins once all required plugins have been installed.

447. **What do you need to do if Git source code is needed in Jenkins?**
☐ By default, Git SCM is not available in Jenkins. To get Git, install the GitHub or related Git plugin before using the Git in the Job configuration.
☐ Once installed, then you can see Git under Source Code Management.

448. **What is the Jenkins dashboard? And what actions you can perform?**
☐ The Jenkins dashboard is what you will see when you first login to the master URL.
☐ The below functions can be found on the Master dashboard right side of the page.
  ☐ List of Views (All and other custom view tab names)

☐ List of jobs
☐ For each job, you can find the below as a table.
- Job name
- Status (S)
- Weather report (W) to show aggregated status
- Last Success time
- Last Failure time
- Last duration
- Build execution icon (does not appear when the job is disabled).

☐ The left side, you can find the menu and list of builds running.

449. How do you configure ANT build file and target to be executed?

☐ In the Jenkins job configuration (edit the job if already exists or else during the first time creation), add the "Build" step as "Invoke ANT". Then enter the ANT target name. Also, change the build file name if the corresponding build file is different than default build.xml.

450. How do you archive the results? And send the build artifacts or results in an email?

☐ The build artifacts should be saved and notified in the email to the stakeholders.
☐ For this, edit the job configuration and perform the below actions.

☐ Add the Post-build action step as "Archive build artifacts" and enter the files/directories to archive. Files are with reference to workspace directory (click ? for help).

☐ Add E-mail notification Post-build action step for email.

☐ NOTE: Install Editable email plugin, which has more flexibility to create the email with attachments of body content in text/html format.

☐ Also, make sure the global settings or email plugin settings of Jenkins have the mail server and email account configuration.

451. What happens when multiple jobs or same job scheduled multiple times?

☐ When multiple builds from different jobs triggered, then those jobs get scheduled for runtime if slaves are free. Otherwise, the later build in the order will wait for the next available slave unless more executors configured in the slave nodes. You will see message "(pending - Waiting for next available executor)" in the left panel.

☐ If the same job is triggered while its build is already running, then the build will wait (you will see the message "pending - Build #? is already in progress (ETA:..)") until the previous build is completed. The parallel execution is allowed and you can see the multiple running jobs if "Execute concurrent jobs if necessary" option is selected in the job configuration.

☐ To configure the parallel builds, edit the job configuration and select "Execute concurrent jobs if necessary" option. Then enter the total number (like 5 or more) based on the slaves capacity or master node.

452. How to see the console output while a job is running?

☐ It is common to see the job console output during the initial stages of the job stabilization and also during the build failure analysis. The console output gives the output of the commands being executed.

☐ For this, go to the particular job (click the job name link) and see the build history on the left panel. Then, click on the specific build number (link) and after that click on the "Console Output" link or the progress bar link. That will give the last part of the console output if the console output is too big. To see the new full console output, click on the Full Log link at the top of the page.

453. How do you configure JDK, ANT, Maven in Jenkins?
- ☐ To make the common configuration across the Jenkins, then System configuration should be modified.
- ☐ Below is the sequence of steps to configure JDK/ANT/Maven or other like mail server etc.
    - ☐ Go to Manage Jenkins link on the Jenkins dashboard.
    - ☐ Click on Configure System link
    - ☐ Add JDK and configure the path/install.
    - ☐ Add Ant and configure the path/install.
    - ☐ Add Maven and configure the path/install.

454. How does one can extend the Jenkins functionality?
- ☐ The Jenkins has been designed to extend the functionality using the plugins. These plugins can do specialized tasks. In summary, the plugins are the heart of Jenkins and one can extend the functionality through new plugins. Jenkins provides plugin Java API to create new plugins and then install it to get the functionality.

455. How many plugins are there in Jenkins? Can you list some?
- ☐ There are more than 600+ plugins in Jenkins. See the of the plugins at https://wiki.jenkins-ci.org/display/JEN-KINS/Plugins
- ☐ Some of the useful plugins are like below.
    - ☐ Email Extension Plugin
    - ☐ Groovy Plugin
    - ☐ S3 publisher plugin
    - ☐ Amazon EC2 plugin

456. How do you get the help while creating job?
- ☐ In the job configuration, the context sensitive help can be seen. By clicking on the "?" link that is visible on the side

of the form-field would give more help. Clicking it again will minimize or close the help part.

457. How do you do distributed builds? What are Jenkins master and slave nodes?

☐ Jenkins Master is the Jenkins installation machine where the jobs have been created, configured and scheduled.

☐ Slave or node is the worker machine. On this machine, the Jenkins agent is going to be executed and which then run the project as delegated by the master. The slave nodes are your test execution nodes where different OSes will be installed as required.

☐ Based on the client needs (like browser types, operating systems, JDK versions, etc.), different slaves would be prepared and added to Jenkins master as slaves. The slaves would be given labels (names), and the same label would be given to all slave if pooling or grouping of slaves needed.

☐ The jobs would be restricted (in the job configuration) to execute on slave nodes by entering the label.

☐ Please see more details at https://wiki.jenkins-ci.org/display/JENKINS/Distributed+builds

☐ Setup details at https://wiki.jenkins-ci.org/display/JENKINS/Step+by+step+guide+to+set+up+master+and+slave+machines

← End: Skill#14. Hudson/Jenkins ←

Good!
Keep going and never give up!!
Please re-read again for more clarity and feel free to contact for help!!!

→ Start: Skill#15. Web Applications Testing and Selenium →

Skill#15. Web Applications Testing and Selenium

The Selenium is a browser-based website testing automation framework. Many of the organizations need this skill to create automated test suites going through the browser. This framework acts as a remote to the browser. The selenium automation hands-on experience is a must for QA automation engineers.

458. What is the Web Application/UI testing means to you?
Web UI testing is the testing of web pages (html elements), URL links, web contents and resources for a given website that can be accessible with a browser. It should be tested for functional and integration with an end-to-end flow of use cases. In specific, the below are the checks:
□ Check for correct page titles
□ Check for expected page content
□ Check the images properly displayed
□ Check for any broken hyperlinks
□ Check for submission and cancel of forms and tab navigation
□ Validation of all input fields
□ Check for proper page navigation
□ Check for any tabular data with proper headings and data columns
□ Check for frames switch and navigation to windows
□ Check for alerts and popup dialogs
□ Check for mouse position appropriately in a given page especially in the forms
□ Check for any ajax functionality such as auto completion/suggestion
□ Check for any background event handling, like bulk report generation or asynchronous events
□ Check for any composite UI components such as drag-and-drop and adobe flash etc.

☐ Check for any other web application features such as usability, performance, and errors or exceptions in the server logs.

459. **What are the key challenges in Web UI testing?**
The below are some of the challenges with web UI automation testing.

☐ Mimic the real user interaction with the universal client, browser.

☐ Cross-browser testing with many browsers (Firefox, Chrome, IE, Safari, Opera, etc.).

☐ Test coverage for many platforms (Windows, Linux, Unix, Mac, iOS, Android, etc.).

☐ Modern Rich UI such as Ajax requests, custom composite components (like JQuery) testing.

☐ The load is not much predictable and should mimic to find bottlenecks with web apps. Different parts of the World would join at different timings.

460. **What automation framework(s) have you used?**

☐ Test automation framework is the software that supports the test development, test execution driver/harness and test results reporting.

☐ Some of the common Java based software testing and automation frameworks, tools are as below:

    ☐ JUnit, a default Unit test framework is used for developing simple unit level and independent tests with assertions and test report. It is simple and easy.

    ☐ TestNG, a Unit and integration test framework used along with Selenium to automate the web apps tests. It provided data-driven capabilities with DataProvider class, which can be applied to the method or test level. Also used for covering integration scenarios by grouping and also adding the dependencies between the test methods.

    ☐ Selenium Webdriver framework has been used for

15. Web Applications Testing and Selenium

automating the browser-based user functionally, and integration uses cases or flows across multiple browsers.

☐ ANT is used for automating the build system for the test environment, which includes Java code compilation, setup of the environment, execution of tests, report generation and archiving the results.

☐ Maven is used for automating the build system with dependency resolution of various third party and common internal libraries.

☐ Jenkins is used for continuous integration with periodically and also the on-demand execution of regression tests.

461. What is Selenium and why do we use? Any alternatives?
Selenium is an open source framework to automate the browser actions to mimic the end user browsing operations. In fact, it is a simple robot for the browser. Selenium itself is a set of tools and APIs. The major components Selenium IDE, Selenium Remote Control, Selenium WebDriver and Selenium Grid.

462. What are the differences between Selenium IDE, Selenium RC, Selenium1.0, Selenium2.0, WebDriver?

• Selenium IDE is a Firefox add-on that facilitates the development of tests using the recording of web events. The overall mode of automation is record and playback. Also, it supports to export the tests into different languages like Java, Ruby, etc. The IDE store tests in html report with a table in 3 columns named selenese command, target, and value. The tests can be loaded back and re-run again. The major advantage of IDE is its simplicity and no programming skill is required.

• Selenium RC is the Remote Control and also called as Selenium 1.0. The RC is the first Selenium API version with

Selenium server running on a separate machine and the framework API interacts with Server, which in turn interacts with the Browser. RC uses JavaScript to interact with browser's DOM and perform the actions. In RC, the functionality limited by the JavaScript. The major drawback of RC is its slowness as there is no native & direct control of the browser.

- Selenium WebDriver is also commonly referred as Selenium 2. WebDriver is the new Selenium API that natively controls the browser. The WebDriver APIs are available in different languages like Java, Ruby, etc. The WebDriver is much faster, simpler and it overcomes the limitations of RC as there is no need for a separate server. The WebDriver is like a complete robot for the browser. Also, WebDriver can run the existing RC code with few migration changes.

- In summary, Selenium 1.0 (RC) + WebDriver = Selenium 2.0

- The current trend is to automate Web UI with WebDriver APIs. The Selenium design patterns like PageObject, and BotStyle design patterns are widely used in the automation. Using IDE, one can automate simple static websites without much programming effort but dynamic sites are hard to maintain with IDE.

463. What Selenium versions and drivers you had used?
- ☐ The latest used Java based WebDriver version is 2.48.2 and also used 2.45 version before. See the current latest drivers at Selenium download page: http://www.seleniumhq.org/download/.
- ☐ The latest used IDE version is 2.9.0 and also used 2.0 version earlier. See IDE releases at http://release.seleniumhq.org/selenium-ide/.

464. How to do you develop automated tests for a given web site? Explain end-to-end process flow.

☐ First, identify the web pages to be tested, the pages navigation and use cases/user flows to test.

☐ Check the HTML pages design and select the best Selenium WebDriver locator strategy such as based on ids or names or xpath or cssselector or any other. All locators can be kept in a separate file like .properties so that it is easy to maintain the changes when UI changes happen.

☐ Next, create one PageObject class per page (following PageObject design pattern) and have the methods corresponding to the services or functionality provided by that page. These Page Objects are the common classes used by the actual test classes. Also, reference the locators from a properties file instead of hard-coded in the test or PageObject.

☐ Create common helper classes to abstract the common actions (following BotStyle design pattern) to leverage the code further.

☐ Using TestNG test framework, create test classes by including each test method per test scenario. Please note Selenium itself doesn't provide any test framework and instead browser controlling API.

☐ Make sure the test data is data-driven, which is automatically populated by writing the DataProvider methods or separate DataProvider class to read from .csv or .json or .xml files.

☐ Integrate with ANT or Maven to build the tests and execute as the command line.

☐ Finally, setup a Jenkins/Hudson CI job for daily or on-demand runs for regressions.

☐ Please note that the test machines or slaves should have the Graphics support (like VNCServer) to bring up the browser. For this, execute VNCServer like software, and set the display numbers.

465. **Can you briefly explain on how to write a simple Selenium test?**

☐ Using Java IDE (Eclipse/Netbeans etc.), create a TestNG test class. In this class, do the following at high level.

☐ To open the browser, simply create the WebDriver object for the specific browser under test. For this, in @Before-Class annotated method of TestNG class, add code similar to below.

   ☐ Firefox browser (using Firefox driver, which is included in the Selenium WebDriver):

   FirefoxBinary fb = new FirefoxBinary("path to browser executable"); FirefoxDriver driver = new FirefoxDriver(fb,null);
   //(or)
   WebDriver driver = new FirefoxDriver(fb,null); // set to interface type

   ☐ Chrome browser (using Chrome driver, which is not included in the Selenium WebDriver jar and needs to be downloaded separately - third party driver):

   System.setProperty("webdriver.chrome.driver", "path to driver executable");
   ChromeDriver driver = new ChromeDriver();
   // (or)
   WebDriver driver = new ChromeDriver(); // set to interface type

   ☐ IE specific (using IE driver, which is not included in the Selenium WebDriver jar and needs to be downloaded separately - third party driver):

   System.setProperty("webdriver.ie.driver", "path to driver exe");
   InternetExplorerDriver driver = new InternetExplorerDriver();

///(or)
WebDriver driver = new InternetExplorer-
Driver(); // set to interface type

☐ For each test scenario, create a @Test annotated method
and have the similar code as below.
  ☐ To open the URL, invoke get() method on the
  driver object.

driver.get("url");

  ☐ To locate particular HTML DOM element(s), use
  the findBy methods with appropriate locators
  (By.id() or By.name() etc).

WebElement element = driver.findByxxx(By.xxx);

  ☐ To add explicit wait for the visibility of elements
  or with expected conditions to be met, use the
  WebDriverWait object similar to below code snippet.

WebDriverWait wdw = new WebDriver-
Wait(driver,10);
wdw.until(ExpectedConditions.presenceOfEle-
mentLocated(By.id("username"))); //this one is
same functionality
wdw.until(ExpectedConditions.elementToBeClick-
able(By.id("username"))); //element displayed
and enabled

  ☐ To perform specific actions like click, enter text,
  etc. on elements found in the above like buttons,
  form text input fields, etc., call the appropriate
  methods on WebElement object.

element.xxx();
Example: *element.sendKeys("...");*

☐ Then, perform the assertions based on the actions as above to complete the test scenario (validate if proper text found or no exceptions etc.)

☐ Add other test code similar to above for related steps in the current test scenario.

☐ To close the browser windows, call close() or quit() methods on the driver object in the @AfterClass annotated method of the TestNG class.

driver.close(); //to close the current/main window
driver.quit(); // to close all windows associated with driver

☐ After adding the base test methods, create the dependencies and grouping among the test methods in the TestNG class.

☐ Add the data-driven support for all test data to the above test methods.

☐ Finally, integrate the test classes with ANT/Maven and then host the jobs on Jenkins/Hudson for regression testing.

466. What are the different web elements that you can find from Selenium and the list of actions performed?

☐ Most of the Web Elements can be accessed from Selenium API on the Web pages. Some of those include links, buttons, text fields, text area, form fields, select, etc. of HTML elements, nested elements or any HTML DOM element.

☐ The following action methods can be invoked on the WebElement. See the WebElement API Javadoc for more details.

  ☐ clear(): If the element is a text entry element, then this will remove the value.

  ☐ click(): Clicks this element.

  ☐ sendKeys(): Use this method to type the value.

☐ submit(): If this current element is a form or an element within a form, then this simulates the form submission.

☐ findElement(By by): Finds the first WebElement using the given By locator.

☐ findElements(By by): Find all elements within the current context using the provided By locator.

☐ getAttribute(name): Get the value of a given name attribute of the element.

☐ getCssValue(propertyName): Gets the value of a given CSS property.

☐ getLocation(): Gets the location w.r.t top left-hand corner of the rendered element.

☐ getSize(): Gets the width and height of this element.

☐ getTagName(): Gets the tag name of the element.

☐ getText(): Gets the visible (i.e. not hidden by CSS) innerText of this element, including sub-elements without any leading or trailing whitespace.

☐ isDisplayed(): Checks if this element is displayed or not.

☐ isEnabled(): Checks if this element is enabled and return true for everything but disabled input elements.

☐ isSelected(): Checks if this element is selected or not.

467. How does the page loading happen in WebDriver? How long does the test code to wait?

☐ The WebDriver itself would wait for the page to load automatically. There is no need to wait explicitly for the page to be loaded.

☐ For particular element(s)'s visibility or wait for expected conditions, use an explicitWait approach or implicit wait not to throw the NoSuchElement exception immediately while finding the elements.

468. What are different WebElement locators? How do you find those elements? What tools or strategies do you use?

☐ The general API usage for the web element locator is as below.

WebElement e = driver.findElement(By.xx("yyyy"));
List<WebElement> es = driver.findElements(By.xx("yyyy"));

☐ There are about 9 locators (By.xxx) available and see their usage snippets.

   ☐ ByID in the DOM

      ● *WebElement e = driver.findElement(By.id("username"));*

   ☐ By Name in DOM

      ● *WebElement e = driver.findElement(By.name("login"));*

   ☐ By Xpath in DOM

      ● *WebElement e = driver.findElement(By.xpath("//a[1]"));*

   ☐ By CSS Class Name in DOM

      ● *WebElement e = driver.findElement(By.className("small"));*

      ● *List<WebElement> e = driver.findElements(By.className("large"));*

   ☐ By Tag Name

      ● *WebElement frame = driver.findElement(By.tagName("iframe"));*

   ☐ By Link Text or anchor text in DOM

      ● *WebElement e = driver.findElement(By.LinkText("Contact"));*

   ☐ By Partial Link Text or partial anchor text in DOM

      ● *WebElement e = driver.findElement(By.partialLinkText("Selenium"));*

   ☐ By CSS Selectors

      ● *WebElement e = driver.findElement(By.cssSelector("#id.class"));*

15. Web Applications Testing and Selenium

- *Webelement e = dirver.findEle-*
  ment(By.cssSelector("[name*=dy-
  namic]"));
☐ By JavaScript function to return the element
   from DOM
- *WebElement element = (WebElement)((Ja-*
  vascriptExecutor)driver).executeScript("re-
  turn $('.cheese')[0]);
☐ Related to tooling/strategy on ease of identifying the elements using locators (especially xpath, id, names and
   other attributes, etc.), use FireBug and FirePath add-ons
   on Firefox browser. It is easy to find the elements and navigate the objects in the DOM by clicking on the desired
   HTML element on the page. Using FirePath, the XPath is
   automatically determined by the plugin, and also it can
   locate the element, if the XPath expression is entered. Using FireBug, the JavaScript debugging can be done, and
   also URLs/Headers can be identified.

469. How to maximize the browser window?
☐ The API to maximize the window is
   driver.manage().window().maximize();

470. How to switch between windows and frames?
☐ To switch a window (for the window name, look for target
   attribute in html), use the API as below.
   driver.switchTo().window("window-name");
☐ (or) navigate through each window as below.
   for (String handle : driver.getWindowHandles()) {
   driver.switchTo().window(handle);
   }
☐ To switch to a frame, use the below API.
   driver.switchTo().frame("frame-name");
☐ (or) to switch subframe in a framename, use below code
   snippet.
   driver.switchTo.frame("framename.0.child");

471. **What are the challenges that you had faced with Selenium automation?**

□ The following are some of the problems observed during the automation of Web UI tests:

   i. NoSuchElementFoundException while finding the elements (typically in the different network bandwidths): The solution is to set proper wait conditions before locating the elements than just adding wait times. Also, adjust the max timeout periods. Use explict wait like WebDriverWait.until (ExpectedConditions.presenceOfElementLocated())

   ii. StaleElementException: Many times in getting this exception during the navigation of elements. This exception is because of cache clearance. The solution is to find the elements again by catching the StaleElementException.

   iii. Locators identification for the dynamically generated IDs: The solution is to use xpath/css in relative to stable elements in the UI.

   iv. Cross browser issues: The solution is to adjust the locators as xpath or css based on the reliable test results among different browsers (like firefox, IE, chrome). For example, the Firefox is good at xpath and IE is good at css.

   v. Sometimes, getting unreliable actions like click() operation doesn't actually click the element. To mitigate this, add retries and timeout (put a loop and make sure click is indeed performed).

472. **How do you test Ajax requests?**

□ Ajax stands for Asynchronous JavaScript and XML. Using the Ajax technique, the elements in the web page refreshed without reloading/refreshing of the entire page.

□ The Ajax elements are going to be identified as usual with right locators, but these must have appropriate wait conditions with timeouts before locating the elements. Otherwise, these elements get refreshed asynchronously without waiting for the entire page reload, and NoSuchElement exception raised.

☐ For example, to wait for the presence of the element and timeout after 10secs, see the following snippet.

WebDriverWait wdw = new WebDriverWait(driver, 10);

wdw.until(ExpectedConditions.presenceOfElementLocated(By.id("username")));

473. **What is implicit wait and explicit wait?**

☐ The wait time is the elapsed time to be set before continuing to the next step (such as action on the web element) in the automation flow so that expected behavior can achieved.

☐ In Selenium, use either implicit wait or explicit wait techniques during the automation.

☐ Selenium's Implicit wait usage as below.

    i. Use the API with required timeout period.

    driver.manage.timeouts().implicitlyWait(timeout-period, TimeUnit.SECONDS);

    ii. Driver will not throw NoSuchElementException immediately if the element is not available and waits until element is found or timeout period reached (say for 10 secs as timeout period.)

    iii. The implicit wait is applied for entire life of webdriver.

    iv. Recommended to use this immediately after the driver creation (in @BeforeClass annotated method).

☐ Selenium's Explicit waits (for Ajax calls) usage is as below.

    i. Use the API with required expected condition.

15. Web Applications Testing and Selenium

> *WebDriverWait wdw = new WebDriver-*
> *Wait(driver, 10);*
> *wdw.until(ExpectedConditions.presenceOfEle-*
> *mentLocated(By.id("username")));*
> *wdw.until(ExpectedConditions.elementToBeClick-*
> *able(By.id("username"))); // elementTo-*
> *BeClickable means displayed and enabled.*

ii. WebDriverWait polls every 500 milliseconds to determine if condition satisfied.

iii. Waits until condition met and then return true or timeout (10 secs) TimeoutException.

iv. Recommended for Ajax calls or most of the elements.

474. **What happens if we have both explicit wait and implicit wait together in the same test?**
☐ It will result in unexpected wait times if both are set. So, don't use together and instead, nullify the implicit wait before setting the explicit wait. Later, you can set it back to implicit wait.

475. **What is the default wait time while finding an element?**
☐ The default wait time is 0 in finding an element. So, if the element is not available during finding of the element, then it will throw NoSuchElementFoundException.

476. **What are different expected conditions to be used in the explicit wait?**
☐ The following are some of the expected conditions and available in ExpectedConditions class:
☐ *ExpectedConditions.elementToBeClickable(loca-*
tor);
ExpectedConditions.elementToBeClickable(ele-
ment);

☐ *ExpectedConditions.elementSelectionState-*
   ToBe(locator);
   ExpectedConditions.elementSelectionStateToBe(el-
   ement);
☐ *ExpectedConditions.elementToBeSelected(loca-*
   tor,boolean);
   ExpectedConditions.elementToBeSelected(ele-
   ment,boolean);
☐ *ExpectedConditions.visibilityofElement-*
   Located(locator);

477. Does Selenium WebDriver supports any test re-
port/driver framework?
☐ No. The Selenium WebDriver doesn't provide any test
report/harness/driver framework. WebDriver is merely an
API or library to use with any other test frameworks such
as JUnit or TestNG to automate the UI tests. The selenium framework is more for functional and end-to-end
testing, and thereby it is better to use TestNG framework
along with WebDriver APIs in the automation.

478. What automation test report/driver framework that you
had used with Selenium?
☐ Most of the time, TestNG framework has been used in the
functional test automation.

479. How do you automate Ajax auto-suggestion or auto-com-
plete UI?
☐ The below are the simple steps to automate auto-complete
UI:
   ☐ First, find the main element using a locator (By.id).
   ☐ Next, send the text (sendKeys()) to the above main
     element.
   ☐ Then, find the auto-suggested elements using de-
     sired locator (note: this locator is different than

above as dynamically generated ids) (use By.cssSe-lector()).

☐ Introduce some wait time if needed to see on the screen.

☐ Later, find the auto-suggested elements to refresh the object.

☐ Use Actions class to move to the desired suggested element using moveElement() and then click().

☐ Here is the sample code snippet:

```
@Test (enabled=true)
public void autoTest6() throws Exception{
 driver.navigate().to(url6);
 WebElement tags = driver.findElement(By.cssSe-
lector("#tags"));
 tags.sendKeys("a");
 List<WebElement> newtags =
 WebDriverWait(driver,WAIT_TIME).until(Ex-
pectedConditions.presenceOfAllElementsLocat-
edBy(By.cssSelector("[id*= \"ui\"]")));
 Thread.sleep(1000); //wait for 1 sec to see on the
screen

 newtags = driver.findElements(By.cssSelec-
tor("[id*=\"ui\"]"));
 System.out.println("Size="+newtags.size());
 assertEquals(11, newtags.size());
 newtags = driver.findElements(By.cssSelec-
tor("[id*=\"ui\"]"));
 System.out.println("Size="+newtags.size());
 assertEquals(11, newtags.size());

 for (WebElement newtag: newtags ) {
  System.out.println("Auto value="+new-
tag.getText()+";");
 }
 Actions actions = new Actions(driver);
 actions.moveToElement(new-
tags.get(5)).click().build().perform();
```

Thread.sleep(500);
String sValue = driver.findElement(By.cssSelec-
tor("#tags")).getText();
System.out.println("Selected value="+sValue);
}

480. How do you trace or log the web requests access? Can we have event listeners? How?
☐ Using the WebDriverEventListener, one can trace or log the request flows. Here are the basic steps.

☐ First, write the Listener class by implementing the WebDriverEventLister interface as below. This class will have all the callback methods implemented and get executed whenever requests processed.
public class MyEventListener implements Web-
DriverEventListener{ .. }

☐ Next, create EventFiringWebDriver object using the already created webdriver object.
EventFiringWebDriver efdriver = new EventFir-
ingWebDriver(driver);

☐ Then, register the listener object with event firing driver.
WebDriverEventListener eventListener = new
MyEventListener();
efdriver.register(eventListener);
☐ Use the event firing driver object than the regular driver object for all requests to be traced in the automation.

481. What is WebDriver Actions class? How to use it?
☐ The Actions class is used to perform the chain of actions together.

☐ For use cases like drag&drop or move and then click etc. actions to be performed together, then Actions class help in the automation.

☐ Below the sample snippet code:

Actions actions = new Actions(driver);
actions.moveToElement(new-
tags.get(5)).click().build().perform();

482. What are the common issues with cross browser testing?

☐ Here are some of the common cross browser issues come across:

   ☐ Mismatch with locators (specially with xpath locations)

   ☐ CSS and HTML validator compatibility issues.

   ☐ DOM implementation differences causing unknown elements

483. What is meant by headless driver and an example?

☐ Headless means no graphical user interface (GUI). The headless driver is for automating on nongraphical terminal environment. One of the headless driver from Selenium is HtmlUnitDriver, which can work on systems (most of the time, remote systems) without GUI. The regular drivers (like FirefoxDriver) would not work on such Non-GUI environments. In this HtmlUnitDrive headless driver, it is going to use the HTMLUnit framework, which is a non-browser way of mimicking the HTTP requests.

484. How do you set the browser specific settings?

☐ Using the WebDriver's DesiredCapabilities API, one can configure the browser specific and startup settings.

☐ The usage is as below.

DesiredCapabilities capabilities = new DesiredCapa-
bilities(); // Use the above capabilities object while creating the driver object.

☐ Examples:

☐ To enable JavaScript (JS):
DesiredCapabilities capabilities = new Desired-Capabilities();
capabilities.setJavaScriptEnabled(true);
WebDriver driver = new FirefoxDriver(capabilities);

● To set the proxy settings:
Proxy proxy = new Proxy();
proxy.setHttpProxy(proxyHost); //proxy-Host=host:port
DesiredCapabilities caps = new DesiredCapabilities();
caps.setCapability("proxy",proxy);
WebDriver driver = new FirefoxDriver(caps);
See more details at https://github.com/SeleniumHQ/selenium/wiki/DesiredCapabilities

485. What is a proxy server and how to configure it in the automated tests?

☐ The proxy server is an intermediate server, which connects users from intranet to internet through various filters while doing the traffic analysis. It mainly protects the internal users and will be allowed only through firewall. Most of the organizations use the proxy servers while connecting to internet.

☐ To set the proxy settings in the automated test code, use the Proxy and DesiredCapabilities APIs as below.
Proxy proxy = new Proxy();
proxy.setHttpProxy(proxyHost);   //proxy-Host=host:port
DesiredCapabilities caps = new DesiredCapabilities();
caps.setCapability("proxy",proxy);
WebDriver driver = new FirefoxDriver(caps);

486. What are the selenium design patterns? What design strategies that you had used?

☐ The Design Patterns helps in writing solutions with maintainable code for re-occurring problems.

☐ There mainly 4 main selenium design patterns that selenium users use with WebDriver.

i) DomainDrivenDesign: In this pattern, the goal is to express tests in the same language as end user of the app. That is the same domain as the end users.
For example, express the test as "Create a new Account" rather than expressing as "Click third element".

ii) PageObjects: In this pattern, the goal is to create the abstraction of the web pages as objects. This pattern is mostly widely used useful Selenium pattern.
– Create public methods as Services that the page offers.
– These methods would return other PageObjects.
– There is no need to create one object for the entire page but make sure no duplicates for the page or parts of pages (HTML).
– Note that these objects are general/common objects to be used in the actual test classes and thereby don't make assertions and also not expose the internals of the objects outside.
– Also one can use the PageFactory class and initElements() method to have auto-initialization and @FindBy, @FindBys for searchable WebElement instance fields.

iii) LoadableComponent: In this pattern, model the PageObjects as components.
– For this, extend LoadableComponent<?> class and then override load() and isLoaded() methods.
– Also, it is possible to have nested components.

iv) BotStyleTests: In this pattern, use the actions as commands in the automation rather than using PageObjects style.

– Here bot is an action oriented abstraction on top of Selenium APIs.

– It is easy to change the commands as needed elements.

☐ Overall, PageObject pattern is more popular. BotStyleTests is also somewhat familiar. Both of these have been used in the automation independently and also together in the same project.

☐ See more details at https://github.com/SeleniumHQ/selenium/wiki/Design-Patterns

487. What is PageObject? How to write design PageObject based tests?

☐ PageObject is a well known and commonly selenium design pattern used in the Web UI automation. In this pattern, the goal is to create the abstraction of the web pages as objects and then utilize in the test code as per test scenario.

☐ In these page objects, create public methods as Services that the page offers. These methods would return other PageObjects.

☐ There is no need to create one object for the entire page but make sure no duplicates for the page or parts of pages (HTML).

☐ Note that these objects are general/shared objects to be used in the actual test classes and thereby don't make assertions and also not expose the internals of the objects outside.

☐ Also one can use the PageFactory class and initElements() method (PageFactory.initElements(driver,class);) to have auto-initialization and @FindBy (@FindBy(name="username");), @FindBys for searchable WebElement instance fields.

15. Web Applications Testing and Selenium

488. What are the different browser versions and platforms you have used in your environment?

☐ In various projects, the below browser versions and platforms used (Please note the latest release versions from the internet).

  ☐ Firefox browser (versions: 27 to 43) on Windows 7, Mac OS X and RedHat/Ubuntu Linux platforms (See the releases history at https://en.wikipedia.org/wiki/History_of_Firefox)

  ☐ Chrome browser (versions: 26 to 49) on Windows 7, Mac OS X and Redhat/Ubuntu Linux platforms (See the releases history at https://en.wikipedia.org/wiki/Google_Chrome_release_history)

  ☐ Internet Explorer browser (versions: 8 to 11) on Windows 7 platform (See the releases history at https://en.wikipedia.org/wiki/Internet_Explorer_versions)

  ☐ Safari browser (versions: 6.x to 9.x) on Mac OS X platform (https://en.wikipedia.org/wiki/Safari_version_history)

☐ The automation might have used the old browsers because of the compatibility with the Selenium WebDriver. The latest used Java based WebDriver version is 2.48.2 and also used 2.45 version before.

☐ See the current latest drivers at Selenium download page: http://www.seleniumhq.org/download/.

489. How did you integrate Selenium tests with continuous integration system?

☐ The Continuous Integration (CI) server, Hudson/Jenkins used for all automated regression tests including the Selenium tests execution on a daily basis.

☐ Create the Jenkins jobs after the tests can be executed with Maven or ANT build scripts to run TestNG selenium tests.

☐ For the UI tests, the significant change is to have the VNCServer kind of GUI supported server should be started on a port and set the DISPLAY to that port. Otherwise, the selenium tests will fail in launching the browser.

☐ To debug or to check while running the tests, one can log in separately to the server using VNCViewer kind of software to see the browser and actions on it as per the automated tests.

☐ Also, create multiple jobs so that one per browser type/version and one per platform so that execute the tests in parallel on a pool of slaves or client or test execution machines.

☐ Monitor the results on the Jenkins/Hudson Web UI dashboard for all these jobs with selenium tests.

490. What is Selenium Grid2 and why do we need?

☐ Selenium Grid2 is a component of the Selenium2.0 suite, and the main purpose is to do the distributed execution of tests onto several machines in parallel.

☐ It extends RC functionality to run a larger number of test suites to reduce overall execution time.

☐ In this architecture, Hub (central machine) is a host that controls actual test execution Nodes (or machines)

☐ Typically, the test nodes will have different OS platforms and browsers w/various versions so that coverage the test matrix in browser testing. Please note that one can use the Jenkins/Hudson for similar parallel runs execution with each job allocated to a separate slave machine.

491. How do you configure the Selenium Grid and run tests in parallel?

☐ The Grid configuration steps are as below.

☐ First, copy selenium standalone server jar (say selenium-server-standalone-2.xxx.jar) to Hub node and all test nodes in a path. Please note that you can find this jar in the earlier downloaded selenium zip.

15. Web Applications Testing and Selenium

☐ Next, start the Hub server process on the hub machine (replace xxx with original jar version) on default 4444 port (or choose some other port if needed as -port xxxx).

java -jar selenium-server-standalone-2.xxx.jar - role hub

☐ Then, verify that if grid console is accessible using hub URL with hub host and port.

http://localhost:4444/grid/console

☐ Finally, register all of the test nodes with the hub using similar to below command (replace xxx with original jar version).

java -jar selenium-server-standalone-2.xxx.jar - role node -hub http://localhost:4444/grid/register

☐ To recognize the grid, perform the below code changes in the tests so that Hub can match the test node and send to it.

☐ Create the desired capabilities object to configure the browser version or platform you want to use for the test matrix.

☐ Then, pass the desired capabilities object to the RemoteWebDriver. Please note that you can't use the regular WebDriver object for the grid.

☐ Here is the code snippet.

DesiredCapabilities capability = DesiredCapabilities.firefox();
WebDriver driver = new RemoteWebDriver(new URL("http://localhost:4444/wd/hub"), capability);

Also, you can find more details at
https://github.com/SeleniumHQ/selenium/wiki/Grid2

492. How do you test Flash objects with Selenium WebDriver?

☐ There is no direct support in Selenium API to do the Adobe's flash testing automation.

☐ But the technique to automate any functionality that is not directly in Selenium API is to write JavaScript functions and then use Selenium's JavaScriptExecutor API to achieve the automation.

☐ See some sample code to do the fash automation at http://seleniumonlinetrainingexpert.word-press.com/2012/12/02/how-to-do-flash-testing-using-se-lenium-webdriver

493. Explain and differentiate Data Driven, Keyword Driven, Hybrid test design frameworks.

☐ The Data Driven test design framework is a paradigm where test logic is fixed but varies the test data. That means to create the test methods and supply the data to them automatically. For example in TestNG, the data is provided by the data provider and TestNG would execute those tests methods with various input data to cover different combinations, conditions, boundaries, etc. This methodology is so popular and useful to separate the data from the test code rather than hard-coded test data for maintenance and to add more test data later. The data itself can be in different repositories like a simple .csv file, .json file or .xls sheet, or database and can add the tests merely updating those external files or DB (instead of placing in test code itself).

☐ The Keyword driven framework is a methodology where actions or steps are treated as keywords. These keywords (like click, move, type etc.,) are stored in some external repositories along just like data (in .csv/.json/.xls/DB). The API methods would be created to perform operations matching for those keywords. The best way to understand this is to review Selenium IDE where Selenese commands used in the .html file as a test. In a similar way, one can create test framework so that test flows can be automated by simply updating the external files or DB than test code. The framework driver would handle the keywords/operations/instructions and execute the tests.

☐ The hybrid framework is the combination of Data Driven

and Keyword driven. Here the operations/instructions/keywords in a separate repository (.csv/.xls/.json/DB) and data is in separate (.csv/.xls/.json/db from data provider) and the tests/driver would read both and perform the actual tests automatically. In this design, we get the best of both methodologies, and it is kind of practical in most of the automation cases.

494. Can you explain the high-level design process for the test automation?

☐ First, decide the test development strategy & framework.
    ☐ Choose the test framework like TestNG.
    ☐ Choose the build framework like Maven.

☐ Identify and work with the dev team to make the consistent web page elements locators. Decide the locators strategy. Please note that you can have multiple locators. As an example, here is the order of preferred locators.
    ☐ Ids
    ☐ Names
    ☐ XPath
    ☐ CSS

☐ Develop a generic/wrapper code with Selenium APIS to cover the basic functionality by Web Driver. Crete code for some of the below tasks as utilities.
    ☐ Create a generic layer for common functionality.
    ☐ Reading test data repositories.

☐ Decide the design pattern such as Page Objects model and write the code for all targeted web pages as PageObjects.

☐ Add Data Driven approach by creating TestNG Data Providers to support some of the repositories like:
    ☐ Properties files
    ☐ CSV files
    ☐ XSL
    ☐ DB

☐ Some of the below considerations can be used for modular and code maintenance

☐ Place all the runtime configuration in a properties file.

☐ Isolate all the html locators in a single place (say properties) for maintenance.

☐ Use the values from properties file rather than hardcode in the test class

☐ The above code would become your Selenium UI test automation framework.

495. **How to read the properties file from Java code?**

The below code snippet can be used for reading properties file.

Properties p = new Properties();
//NOTE: The below commented line need to know the exact path for file.
// p.load(new FileReader(new File(BROWSER_PROPER-TIES)));

//NOTE: The below way to read file from any path as long it is in the classpath.
p.load(this.getClass().getResource-
AsStream(BROWSER_PROPERTIES)
String proxyHost = p.getProperty("proxy.host");

496. **How do you take the screenshots/images for the failed tests? Give the code snippet.**

☐ Taking the screenshots is very useful for debugging the UI test failures. Otherwise, it is hard to see what happened on the browser at the time of failure. Selenium made easy for taking the screenshots.

☐ To take the screenshots, use the TakesScreenShot class from WebDriver API. Please follow the below 2 simple steps.

i) Simply cast the driver object to (TakesScreen-shot)driver (or) create AugmentDriver object for RemoteWebDriver and then cast to TakesScreenshot class.

ii) Use getScreenshotAs(OutputType.File) method to save as file.

See the sample below code for taking the screenshots for failed tests. This method gets executed all the time and finds out if the test is failed or not. If failed, then does the above steps. Using Apache's FileUitls, it does copy to the destination file (with timestamp) or simply can use the Java core APIs instead of Apache utilities.

```
/*
* Take snapshot
*/
@AfterMethod (alwaysRun=true)
public void catchFailure(ITestResult result) throws Exception{
  String dateSuffix = new SimpleDateFormat("MM_dd_yyyy_hh_mm_ss").format(
  Calendar.getInstance().getTime()).toString();
  String methodName = result.getName();
  if (!result.isSuccess()) {
    TakesScreenshot screenshot = (TakesScreenshot)driver;
    assertNotNull(screenshot,"Can't get TakesScreenshot object from driver!"+screenshot);
    File("failed_screens"+File.separator+methodName+"-"+dateSuffix+".png");
    File srcFile = screenshot.getScreenshotAs(OutputType.FILE);
    File destFile = new FileUtils.copyFile(srcFile, destFile);
    org.testng.Reporter.log(destFile.getCanonicalPath(),true);
  }
```

}

- To take from remote webdriver (for Grid environment):
Note that the RemoteWebDriver does not implement the
TakesScreenshot class.
If the driver does have the Capabilities to take a screen-
shot, then Augmenter will add the TakesScreenshot meth-
ods to the instance. Here is the code snippet.

*WebDriver driver = new RemoteWebDriver(new
URL("http://localhost:4444/wd/hub"), DesiredCapabili-
ties.firefox());
driver.get("http://www.google.com");
WebDriver augmentedDriver = new Augmenter().aug-
ment(driver);
File screenshot = ((TakesScreenshot)augmentedDriver).
getScreenshotAs(OutputType.FILE);*

497. How do you handle drag-and-drop web UI scenario in the
automation?
   ☐ The drag-and-drop involves multiple elements and actions together. The automation steps are as follows.
      ☐ First, find the draggable element (say draggable)
using a locator (say By.id).
         *WebElement source = driver.findEle-
ment(By.id("draggable"));*
      ☐ Next, find the droppable element (say droppable)
using a locator (say By.id).
         *WebElement target = driver.findEle-
ment(By.id("droppable"));*
      ☐ Then, create Actions object with driver (new Ac-
tions(driver)) to create chained events.
      ☐ Perform the drag and drop using dra-
gAndDrop(source,target) method.
         Actions.dragAndDrop(source,target);
      ☐ Build the chained actions by using build(), which
will pop-out all of actions and ready for execution.

☐ Finally, trigger the actions by calling perform() on Actions object.

☐ Couple of other ways of doing the same drag&drop action.

    ☐ Using below API.

    clickAndHold(source).moveToElement(target).release(target).build().perform();

    ☐ Write Java Script and use as below.

    ((JavascriptExecutor)driver).execute('script');

☐ Here is the sample code snippet.

```
@Test (enabled=true)
public void dragTest() {
  driver.navigate().to(url);
  WebElement source = driver.findElement(By.id("draggable"));
  WebElement target = driver.findElement(By.id("droppable"));
  Actions builder = new Actions(driver);
  Action dragAndDrop =
  builder.clickAndHold(source).moveToElement(target).release(target).build();
  dragAndDrop.perform();
  builder.dragAndDrop(source, target).build().perform();
}
```

498. **How do you do handle html SELECT element automation?**

☐ For the html SELECT element to be automated, the below are the general steps:

    ☐ First, find the main SELECT element in the web page using a locator (say By.id).

    ☐ Next, create selenium's Select object (like new Select(WebElement);).

    ☐ Then, select the required option or an element (by index or value) using selectByIndex(index).

    ☐ For example to get a selected first option, use the

below API. *select.getFirstSelectedOption();*
- ☐ After that assert the selected option's text with expected value.
- ☐ To get all options in the SELECT, use select.getOptions() api.
☐ Here is the sample code snippet:

```
@Test (enabled=true)
public void autoTest5() {
driver.navigate().to(url5);

/*
// Method 1
WebElement source = driver.findEle-
ment(By.id("city"));
source.click();
Actions actions = new Actions(driver);
actions.click(source).keyDown(Keys.EN-
TER).click().keyDown(Keys.AR-
ROW_DOWN).build().perform();
*/
// Method 2
Select selectBox = new Select(driver.findEle-
ment(By .cssSelector("select#city")));

// Select 2nd option and select
selectBox.selectByIndex(2);
String optionValue = selectBox.getFirstSelectedOp-
tion().getText();
assertEquals("Santa Clara", optionValue);

// Check all options
List<String> cityOptions = new Ar-
rayList<String>();
cityOptions = Ar-
rays.asList("Fremont","Sunnyvale","Santa
Clara","Cupertino","Newark");
List<WebElement> options = selectBox.getOp-
tions();
```

```
 for (WebElement option: options ) {
    System.out.println(option.getText());
    assertEquals(true,cityOptions.contains(op-
    tion.getText()),"Expected City");
    }
 }
```

499. What is HTTP protocol? Please explain.

☐ HTTP stands for Hyper Text Transfer Protocol in use
   since 1990.

☐ HTTP is an application-level protocol to communicate the
   HTTP messages between the client (say Browser) and
   servers (say Web Server) over the TCP/IP.

☐ HTTP is a stateless and connection oriented protocol.

☐ HTTP W3C standard web protocol, and default port is 80.

☐ HTTP is a request/response protocol. The client sends the
   HTTP request to Server and Client receives HTTP response from Server.

☐ HTTP request is requesting method (GET/POST/PUT
   etc.), URI (/index.html), protocol version (HTTP/1.0) followed by MIME-like messages containing request modifiers, client information, and body content if any.

☐ HTTP response is the status line with protocol version,
   success or error status code, followed by a MIME-like
   message containing server information, meta information,
   and body content if any.

☐ HTTP is being used for WWW (World Wide Web) since
   first version HTTP/0.9, HTTP/1.0, and the HTTP/1.1 is
   the latest.

☐ HTTP allows hypermedia access to resources available
   from diversified applications.

☐ HTTP is also a generic protocol that communicates messages between user agents/proxies to other internet systems.

500. What are different HTTP status codes?

☐ The HTTP status code element is a 3 digit integer result code sent by the server to the requested client.

☐ The first digit of the 3 digit status code defines the class or category of response. See the below for codes (xx mean any other digits) and brief details.

☐ 1xx is Informational, which means request received and continuing the process.

    ☐ Example: 100 Continue

☐ 2xx is Success, which means the actual has been received successfully, understood and accepted.

    ☐ Example: 200 OK

    ☐ Example: 201 Created

    ☐ Example: 202 Accepted

☐ 3xx is Redirection, which means further action must be taken to complete the request.

    ☐ Example: 301 Moved Permanently

☐ 4xx is Client Error, which means the request contains bad syntax and can't be fulfilled.

    ☐ Example: 400 Bad Request

    ☐ Example: 401 Unauthorized

    ☐ Example: 403 Forbidden

    ☐ Example: 404 Not Found

    ☐ Example: 405 Method Not Allowed

☐ 5xx is the Server Error, which means the server failed to fulfill the validated request.

    ☐ Example: 500 Internal Server Error

    ☐ Example: 501 Not Implemented

    ☐ Example: 502 Bad Gateway

    ☐ Example: 503 Service Unavailable

501. Can we get HTTP status codes from Selenium Web-Driver?

☐ No. The Selenium doesn't provide the HTTP status codes. In fact, this is one of the limitations of Selenium. The validation should be done through the content valuation and web element assertions. If required, some other HTTP

API to use.

502. **Can you explain the end-to-end process for a given website testing with selenium?**
    ☐ To test any given website, I would use the browser as the client because it is the universal client that end users like to use in general. For creating the browser automated tests, I would use Selenium, which is a free and open source framework to use the exact browser interface as users.
    ☐ Using Selenium, all the browser actions can be controlled directly using Java APIs. But selenium itself doesn't provide any test harness and thereby TestNG also used along with Selenium WebDriver API.
    ☐ TestNG supports data-driven framework, and once the scenario is automated, then test data will be provided to apply for each scenario with DataProvider functionality of TestNG.
    ☐ The driver for each browser initialization can be done using WebDriver d = new FirefoxDriver() or other browsers specific driver in the @BeforeClass annotated method. Quitting of browser (driver.quit()) will be done @AfterClass annotated method.
    ☐ Then, create all the test methods would be created for each test scenario in all @Test annotated methods. Within each test method, browser URL is open, element (WebElement) is going to be located using one of the available locators such as By.id or By.xpath etc. The actions such as click or sendkeys applied on top of the web elements. Then assertions would be added based on the checks such as title, content, position verification. Multiple actions can be chained for features like Drag-and-drop, dynamic list selection using Action class. Any flash object and other not directly supported features can be tested with JavaScriptExecutor class in WebDriver API.
    ☐ Later, the test data is formulated by reading the reposito-

ries such as csv files, xls sheets or DB with @DataProvider annotated method. If there are any Ajax components, the time waits should be explicitly applied to those elements to satisfy the conditions such as visible or clickable. For all other elements collectively implicit wait on the driver can be applied to wait until timeout for an element to load. Some of the design considerations are PageObjects design pattern, where Java objects created per web page and then write the test classes to formulate the test scenario with assertions.

☐ Once the basic scenarios automated, the tests need to be compiled, and dependents jars created and then need to execute the tests. These build steps can be automated using ANT or Maven build framework.

☐ As part of giving the highly automated and quick feedback on the regression testing for the website, it is better to integrate the tests into Continuous Integration (CI) systems such as Jenkins/Hudson. The test jobs can be executed on-demand or schedule at a particular time or continuously after product build completed.

☐ Finally, keep monitoring the regression runs and add more tests as need.

← End: Skill#15. Web Applications Testing and Selenium ←

Good!
Keep going and never give up!!
Please re-read again for more clarity and feel free to contact for help!!!

→ Start: Skill#16. Web Services (SOAP&REST API) Testing and
SoapUI Tool →

Skill#16. Web Services (SOAP&REST API) Testing and SoapUI Tool

The Web Services are loosely coupled and distributed technology that is widely used. The WS are being used in Service Oriented Architecture (using SOAP-based web services), or with the Internet resources addressed as RESTful WS or REST API or REST endpoints. Nowadays, the REST is very popular and is everywhere. It is essential to understand and test these REST APIs. This skill is a must for both developers and QA engineers to survive in the development of current software and IT services.

503. How do you describe Web Services? What are key elements?
- ☐ The Web Services are loosely coupled, remote and distributed component technology that communicate over the internet protocol using XML based messages along with other web-related standards.
- ☐ These are self-describable and discoverable services.
- ☐ Two parties involved in this are Service Provider providing the service and Service Consumer consuming the service.
- ☐ Key elements are communicating protocol - IP, describable WSDL, discoverable protocol as UDDI, Application protocol as SOAP or HTTP, Payload as XML or JSON data.

504. What are some of the distributed technologies?
- ☐ CORBA (Common Object Request Broker Architecture)
- ☐ Java RMI
- ☐ DCOM
- ☐ EJB (Enterprise Java Beans)
- ☐ Web Services

505. What are the benefits or key advantages of web services?

☐ Web Services are simple, easy to understand and implement both service providers and consumers.

☐ These are loosely coupled, which means no tight binding between service providers and consumers.

☐ The key advantages are as below.

　☐ WS are platform independent where the provider can be on one platform like Linux and consumer can be on a different platform like Windows.

　☐ WS are language neutral where provider implementation can be in Java and consumer implementation can be C#.

　☐ WS are transport neutral where provider and consumer can communicate using different protocols (for example - SOAP WS)

☐ WS have become so popular, and now the RESTful WS are simply termed as APIs.

506. What are key elements in web service architecture? How is it different from traditional client/server?

☐ Web services are built with multi-tier architecture, and the key elements are the service provider/producer, service requester/consumer, service broker, XML, protocols - HTTP protocol, UDDI, WSDL.

　☐ SOAP (Simple Object Access Protocol)

　☐ UDDI (Universal Description, Discovery and Integration)

　☐ WSDL (Web Services Description Language)

　　• External interface to services describing how to use

　　• Analogy to Java Interfaces

　　• Guideline for constructing SOAP message

☐ Typically, client/server have tight binding w.r.t language and transport protocols whereas the Web Services are language and transport protocol neutral. Thereby Web Services architecture provides flexibility and easy maintenance with different types of clients (like Web UI, Mobile

UI, Standalone or Desktop UI) serving to the same backend service without any changes/replicating the service code.

☐ Examples of process flows in both Client/server and WS:

    ☐ Client/server:

        ● Browser → Web/AppServer (WebApp) →(jdbc) → DB

        ● Standalone client → (jdbc) → DB

    ☐ WS:

        ● Browser → Web/AppServer (WebApp client with WSDL) → (XML over HTTP) → AppServer (WSDL/service provider) →(jdbc) → DB

        ● Mobile client → (XML over HTTP) → AppServer (WSDL/service provider) →(jdbc) → DB

        ● Standalone client → (XML over HTTP) → AppServer (WSDL/service provider) →(jdbc) → DB

507. What are different kinds of web services?

☐ There are two major WS types:

i) SOAP (Simple Object Access Protocol) Web Services

ii) RESTful (REpresentational State Transfer) Web Services

508. What kind of protocol used between the service provider and consumer?

☐ In SOAP-based web services, it is XML over HTTP over TCP/IP protocol and in RESTful, it could be XML or JSON payload over HTTP over TCP/IP protocol.

509. What is a de-facto standard web service?

☐ The SOAP WS are the de-facto standard for web services.

510. **What is a SOAP based web service?**
☐ SOAP stands for "Simple Object Access Protocol."
☐ The SOAP WS are Platform, Language and transport neutral.
☐ These are the de-facto standard for distributed Web Services.
☐ SOAP WS are more secure and reliable used in SOA (Service-Oriented Architecture)
☐ The SOAP-based WS were started with the goals of simple and easy use. But became heavyweight and complex because of more and more extensions like WS-* (WS-Security, WS-Addressing, etc.) were added to the standards.
☐ SOAP WS are the true alternative to old CORBA, DCOM and EJB distributed technologies.
☐ Key elements are WSDL, SOAP XML as payload, UDDI for publishing and discovery the services.

511. **What is the transport protocol used for SOAP web services? And what is the Payload?**
☐ The SOAP protocol is XML over HTTP (over TCP/IP).
☐ The default SOAP WS payload is SOAP XML.

512. **What are different versions available in SOAP? What is the latest?**
☐ There are two major versions and SOAP 2.0 is the latest version.
  i) SOAP 1.1
  ii) SOAP 2.0

513. **What are some of the WS implementations around?**
☐ The WS implementations are the framework APIs to create, deploy, and consume the WS resources as services. Some of the common WS frameworks are as below.
  ☐ JAX-WS/JavaEE on Java platform
  ☐ .NET platform
  ☐ Apache Axis on Java platform

514. What is meant by API? How do you describe APIs or characteristics of APIs?

☐ The API stands for "Application Programming Interface."

☐ These are in the form of classes and libraries (jar files in Java). The objective of APIs is to share the common functionality for building some other end-user applications software.

☐ Most of the time, these APIs provide generic and specific targeted services and require programming skills to use the APIs. For example, Java APIs, C APIs, C++ APIs for targeted services/functionality/use cases. Another example is Selenium WebDriver API is to automate the browser actions.

☐ There is no GUI interface in APIs. That means the end user of the applications can't interact directly with APIs.

☐ From the testing point of view, API tests are functional and end-to-end test scenarios and not unit testing scenarios.

☐ Typically, the APIs will be tested by Quality Team because of end-to-end scenarios.

☐ Even though, these are low-level APIs but are mostly considered as black box because these are consumed by other vendors/customers who will be using in their software solutions.

☐ Test Frameworks for API testing are similar to unit testing because APIs testing falls in similar requirements as unit testing. Examples frameworks are TestNG and JUnit for Java programming environment.

☐ The APIs can produce either direct results, perform updates, create data structures, generate events, exceptions, etc.

☐ In testing, the focus would be more on the API method parameters, conditions, scenarios, procedures, triggers, exceptions, etc. based on the APIs functionality.

515. Why are Web Services called as APIs?

☐ The Web Services have the similar characteristics as APIs and thereby referred them as APIs. Some of these features are providing loosely-coupled services used by some other end-user software, no GUI involved, requires programming skills to consume the services, etc.

516. How would you test an API (say for address validation)? How many tests do you write? Can you write single test case covering all different scenarios?

☐ For any API, create the test scenarios covering both positive and negative tests that include the functional correctness, parameters validation, boundary conditions, exceptions, events and any data structures updated, etc.

☐ Also create the test scenarios for the other nonfunctional testing that includes security testing, stress testing, and performance testing.

☐ It is not advised to have one test case for all the API test scenarios and instead, create a separate test for each test scenario.

☐ The number of tests depends on the number of test scenarios/flows.

☐ Typically, each test scenario would be written a single test method in TestNG. If more assertions to be covered for a use case, then add all those assertions in the same test method. After that, make the method as data-driven covering the right data for both +ve and -ve tests.

517. What are the things to be tested in Web Services API testing?

☐ The first focus is on the testing of responses for functionality correctness.

☐ Validate all of the parameters, payload variations, and data boundaries for both positive and negative cases.

☐ Also focus more on method parameters, conditions, scenarios, procedures, triggers, etc. based on the APIs functionality.

518. **What is a RESTful Web Service? How do you describe these services?**
- ☐ RESTful stands for REpresentational State Transfer, which is an architectural style for designing software. These WS are popular, easy to implement and use. These are called popularly as REST APIs.
- ☐ REST APIs are mainly to provide loosely-coupled services over the Web/HTTP over the TCP/IP. It means that the resources can be accessed and actions performed by standard HTTP methods.
- ☐ The typical REST access flow is as below:
    - ☐ A REST client is making HTTP Request to the hosted REST resource/ REST API.
    - ☐ A REST client gets the HTTP Response from REST resource/REST API.
- ☐ Also, RESTful WS are purely HTTP-Oriented, and the communication is stateless.
- ☐ REST WS supports the payload and content negotiation with multiple formats in XML or JSON.
- ☐ The HTTP request/responses headers include,
    - ☐ Accept: application/json, application/xml
- ☐ The RESTFul Web Services are platform, language neutral and tied with HTTP transport.
- ☐ These are much simpler than SOAP WS and closure to the Web.
- ☐ The REST APIs are more of point-to-point services and not meant for distributed/intermediates like in SOA architecture(or SOAP WS).
- ☐ The key elements of REST WS are
    - ☐ Resources or URI (Uniform Resource Identifier). Here everything is represented with unique service id.
        - Some examples of resources are as below.
            - o http://www.everydayon.com/products/10

: Represents product
o   http://www.everydayon.com/or-
    ders/2013/: All orders in 2013
☐   REST APIs use the HTTP standard methods.
 • HTTP verbs: GET, POST, PUT, DELETE
 • HTTP verb is the action to be performed on
    the Resource
 • Example:
    o   GET http://www.everydayon.com/prod-
        ucts/10 HTTP/1.1

☐ The resource CRUD operations are mapped to HTTP
   methods/verbs.
   ☐   Create operation is mapped to HTTP POST
       method for creating new resources.
   ☐   Retrieve operation is mapped to HTTP GET
       method for retrieving resources identified by URI.
   ☐   Update operation is mapped to HTTP PUT for up-
       dating existing resources.
   ☐   Delete operation is mapped to HTTP DELETE for
       deleting resources identified by URI.

519. What are the key elements in REST APIs?
   ☐ The key elements of REST WS are as below.
      ☐   Resources or URIs (Uniform Resource Identifier)
          and HTTP methods. In REST, everything is repre-
          sented with unique resource id.
       • Some of the examples are as below.
          o   http://www.everydayon.com/prod-
              ucts/10 : Represents product.
          o   http://www.everydayon.com/or-
              ders/2013/: All orders in 2013
      ☐   HTTP standard verbs/methods.
       • HTTP verb: Action to be performed on the
          Resource
          o   GET, POST, PUT, DELETE

- Example:
  - GET http://www.everydayon.com/products/10

520. **What are the different message formats supported in SOAP and REST WS?**
   □ The below are the WS supported payload formats.
       □ SOAP WS: XML (in specific, it is SOAP XML)
       □ REST WS: JSON or XML

521. **How is a SOAP envelope and what it contains?**
   □ SOAP Envelope contains the SOAP header and body for requests/responses xml.
       □ SOAP Header
           - WS-* Extensions like WS-Security, WS-Addressing, etc.
       □ SOAP Body
           - Request/response XML payload.

522. **How do the REST API request and REST API responses look (give a snippet)?**
   □ The below is the sample REST API request and responses for youtube search REST API. One can use curl command to check the provided REST API for basic functionality.
   □ The general REST API request syntax is as below.
       <http-method> <uri> <http-protocol/ver>
       <headers>

       <json/xml payload>

   □ The general REST API response syntax is as below.
       <http-protocol/ver> <code>
       <headers>

       <json/xml payload>

☐ Example:
curl -v 'https://www.goog-
leapis.com/youtube/v3/search?part=snip-
pet&q=Jagadesh+Munta&key=YOUR_KEY'

*GET /youtube/v3/search?part=snip-
pet&q=Jagadesh+Munta&key=YOUR_API_KEY
HTTP/1.1*
Host: www.googleapis.com
User-Agent: curl/7.43.0
Accept: */*

HTTP/1.1 200 OK
Expires: Sat, 18 Jun 2016 22:02:03 GMT
Date: Sat, 18 Jun 2016 22:02:03 GMT
Cache-Control: private, max-age=120, must-revalidate,
no-transform
ETag: "5g01s4-wS2b4VpScndqCYc5Y-8k/SBiMtK-
waTVlsmlEX6_uBvu_ydt4"
Vary: Origin
Vary: X-Origin
Content-Type: application/json; charset=UTF-8
X-Content-Type-Options: nosniff
X-Frame-Options: SAMEORIGIN
X-XSS-Protection: 1; mode=block
Content-Length: 4743
Server: GSE
Alternate-Protocol: 443:quic
Alt-Svc: quic=":443"; ma=2592000;
v="34,33,32,31,30,29,28,27,26,25"

{
"kind": "youtube#searchListResponse",
"etag": "\"5g01s4-wS2b4VpScndqCYc5Y-8k/SBiMtK-
waTVlsmlEX6_uBvu_ydt4\"",
"nextPageToken": "CAUQAA",
"regionCode": "US",
"pageInfo": {

```
"totalResults": 42,
"resultsPerPage": 5
},
...
}
```

(Or) Directly as below using request's XML payload and JSON response payload.
REST request/REST API request:

```
POST /stock/
Accept: application/json
Content-Type: application/xml
Content-Length: 1000

<stock>
    <symbol>IBM</symbol>
    <value>40.00</value>
</stock>
```

REST API response

```
HTTP/1.1 200 OK
Accept: application/json

{"status":"successful"}
```

523. **What is WSDL? And it's significance?**
   □ WSDL stands for "Web Services Description Language."
   □ The WSDL is an external interface to the hosted services by describing the services on the supported operations, operation parameters, security, etc. and guides on "how to use" the service.
   □ WSDL can be understood better as an analogy to Java interfaces in Java programming.

16. Web Services Testing and SoapUI Tool

   ☐ At a high level, WSDL provides a guideline for constructing SOAP request message and expected SOAP response
message.

   ☐ Typically, the WSDL can be retrieved from a hosted Web
Service by appending "?wsdl" to the URL.

524. What is UDDI, and its significance?

   ☐ UDDI stands for Universal Description, Discovery, and
Integration.

   ☐ The UDDI is a standard protocol to publish a web service
(WSDL) by the Service Provider and to discover and retrieve the WSDL by the Service Consumer.

   ☐ UDDI server is like yellow pages for Web Services.

525. What is WADL, and its significance?

   ☐ WADL stands for Web Application Description Language.

   ☐ Th WADL is evolving as a standard for the RESTful Web
Services description, in similar to WSDL for SOAP Web
Services.

526. What is Service Oriented Architecture (SOA)?

   ☐ SOA stands for Service Oriented Architecture.

   ☐ In SOA, all the services would be formed as a network to
accomplish a business solution/use cases. The primary entities are SOAP Web Services, which serve the useful part
of the solution to entire business flow/solution.

   ☐ Initially, Amazon made the SOA as popular with their
Elastic Compute (EC2) Web Services.

   ☐ Another example of SOA applications includes the automation of a Bank Loan process. In this, one SOA service
would serve the validation of customer application and
then pass with some additional data to next service in the
flow to do some credit checks. After that do approval process with another web service in the chain, and continue
with remaining actions/services and finally notify to the

end customer.

☐ In SOA, the SOAP Web Services are provided with distributed and intermediates in the solution (like act as some modifications and pass on the updated data/context).

527. **How do you compare SOAP web services with RESTful web services? Which one is more secure/standard/reliable? Which one is more simple to use?**

☐ The "SOAP" stands for "Simple Object Access Protocol" and REST stands for "REpresentational State Transfer."

☐ The SOAP WS are Platform, Language and transport neutral; RESTful WS are platform and language neutral and bound to HTTP transport.

☐ SOAP WS are the de-facto standard for distributed Web Services whereas RESTful WS are not standard but merely architecture style based on original Ph.D. thesis.

☐ The SOAP WS are more secure, reliable and used in SOA (Service-Oriented Architecture) whereas the RESTful WS are used in point-to-point services. REST APIs were popularized mainly through social network websites.

☐ The SOAP WS have been started with a simple goal of simplicity and easiness. But slowly became complicated because of more and more extensions like WS-* (WS-Security, WS-Addressing, etc.) were added to the standards. The RESTful WS are simple, easy to understand and implement.

☐ The SOAP WS are the true alternative to old CORBA, DCOM and EJB distributed technologies whereas RESTful WS became as default synonym to APIs, called REST APIs for almost all new sites and commonly for any web interactions.

☐ The key elements in SOAP WS are WSDL, SOAP XML as payload, UDDI for publishing and discover services whereas the RESTful WS have Resource URIs and HTTP standard methods.

☐ It is recommended to use REST APIs for your web applications backend interaction or programming because of their simplicity and easy to implement and share.

528. What are some of the example SOAP web services and RESTful APIs?
- ☐ SOA WS examples are as below.
  - ☐ Amazon EC2 SOAP Web Services - http://docs.aws.amazon.com/AWSECommerce-Service/latest/DG/SOAPEndpoints.html
- ☐ REST APIs examples are as below:
  - ☐ Google Search REST APIs - https://developers.google.com/custom-search/json-api/v1/using_rest
  - ☐ Twitter REST APIs - https://dev.twitter.com/rest/public
  - ☐ Facebook REST APIs - https://developers.facebook.com/docs/graph-api
  - ☐ LinkedIn REST APIs - https://developer.linkedin.com/docs/rest-api
  - ☐ GIT APIs - https://developer.github.com/v3/
  - ☐ JIRA REST APIs - https://docs.atlassian.com/jira/REST/cloud/
  - ☐ See more programmable REST/Web APIs at http://www.programmableweb.com/category/all/apis

529. What are some of SOAP based WS-* specifications?
- ☐ Some of the SOAP WS standards are as below.
  - ☐ WS-I (WS- Interoperable)
  - ☐ WS-S (WS - Security)
  - ☐ WS-Addressing
  - ☐ WS-Trust
  - ☐ WS-Notification
  - ☐ WS-Federation
- ☐ See nice graphical chart at https://www.innoq.com/soa/ws-stand-

ards/poster/innoQ%20WS-Stand-
ards%20Poster%202007-02.pdf

530. **What is a protocol or protocol stack? What is meant by over HTTP protocol?**

☐ The protocol is a set of rules, syntax, and semantics to be agreed and followed between all communicating entities. These protocols can exist at different layers one over another.

☐ The protocol stack is a set of protocols where one protocol functions on top of another, which can form a stack to achieve the full communication/message transfer.

☐ Over HTTP means, the current protocol on top of the HTTP protocol. Again, the underlying protocol for the current communication will be the HTTP and then do follow another set of rules. Example SOAP-XML over HTTP.

531. **What is HTTP protocol? What are different HTTP methods?**

☐ In summary, the HTTP protocol can be described as below.

   ☐ HTTP stands for Hyper Text Transfer Protocol in use since 1990.

   ☐ HTTP is an application-level protocol to communicate the HTTP messages between the client (say Browser) and servers (say Web Server) over the TCP/IP.

   ☐ HTTP is a stateless and connection oriented protocol.

   ☐ HTTP W3C standard web protocol and the default port is 80.

   ☐ HTTP is a request/response protocol. The client sends the HTTP request to Server and Client receives HTTP response from Server.

   ☐ HTTP request is a string with request method

(GET/POST/PUT etc.), URI (/index.html), protocol version (HTTP/1.0) followed by MIME-like
messages containing request modifiers, client information, and body content if any.

☐ HTTP response is the status line with protocol version, success or error status code, followed by an
MIME-like message containing server information, meta information, and body content if any.

☐ HTTP is being used for WWW (World Wide Web)
since first version - HTTP/0.9, later HTTP/1.0, and
HTTP/1.1 is the latest.

☐ HTTP allows hypermedia access to resources
available from diversified applications.

☐ HTTP is also a generic protocol that communicates
messages between user agents/proxies to other internet systems.

☐ The following are the HTTP request methods defined in
HTTP 1.0 and HTTP 1.1 specifications. Here the resource
is identified as URI. Also, most of the Web Servers do
support GET/HEAD/OPTIONS methods.

☐ GET is a Request method to retrieve the representation of a resource as response. It is like a read operation on a resource.

☐ HEAD is a Request method same as GET except
that the response contains only the headers section
and no body part.

☐ POST is a Request method to create the the representation of a resource with supplied data in the
payload. It is like a write operation of a resource.

☐ PUT is a Request method to update an existing resource or to create a new resource if the resource
doesn't exist.

☐ DELETE is a Request method to delete a resource.

☐ OPTIONS is a Request method to retrieve the list
of HTTP request methods supported by the Server.

☐ TRACE is a Request method to indicate that the
response should contain the originally received re-

quest so that client would know if any modifications done by the intermediate servers.

☐ CONNECT is a Request method that is going to convert the request connection to a transparent TCP/IP tunnel for proxying.

☐ PATCH is a Request method to do the partial modifications for a resource.

532. **How do you map HTTP methods with CRUD operations in REST?**

☐ The REST resource CRUD operations have been mapped to HTTP methods/verbs as below:

☐ HTTP POST method is mapped to Create operation for creating new resources.

☐ HTTP GET method is mapped to Retrieve operation for retrieving resources identified by URI.

☐ HTTP PUT method is mapped to Update operation for updating existing resources.

☐ HTTP DELETE method is mapped to Delete operation for deleting resources identified by URI.

533. **What are some of the web services testing tools or frameworks available for the automated testing?**

☐ Below three frameworks are widely used in the Web Service testing.

i) SoapUI tool/framework is a popular open source Web Services Testing tool in use since 2005.

☐ SoapUI is one of the initial testing tools for WS and has an active and vibrant community.

☐ This framework supports cross platform as it is written in Java.

☐ SoapUI is a simple and easy to use GUI based tool to develop test suites across the SOAP and RESTful Web Services. It also supports command line (CLI) to execute the tests.

☐ SoapUI does support other languages such as

Groovy and Javascript.

ii) Jersey client API is an open source implementation of JAX-RS (Java API for XML REST Services) that is used for developing RESTful Web Services. It is created by Oracle (earlier Sun Microsystems). This framework is not a test framework but instead a simple WS client Java APIs to consume in TestNG/JUnit frameworks while developing the tests. A wrapper test framework with common functionality can be created on top of Jersey.

iii) REST Assured framework is a free and open source Java library to work with REST APIs. This framework specialty is that it is very easy to send requests and parse the JSON responses.

534. **What is SoapUI tool? Why do you choose SoapUI tool? What are latest versions?**
   - ☐ The SoapUI tool/framework is a popular open source Web Services Testing Tool. Ole Lensmar from Smartbear (formerly Eviware) developed this framework while working on SOA project.
   - ☐ This tool is easy and straightforward GUI based tool to develop test suites across the SOAP and RESTful Web Services. Using SoapUI, the productivity is high with SoapUI tool for testing and automating the Web Services testing.
   - ☐ The first release of SoapUI is 1.0 as an open source in 2005 and the latest version SoapUI 5.2.1 /NGPro 1.8.0 in 2016. It has both community and commercial edition - SoapUI Pro/SoapUI NG Pro (14-day trial).

535. **What are different platforms supported?**
   - ☐ The SoapUI tool is written in Java and thereby supports cross platform, like Windows or Linux or Mac OS.

536. **What kind of testing can be done with SoapUI tool? What are some of the key features of SoapUI tool?**
   - ☐ The SoapUI tool is mainly to perform functional and load testing of SOAP and RESTful Web Services.
   - ☐ The SoapUI tool helps for the following tasks.
     - ☐ Inspection of Web Services (WSDL/WADL)
     - ☐ Generation of test skeleton automatically
     - ☐ Supporting Data-Driven test development
     - ☐ Creation of mock services if Web Services are not ready while developing the tests.
   - ☐ Available as a plugin to IDEs (Eclipse/Netbeans/IDEA etc.).
   - ☐ Integration of SoapUI tests with ANT/Jenkins for automated regression testing.

537. **Does the SoapUI tool support the data-driven framework?**
   - ☐ Yes. But it is supported only in the Pro edition but not supported in the community edition.
   - ☐ For the data driven, multiple data repositories like .csv, .xsl, many databases are supported.

538. **How do you do the data driven in SoapUI tool?**
   - ☐ In SoapUI, at the test case level of project hierarchy, do the below three steps.
     - ☐ First, add the DataSource TestStep.
     - ☐ Next, add all required Test logic steps.
     - ☐ Finally, add the DataSource Loop TestStep.
   - ☐ Please note that the DataSource should be created first using the desired data repository (CSV file, DB or XSL sheet).

539. **Describe the end-to-end steps for testing of web services using SoapUI tool?**
   - ☐ The following are the high-level steps to perform the WS

testing using SoapUI tool.

☐ First, get the WSDL or WADL or REST API URL for the Web Service to be tested.

☐ Then, launch the SoapUI tool and start creating a new project using the GUI wizard.

☐ Next is to inspect the WSDL and also check for WS-I profile compliance if needed. It will generate a report and see if any errors.

☐ Next, it is to add a new Web Service request. Check this WS if it is functioning ok or not.

☐ Then, create a new TestSuite, and then Test, and then required TestSteps based on the above WS request.

☐ After that keep adding the test steps to match the test scenario and also add test assertions.

☐ Check the project once to see the test scenario is achieved. You can see the results on the GUI.

☐ Later, parameterize the inputs and also add the Data Driven using DataSource and Loop steps in the SoapUI tool.

☐ Finally, execute and save the project. The project itself is going to be saved as XML, which is what to be checked into the source code repository (git).

☐ For complete automated regression testing, the execution can be done ANT or Maven and then hook in Jenkins/Hudson CI.

540. **What are the data stores that can be associated with data sources?**

☐ SoapUI supports the following data stores for data driven support using data sources.

  ☐ CSV (Comma Separated Values) files with any separator between the values and the default is ','.

  ☐ XLS (eXceL Spreadsheet) files (Microsoft specific format) with rows and columns filled with data.

  ☐ Databases like Oracle, MySQL, etc.

541. What is basic input required to test SOAP and RESTful web services?

- ☐ At a minimum, the following information is needed for testing.
  - ☐ WSDL file or URL is required for SOAP Web Service.
  - ☐ WADL or REST API URI and payload information are needed for RESTful APIs.

542. How do the tests developed in SoapUI projects getting saved? What are the different types of SoapUI tests execution?

- ☐ The SoapUI created WS tests are stored in XML format. The entire test suite information is in this XML file and needs to be saved to make modifications in future or to execute the tests later.
- ☐ The following are the common execution types with SoapUI WS tests.

  i) SoapUI GUI: Use GUI tool itself to run the tests directly. Open the project from XML and run.

  ii) CLI: Use the command line testrunner script with appropriate options. See the below console snippet.

```
C:\SmartBear\soapUI-Pro-4.5.1\bin>testrunner.bat
soapUI Pro 4.5.1 TestCase Runner
usage: testrunner [options] <soapui-project-file>
C:\webservicestesting>\SmartBear\soapUI-Pro-
4.5.1\bin\testrunner.bat "C:\users\Jagadesh Babu
Munta\Documents\CurrencyConverter-soapui-pro-
ject.xml"
soapUI Pro 4.5.1 TestCase Runner
..
---------------- Request --------------------------
Request Headers: Host : www.webservicex.net
Content-Length : 325
```

Accept-Encoding : gzip,deflate
User-Agent : Apache-HttpClient/4.1.1 (java 1.5)
Connection : Keep-Alive
Content-Type : application/soap+xml;charset=UTF-8;action="http://www.webserviceX.NET/ConversionRate"
<soap:Envelope
xmlns:soap="http://www.w3.org/2003/05/soap-envelope" xmlns:web="http://www.webserviceX.NET/">
 <soap:Header/>
 <soap:Body>
 <web:ConversionRate>
 <web:FromCurrency>USD</web:FromCurrency>
 <web:ToCurrency>AUD</web:ToCurrency>
 </web:ConversionRate>
 </soap:Body>
</soap:Envelope>

---------------- Response ------------------------
Response Headers: X-AspNet-Version : 4.0.30319
Date : Mon, 06 May 2013 05:24:55 GMT
#status# : HTTP/1.1 200 OK
Content-Length : 380
Content-Type : application/soap+xml; charset=utf-8
X-Powered-By : ASP.NET
Server : Microsoft-IIS/7.0
Cache-Control : private, max-age=0
<soap:Envelope
xmlns:soap="http://www.w3.org/2003/05/soap-envelope"
xmlns:xsi="http://www.w3.org/2001/XMLSchema-instance
" xmlns:xsd="http://www.w3.org/2001/XMLSchema">
 <soap:Body>
 <ConversionRateResponse xmlns="http://www.webserviceX.NET/">
 <ConversionRateResult>0.9725</ConversionRateResult>
 </ConversionRateResponse>

```
</soap:Body>
</soap:Envelope>
```

iii) SoapUI APIs: Use the SoapUI APIs to run the test suites by integrating in the regular TestNG or JUnit tests or any other test framework. The below is the code snippet.

```
public void testRunner() throws Exception
{
// Use this for soapui free edition
//SoapUITestCaseRunner runner = new SoapUITestCaseRunner();
// Use this for soapui Pro edition
SoapUIProTestCaseRunner runner = new    SoapUIProTestCaseRunner();
runner.setProjectFile(projectDir+File.separator+projectFile);
 assertTrue(runner.run());
}
```

In the above, catch the exception as the runner.run() call can throw an exception if an error occurs. To gain more control over the reporting, run a particular TestCase as below..

```
public void testTestCaseRunner() throws Exception
{
WsdlProject project = new WsdlProject( "src/dist/sample-soapui-project.xml" );
 TestSuite testSuite = project.getTestSuiteByName( "Test Suite" );
 TestCase testCase = testSuite.getTestCaseByName( "Test Conversions" );

// create empty properties and run synchronously
TestRunner runner = testCase.run( new PropertiesMap(), false );
```

assertEquals(Status.FINISHED, runner.getStatus());

}

iv) ANT integration: Integrate the SoapUI testrunner into Ant build files by running the tool using exec task as there is no direct SoapUI ANT task. See the below ANT build.xml snippet.

```xml
<?xml version="1.0" encoding="UTF-8" ?>
<!--
Description: SoapUI tests execution build xml file
-->

<project name="soapuiproject1" default="usage" basedir=".">
        <property name="project.dir" value="."/>
        <property name="soapui.files.dir"
        value="C:\\webservicestesting"/>
        <property name="results.dir" value="C:\\web-
servicestesting\soapui_results"/>
        <property name="soapui.xml" value="Curren-
cyConverter-soapui-project.xml"/>

        <property name="soapui.tool"
        value="C:\\SmartBear\\soapUI-Pro-
4.5.1\\bin\\testrunner.bat"/>
        <target name="usage" description="usage">


        <!-- Run soapui tool -->
        <target name="run" description="Run soap ui
test">
                <exec executable="${soapui.tool}">
                <arg line="-f ${results.dir} -r -o -j -a
${soapui.xml}"/>
                </exec>
        </target>
</project>
```

543. **Can you generate JUnit test reports from SoapUI tests? And how?**
   - ☐ Yes. The JUnit reports can be generated for SoapUI based WS tests using the following two ways.
      - ☐ Generate directly from UI itself by selecting the Junit-style option for reports.
      - ☐ Choose the JUnit reporting option in the test runner command (-j option).

544. **How do you integrate SoapUI tests in ANT and Jenkins?**
   - ☐ The ANT integration for SoapUI tests is to invoke the testrunner script and supply as the SoapUI project XML as input. See the below snippet. Here soapui.tool is the property pointing to the full path of SoapUI testrunner executable file.

      <exec executable="${soapui.tool}">
      <arg   line="-f ${results.dir}   -r   -o   -j   -a ${soapui.xml}"/>
      </exec>

   - ☐ For Jenkins integration, once the ANT build file is ready, then invoke the ANT targets directly from the Jenkins job build steps or execute the SoapUI tool directly in from shell script. There is no need for UI interface to integrate and instead only CLI is enough.

545. **Without SoapUI tool, how can you test web services?**
   - ☐ One simple way to test WS without SoapUI tool is to use the Java's net programming APIs for URLConnection. Here are the basic steps.
      - ☐ First, construct the payload request/SOAP request XML as String.
      - ☐ Next, create URL object with the given Web Service URL.
      - ☐ Open the URLConnection from url.openConnection().

- ☐ Set the request and response properties on the connection to write and read from streams.
- ☐ Get the OutputStream from connection object.
- ☐ Write SOAP request XML/REST API JSON payload on the outputstream and flush out buffer.
- ☐ Get the InputStream from connection object.
- ☐ Start reading the response from InputStream buffer until the end of stream or no lines to read.
- ☐ Assert the test by parsing the response string (SOAP XML or JSON file).

☐ See the code snippet as below for SOAP WS.

```
@Test(dataProvider="testData2", enabled=true)
public void testCurrency(String curFrom, String
curTo, String expRes) throws Exception{
        String soaprequest =
                        "<soap:Envelope
xmlns:soap=\"http://www.w3.org/2003/05/soap-en-
velope\" xmlns:web=\"http://www.web-
serviceX.NET/\">"+
                "\n<soap:Header/>"+
                "\n<soap:Body>"+
                "\n<web:ConversionRate>"+
                "<web:FromCur-
rency>"+curFrom+"</web:FromCurrency>"+
                "<web:ToCur-
rency>"+curTo+"</web:ToCurrency>"+
                "</web:ConversionRate>"+
                "</soap:Body>"+
                "</soap:Envelope>";

                System.out.println("\n*** SOAP
REQUEST ***\n"+soaprequest);
                URL url = new
URL("http://www.webservicex.net/CurrencyConver-
tor.asmx");
                URLConnection conn = url.open-
Connection();
```

```
            conn.addRequestProperty("Con-
tent-Length", soaprequest.length()+"");
            conn.addRequestProperty("Con-
tent-Type", "application/soap+xml;charset=UTF-
8;action=\"http://www.webserviceX.NET/Conver-
sionRate\"");
            conn.setDoOutput(true);
            conn.setDoInput(true);
            // Send soap request
            OutputStreamWriter writer = new
OutputStreamWriter(conn.getOutputStream());
            writer.write(soaprequest);
            writer.flush();

            // Read soap response
            BufferedReader reader =
                        new Buff-
eredReader(new InputStreamReader(conn.get-
InputStream()));
            String line = null;
            StringBuffer sb = new String-
Buffer();
            while ((line = reader.readLine())
!= null) {
                //System.out.println(line);
                sb.append(line);
            }
            writer.close();
            reader.close();
            String actualOutput =
sb.toString();
            System.out.println("\n*** SOAP
RESPONSE ***\n"+actualOutput);
            // Check the result
            System.out.println("\n*** ASSER-
TIONS ***\n");
            Assert.assertNotNull(actualOut-
put);
```

```
                    if (actualOutput.indexOf(ex-
pRes)!=-1) {
                            System.out.println("Found
the value...");
                            Assert.assert-
True("Match", true);
                    } else {
                            System.out.println("NOT
Found the value!");
                            Assert.assertFalse("No
match", true);
                    }
        }

        @DataProvider
        public Object[][] testData() {
                return new Object[][]{{"CurrencyConvert-
        erTestProject-soapui-project.xml"}};
        }

        @DataProvider
        public Object[][] testData2() {
                return new Ob-
        ject[][]{{"USD","INR","54"},{"USD","EUR","0.6"},
        {"USD","AUD","1"},
                            {"USD","JPY","100"}};
        }
```

546. **How do you use the properties in SoapUI projects?**
   □ The properties in the SoapUI project helps in making the customization in the test configuration. The Properties can be defined at a different level in the SoapUI project.
      □ Project level properties
      □ Test Suite level properties
      □ Test Case level properties.
   □ To set the property, right click and define a new custom property.

☐ To property can be referenced as ${#project#property} wherever the property value to be substituted.

☐ See more at https://www.soapui.org/functional-test-ing/properties/working-with-properties.html

547. Can you create a mock service from SoapUI tool? And how?

☐ Yes. One of the key features of SoapUI is to create mock services for WS.

☐ To create the mock service, please follow the below steps.

   ☐ First, create the SoapUI project with given WSDL URL as usual.

   ☐ From the Project WS interface, create mock service by right click to get the contextual menu and then click on "Generate SOAP mock service". Then, fill all the details in the wizard.

   ☐ Start the mock service by clicking the green play button.

   ☐ Finally, edit the mock service and update the response as needed.

☐ See more details at https://www.soapui.org/getting-started/mock-services.html

548. How do you assert the responses with xpath in SoapUI project?

☐ In the SoapUI, add an assertion to the test by right click on the response to get a context menu (in Pro edition) and then choose an appropriate option like content.

☐ Later, select XPath Match from the UI wizard, choose the options like wildcards and enter the expected result string along with xpath.

☐ See more details at https://www.soapui.org/functional-testing/validating-messages/validating-xml-mes-sages.html

549. What is the hierarchy of test workspace structure with SoapUI?

☐ The SoapUI project has the workspace structure as below.

Project
-->Test Suite
   -->Test Case
      -->Test Step

550. What kind of automation framework used for both web application and web services testing?

☐ In most of the test automation, the Data Driven Framework has been used.

☐ The Data Driven test design framework is a paradigm where test logic is fixed but varies the test data. Here is the general analogy.

   i. test == test logic (or test assertions) + test data

   ii. test data is input data and expected output data

   iii. test logic is looped through test data

☐ That means the test methods would be supplied with the data from the data provider in TestNG. These methods will be executed with various input data such as conditions, boundaries, etc.

☐ This methodology is popular and useful to separate the data from the test code rather than hard-coded test data for maintenance and test conditions.

☐ The data itself can be in different datastores/repositories like a simple .csv files, .json files or .xls sheets, or database. The new tests can be added merely updating those external files/DB (rather than in test code) with right input data.

Congratulations!

All skills have been completed. Please see next pages for hands-on or Getting Started and then Java sample code!!
Please re-read again for more clarity and feel free to contact for help!!!

All the best!

Hands-on/Getting Started

First of all, congratulations on your new Job!

In many cases, if someone is a beginner to a profession, it would be uncomfortable where and how to get started! Giving confidence in this situation is important for new folks and here is an attempt to put together a hands-on step by step getting started information for the day-to-day work without repeating much information from the above details.

Understand the process, your role and communication channels

The first step is to understand the current process and in specific, the development process (SDLC) being followed in the organization. For this, set up a meeting with lead or manager to get such information and pointers. The process itself could be either Waterfall or Scrum process or mixed mode but identify the exact process. Also, recognize the project stakeholders and your role in the project. Understand your contributions and value-add to the project. Your goal is to exceed those expectations to develop or test a software project.

In this process or after the process identification, one should join the appropriate meetings along with colleagues to understand the expectations of the project work. Also, gain the domain knowledge on the product or IT service that is going to be worked on by going through the related documents and wikis, etc. The domain knowledge is all about understanding at high-level on the team's/group's project. The areas such as features or use cases, end-to-flows, architecture, the design on product engineering side. If it is an IT project (intranet/company/partners related projects), then familiarize on the applications and the related features, etc. During this process, establish a wrap with colleagues or counterparts in QA and Dev teams to make as you might be working on a day-to-day basis and also get the knowledge quickly. If you need more clarity on the process, then go through the SDLC and QA concepts skills in this book as necessary.

As an engineer, your role might be to work as a module development or test owner.

Task#1. Get or Create Test Plan and Test Specs (QA role)

To get started, see if you have already a master test plan or module test plan and test spec. If there is none, then create the Test plan and Test Spec artifacts.

The test plan is a testing artifact in the planning process to plan the testing with details like scoped, non-scoped requirements to test, test strategy, resources, matrix and schedule (estimates) created by the QA team. See Q#54 for more details in QA concepts skill. Take the template and start filling it. Follow the steps in Q#54.

Test design process is more of thinking of the test scenarios and their priority. The Test Specification (TS or TDS) is documenting those scenarios as test cases before actually testing as either manually or automating the tests. See #55 in QA concepts skill. Take the template and start filling it. Follow the steps in Q#55.

Task#2. Perform Manual verification

It is important first to get the scenarios tested and file bugs sooner as soon as the code is available to test. For this, verify the use cases/ test scenarios manually by following step by step as mentioned in the test spec to make sure features are working fine. If not tests failed (means not expected results), then file bugs. Follow the bugs lifecycle (new, fix, verify cycles). If the automation itself helps in quick verification (such as computing actions), then start writing the automated code. Most of the time, manual check is useful to quickly verify the basic product features and understanding of use cases.

Send the status reports on tests executed, passed, failed and bugs information to the QA/Dev managers and leads. Note that the consistent status updates to the key project stakeholders are important.

Task#3. Get handle on the code base and develop automated test code or new dev code

After knowing the project details or manual use cases verification, the next step is to get familiar with existing codebase (dev code for developers and QA automated test code for QA engineers) for if exists. In most of the organizations, this might be the case as you might be joining as a team member to work on current projects.

For QA, it 's hard to scale with only manual testing and need to auto-mate the tests. For development, keep building the main code and unit test code.

For this, identify the source code repository (git or svn) and valid cre-dentials to access the test source code repository. See the steps in Q#163 for getting the source code from git.

To add new code in the local workspace, create a module directory or define the workspace. See if ANT or Maven build framework is being used. Based on this, create a new build file for the sources compile or test project directory in pom.xml or build.xml for the project. See more details on ANT build.xml steps at Q#345. Use the ant targets if any common targets available in the common build files.
In the case of Maven, see the test project's pom.xml and modify it to add the dependencies required for the test code compilation and build.

Test the project locally using "mvn test" or "mvn compile" or "ant build". Verify that REST API test code or Selenium test code works fine. If not working, then analyze the failures on the console output and then fix the java test code or build.xml or pom.xml files. Refer the re-lated questions in the previous on how to work with these skills.

Once the code is successfully verified, then create a module dev/test branch and checkin the code. In the case of dev code, add the JUnit or TestNG unit test code. Make sure that the tests passed. Refer the related questions in the previous on how to work with these skills.

Integrate the tests run into the Jenkins or Hudson CI to verify the code regressions on each project binaries or module code. Refer the related questions in the previous on how to work with these skills.

Mostly, your day-to-day work will continue with repetition of above tasks from #1 through #3. Enjoy and try new technology with making your job as smarter with less effort but big gains rather than doing mun-dane daily work!

Java Samples Code

Learning by an example is a quick way to learn new things. The Java sample code helps developers and QA engineers to get comfortable in Java programming.

551. Write a binary search program.

```
package com.everydayon;

import java.util.Arrays;

/**
 * Binary search method
 * User: jmunta
 */
public class BinarySearch {


    /* Driver program to check above functions */
    public static void main(String []args)
    {
        System.out.println("Searching...");
        int arr[] = {3, 4, 5, 1, 2};
        Arrays.sort(arr); // {1, 2, 3, 4,5}
        int no = 1;
        System.out.println(binarySearch(arr, 0, arr.length,
no));
        System.out.println("Searching...done");
    }


    /* Standard Binary Search function*/
    public static int binarySearch(int arr[], int low, int high,
int no)
    {
        if (high < low)
```

```
        return -1;

        int mid = (low + high)/2;  /*low + (high - low)/2;*/

        if (no == arr[mid])
            return mid;
        if (no > arr[mid])
            return binarySearch(arr, (mid + 1), high, no);
        else
            return binarySearch(arr, low, (mid -1), no);
    }
}
```

552. Recursion - Print Fibonacci series for given count. (start
     with 0 and 1, then each next number is sum of previous 2
     numbers)
     Example: java Fibonacci 10
              0 1 1 2 3 5 8 13 21 34

     Compute factorial of a given number (n!). Use Recursion.
     Example: java Factorial 6
              720

```java
/**
 * Recursion.java
 * User: jmunta
 */
package com.everydayon;

/**
 * @author Jagadesh Babu Munta
 *
 */
public class Recursion {

    /**
     * @param args
     */
    public static void main(String[] args) {
```

```
        int f = 5;
        if (args.length>0) {
                f = Integer.parseInt(args[0]);
        }
        System.out.println(f+ "! = "+factorial(f));

        System.out.println(f+ "th finonacci number =
"+fibonacci(f));

        printTower(f);

}

/*
 * Base : f(1) = 1
 * f! = fx(f-1)!
 *
 * f! = fx(f-1)x(f-2)x(f-3)..x1
 */
public static int factorial(int f) {
        if (f==1) {
                return 1;
        } else {
                return f*factorial(f-1);
        }

}

/*
 * F(0) = 0, F(1) = 1
 * F(n) = F(n-1)+F(n-2)
 * 0 1 1 2 3 5 ...
 *
 */
public static int fibonacci(int n) {
        if (n==0) {
                return 0;
        } else if (n==1) {
```

```
                    return 1;
            } else {
                    return fibonacci(n-1)+fibonacci(n-
2);
            }
    }

    public static void printTower(int n) {
            if (n==1) {
                    System.out.println("*");
                    return;
            } else {
                    for (int i=0;i<n;i++) {
                            System.out.print("*");

                    }
                    System.out.println("");

                    printTower(n-1);
            }
    }

}
```

553. Reverse echo or reverse the given input string.
     Example: java ReverseEcho Programming is Fun if you get
     it! Else it is headache!!
     !!ehcadaeh si ti eslE !ti teg uoy fi nuF si gnimmargorP

```
/**
 * ReverseEcho.java
 *
 */
package com.everydayon;

/**
 * Reverse a String with and without using inbuilt
```

```
java funtions.
 *
 * @author jagadeshmunta
 *
 */
public class ReverseEcho {

        public static void main(String [] args) {
                String input = "Programming is
Fun if you get it! Else it is headache!!";
                System.out.println(input + "-->");
                System.out.println(reverse(input));
                System.out.println(inReverse(in-
put));
        }

        /**
         * Reverse a given string
         * @param s
         * @return
         */
        public static String reverse(String s) {
                int n = s.length();
                char [] chars = new char[n];
                s.getChars(0, n, chars, 0);
                char t;
                for (int i=0; i< n/2; i++) {
                        t = chars[i];
                        chars[i] = chars[n-i-1];
                        chars[n-i-1] = t;
                }
                return new String(chars);
        }

        /**
         * Using inbuilt
         * @param s
         * @return
```

```
                    */
            public static String inReverse(String s) {
                    return new StringBuilder(s).re-
verse().toString();
            }


    }
```

554. Reverse words of the given input string
Example: java ReverseWord "I Love Java"
Java Love I

```
/**
 * ReverseWords.java
 *
 */
package com.everydayon;

/**
 * Reverse words
 *
 * @author jagadesh munta
 *
 */

public class ReverseWords {

        public static void main(String [] args) {
            String input = null;
            if (args.length>0){
                    input = args[0];
            }
            else {
                    input = "I Love Java";
            }
            System.out.println(input + "-->");
            System.out.println(reverseWords(input));
```

```
        }

        /**
         * Reverse words
         * @param s
         * @return
         */
        public static String reverseWords(String s) {
                String [] words = s.split(" ");
                StringBuffer sb = new StringBuffer();

                for (int i=words.length-1; i>=0; i--) {
                        if (i!= 0) {
                                sb.append(words[i]+" ");
                        } else {
                                sb.append(words[i]);
                        }
                }
                return sb.toString();
        }

}
```

555. Write a program to replace a given from word to a word in a
    string
    Example: java Replace "I love Java" "love" "and"
    I and Java

```
/**
 *
 */
package com.everydayon;

/**
 * @author jagadeshmunta
 *
```

```java
*/
public class Replace {

    /**
     * @param args
     */
    public static void main(String[] args) {
        String input = "I Love Java";
        String from = "Love";
        String to = "and";
        if (args.length==3){
            input = args[0];
            from = args[1];
            to = args[2];
        }

        System.out.println(input + "-->");
        System.out.println(replace(input,from,to));

    }

    /**
     * Return new string after replacing the original with
to at from word.
     * @param orig
     * @param from
     * @param to
     * @return
     */
    public static String replace(String orig, String from,
String to) {
        String [] words = orig.split(" ");
        StringBuilder sb = new StringBuilder();
        String w = null;
        for (int i=0; i<words.length; i++) {
            if (words[i].equals(from)) {
                w = to;
            } else {
```

```
                w = words[i];
        }
        if (i!=words.length-1) {
                sb.append(w+" ");
        } else {
                sb.append(w);
        }

    }
    return sb.toString();
}

}
```

556. Write a program to find how many times a given letter is there in a given string
Example: java LetterFind "Java is a cross platform" a
'a' found at 4 places.

```
/**
 *
 */
package com.everydayon;

/**
 * Find how many times a given letter is there in a given string
 * @author jagadeshmunta
 *
 */
public class FindLetter {

        /**
         * @param args
         */
        public static void main(String[] args) {
                String input = "Java is a cross platform";
                String letter = "a";
```

```
        if (args.length==2){
                input = args[0];
                letter = args[1];
        }
        char c = (char) letter.getBytes()[0];

        System.out.println(input + "-->");
        System.out.println(""""+c +"""+ "found at
"+findLetter(input,c) + "places.");

    }

    /**
     * Return the number of times character appeared in
a string
     *
     * @param orig
     * @param c
     * @return
     */
    public static int findLetter(String orig, char c) {
            int n = orig.length();
            int count = 0;
            char [] chars = new char[n];
            orig.getChars(0, n, chars, 0);
            for (int i=0; i<n; i++) {
                    if (chars[i] == c) {
                            count++;
                    }
            }
            return count;
    }

}
```

557. Write a program to convert a given sentence string to Camel case (Capital letter in the beginning of a word if it is a letter)

Example: java PrintCamel "i AM a JAVA program"
I am a Java Program

```java
/**
 *
 */
package com.everydayon;

/**
 * To convert a given sentence string to Camel case (Capital
letter in the beginning of a word if it is a letter)
 * Example: java PrintCamel "i AM a JAVA program"
 *          I am a Java Program
 *
 * @author jagadeshmunta
 *
 */
public class PrintCamel {

        /**
         * @param args
         */
        public static void main(String[] args) {
                String input = "i AM a JAVA program";

                if (args.length>0){
                        input = args[0];
                }

                System.out.println(input + "-->");
                System.out.println(getCamelStr(input));

        }

        public static String getCamelStr(String s) {
                String ns = s.toLowerCase();
                String [] words = ns.split(" ");
                StringBuilder sb = new StringBuilder();
```

```
            for (int i=0; i<words.length; i++ ) {
                if (i!=words.length-1) {
                    sb.append(con-
vertUpper(words[i]) +" ");
                } else {
                    sb.append(con-
vertUpper(words[i]));
                }

            }
            return sb.toString();
        }


        public static String convertUpper(String w) {
            char [] chars = w.toCharArray();
            if (chars[0] > 'a' && chars[0] < 'z') {
                chars[0] -=32; // 'A'=65 and
'a'=97
            }
            return new String(chars);
        }

    }
```

558. Write a program to efficiently concatenate given multiple
     strings into a single string.
     Example: java CatString "Hello" "I know" "Java"
     Hello I know Java

```
/**
 *
 */
package com.everydayon;

/**

 * Efficiently concatenate given multiple strings into a single
```

```
string
*
* @author jagadeshmunta
*
*/
public class ConcatWords {

        /**
         * @param args
         */
        public static void main(String[] args) {
                if (args.length<0) {
                        System.out.println("Please enter
words to get a single string");
                        return;
                }

                System.out.println(concat(args));

        }

        public static String concat(String... words) {
                StringBuilder sb = new StringBuilder();
                for (int i=0; i<words.length; i++) {
                        sb.append(words[i]);
                }
                return sb.toString();
        }

}
```

559. Write a program to compute initials from your full name.
Example: java NameInitial "Jagadesh Munta"
Initial is "JM"

```java
/**
 *
 */
package com.everydayon;

/**
 * compute initials from your full name.
 *        Example: java NameInitial "Jagadesh Munta"
 * Initial is "JM"
 *
 * @author jagadeshmunta
 *
 */
public class NameInitials {

    /**
     * @param args
     */
    public static void main(String[] args) {
        String input = "Jagadesh Munta";

        if (args.length>0){
            input = args[0];
        }
        System.out.println(input + "-->");
        System.out.println(getInitials(input));

    }

    /**
     * Get name initials
     *
     * @param name
     * @return
     */
    public static String getInitials(String name) {
        String s = name.trim().toUpperCase();
        char [] chars = s.toCharArray();
```

```
int beginIndex = s.lastIndexOf(' ');
return chars[0]+""+chars[beginIndex+1];
}


}
```

560. Print prime numbers between 2 given numbers and also total number of primes found.Also write if those given numbers also prime or not. See primes at http://primes.utm.edu/
Example: java com.everydayon.PrimeNumber 2 500
Prime numbers...
2 3 5 7 11 13 17 19 23 29 31 37 41 43 47 53 59 61 67 71 73
79 83 89 97 101 103 107 109 113 127 131 137 139 149 151
157 1
63 167 173 179 181 191 193 197 199 211 223 227 229 233
239 241 251 257 263 269 271 277 281 283 293 307 311 313
317 331 3
37 347 349 353 359 367 373 379 383 389 397 401 409 419
421 431 433 439 443 449 457 461 463 467 479 487 491 499
Total number of primes found=95

Is 2 prime?true

Is 500 prime?false

```
/**
 * PrimeNumber.java
 *
 */
package com.everydayon.PrimeNumber;

/**
 * @author Jagadesh Babu Munta
 *
 */
public class PrimeNumber {
```

```java
/**
 * @param args
 */
public static void main(String[] args) {
    //System.out.println("\nTotal number of
primes found="+printPrimes(Integer.parseInt(args[0])));
    System.out.println("\nTotal number of
primes found="+printPrimes(Integer.parseInt(args[0]), Inte-
ger.parseInt(args[1])));

    System.out.println("\n Is "+args[0] +"
prime?"+isPrime(Integer.parseInt(args[0])));
    System.out.println("\n Is "+args[1] +"
prime?"+isPrime(Integer.parseInt(args[1])));
}

/*
 * Print primes within a given number
 */
public static int printPrimes(int end) {
    System.out.println("Prime numbers...");
    int count = 0;
    boolean prime = false;
    for (int i=2;i<end;i++) {
        prime = true;
        for (int j=2;j<i;j++) {
            if (i%j==0) {
                prime = false;
            }
        }

        if (prime) {
            System.out.print(i+" ");
            count++;
        }
    }
    return count;
```

```java
        }

        /*
         * Print primes with between 2 numbers
         */
        public static int printPrimes(int start, int end) {
                System.out.println("Prime numbers...");
                int count = 0;
                boolean prime = false;
                for (int i=start;i<end;i++) {
                        prime = true;
                        for (int j=2;j<i;j++) {
                                if (i%j==0) {
                                        prime = false;
                                }
                        }

                        if (prime) {
                                System.out.print(i+" ");
                                count++;
                        }
                }
                return count;
        }

        /*
         * Check if a given number is prime or not
         */
        public static boolean isPrime(int number) {
                boolean prime = true;
                for (int j=2;j<number;j++) {
                        if (number%j==0) {
                                prime = false;
                        }
                }
                return prime;
        }
```

}

561. Write Anagram checker. See details and algorithm at URL
http://www.codemiles.com/java/java-anagram-t5455.html
Two words or phrases in English are anagrams if their letters,
rearranged, are the same. We assume that upper and lower
case are indistinguishable, and punctuation and spaces don't
count.

Example: java com.everydayon.Anagram "The eyes" "they
see"
  Anagram: true
Example: java com.everydayon.Anagram "Funny" "fun"
  Anagram: false

```
/**
 *
 */
package com.everydayon;

/**
 * See details and algorithm at URL http://www.codemi-
les.com/java/java-anagram-t5455.html
 * Two words or phrases in English are anagrams if their let-
ters, rearranged, are the same. We assume that upper and
lower case are indistinguishable, and punctuation and spaces
don't count.
 * Example: java com.everydayon.Anagram "The eyes" "they
see"
 * Anagram: true
 * Example: java com.everydayon.Anagram "Funny" "fun"
 * Anagram: false
 *
 * @author jagadeshmunta
 *
 */
```

```java
public class AnagramChecker {

    /**
     * @param args
     */
    public static void main(String[] args) {
        String input1 = "The Eyes";
        String input2 = "They See";
        if (args.length==2){
            input1 = args[0];
            input2 = args[1];
        }
        System.out.println(input1 +" "+ input2 + "--
>");

        System.out.println("Anagram: "+isAna-
gram(input1, input2));


    }

    /**
     * Check if given 2 strings are anagram
     *
     * @param one
     * @param two
     * @return
     */
    public static boolean isAnagram(String one, String
two) {
        boolean isA = false;
        char [] oneChars = one.trim().toLower-
Case().toCharArray();
        String twoS = two.trim().toLowerCase();
        int j = 0;
        for (int i=0; i<oneChars.length; i++) {
            if (oneChars[i]==' ') {
                continue;
            }
```

```
                          if (twoS.indexOf(oneChars[i])== -
1) {
                                  return false;
                          }
                          j++;
                  }
                  char[] twoChars = twoS.toCharArray();
                  int j1=0;
                  for (int i=0; i<twoChars.length; i++) {
                          if (twoChars[i]==' ') {
                                  continue;
                          }
                          j1++;
                  }
                  if (j==j1) {
                          isA = true;
                  }
                  return isA;

          }

  }
```

562. Write a program to calculate GCD.

```
/**
 * GCD.java
 * User: jmunta
 */
package com.everydayon;

/**
 * @author Jagadesh Babu Munta
 *
 */
public class GCD {
```

```
/**
 * @param args
 */
public static void main(String[] args) {

    if (args.length<2) {
        System.out.println("Usage: java
com.everydayon.GCD");
        return;
    }
    long gcd = gcd(Integer.par-
seInt(args[0]),Integer.parseInt(args[1]));
    System.out.println("GCD="+gcd);

}

public static long gcd(int a, int b) {
    if (b==0) {
        return a;
    }
    return gcd(b, a%b);
}

}
```

563. Write a program to do Palindrome Checker.

```
/**
 * PalindromeChecker.java
 * User: jmunta
 */
package com.everydayon;

/**
 * @author Jagadesh Babu Munta
 *
 */
public class PalindromeChecker {
```

```java
/**
 * @param args
 */
public static void main(String[] args) {
    String input = "malayalam";

    if (args.length > 0) {

        input = args[0];

    }

    // characters

    char[] outchars = new char[input.length()];
    //char[] outchars = new char[100];
    input.getChars(0, input.length(), outchars, 0);
    char [] outchars1 = outchars.clone();
    // reverse
    System.out.println(input + "; reverse string is ...");
    for (int i = input.length()-1; i >= 0; i--) {
        outchars[input.length()-1-i] = outchars1[i];
    }
    String str = new String(outchars);
    //System.out.println("\n");
    System.out.println("\n" + str);
    if (input.equals(str)) {
        System.out.println(input + " is a palindrome");
    }
    else {
        System.out.println(input + " is not a palindrome");

    }
```

```
                }
        }
```

564. Write a program to declare a map, add entries and print the entries.

package com.jd;

import java.util.Collection;
import java.util.HashMap;
import java.util.LinkedHashMap;
import java.util.Map;
import java.util.Set;
import java.util.TreeMap;

public class MapExample {

> */***
> ** @param args*
> **/*
> *public static void main(String[] args) {*
> > *map1();*
> *}*
> *public static void map1() {*
> > *System.out.println("*** Hash Map Example*
> ****");*
> > *Map<String, Integer> population = new*
> *HashMap<String, Integer>();*
> > *updateMap(population);*
> > *System.out.println("*** Tree Map Example*
> ****");*
> > *Map<String, Integer> population1 = new*
> *TreeMap<String, Integer>();*
> > *updateMap(population1);*
> > *System.out.println("*** LinkedHash Map*
> *Example ***");*
> > *Map<String, Integer> population2 = new*
> *LinkedHashMap<String, Integer>();*

```java
        updateMap(population2);

    }

    public static void updateMap(Map<String,Integer>
population) {

        population.put("Fremont", 20);
        population.put("San Francisco", 100);
        population.put("Sunnyvale", 10);

        System.out.println(population); // debugging
        Int fremontPop = popula-
tion.get("Fremont").intValue();
        System.out.println("Fremont population="
+ fremontPop);

        Map<String, Integer> calPop = new
HashMap<String, Integer>();
        calPop.putAll(population);
        System.out.println(calPop); // debugging


        Set<String> cities = population.keySet();
        Collection<Integer> vals = population.val-
ues();

        for (String city : cities) {
            System.out.println(city + "=" +
population.get(city));
        }

        long totalPop = 0;
        for (Integer val : vals) {
            totalPop = totalPop + val;
        }
        System.out.println("Total population="+to-
talPop);
```

```
        population.clear();
        System.out.println(population); // debugging
    }
}
```

565. Write a cards deck (playing cards) program to distribute given n cards among given m hands. Use OOPS concepts and Java collections.
    - ☐ See the cards code at http://cs.fit.edu/~ryan/java/programs/enum/Card-java.html
    - ☐ Also see the detailed explaination on cards/deck - http://math.hws.edu/javanotes/c5/s4.html

566. Write a program to search a given element in a given array with time complexity O(log n)
    - ☐ See the algorithm and code at http://www.geeksforgeeks.org/search-an-element-in-a-sorted-and-pivoted-array/

567. Write a program to print words for given number.

```
package com.everydayon.exercises007;

/**
 * Description: Converting numbers to Words (as in dollar check)
 * Example: 123456789
 * Given number 1,234,567 is in WORDS:
 * *** ONE MILLION TWO HUNDRED THIRTY FOUR
 * THOUSAND FIVE HUNDRED SIXTY SEVEN ***
 * @author jmunta
 */
public class NumberText {
```

```java
static String [] ONES = { "ZERO","ONE", "TWO",
"THREE", "FOUR", "FIVE", "SIX",
    "SEVEN", "EIGHT", "NINE","TEN", "ELEVEN",
"TWELVE", "THIRTEEN", "FORTEEN",
    "FIFTEEN", "SIXTEEN", "SEVENTEEN", "EIGHT-
EEN", "NINETEEN", "TWENTY"};
    static String [] TENS = {
"ZERO","TEN","TWENTY","THIRTY", "FORTY", "FIFTY",
"SIXTY", "SEVENTY", "EIGHTY", "NINETY"};
    //static String [] HUNDREDS = { "ZERO","HUNDRED",
"THOUSAND", "MILLION", "TRILLION"};

    /**
     * @param args the command line arguments
     */
    public static void main(String[] args) {

        int n = 156;
        String ns = String.valueOf(n);
        // Take the input
        if (args.length>0) {
            ns = args[0];
        }
        String result = " ";
        String s = null;
        int l = ns.length();
        if (ns.length()>3) {
            s=ns.substring(l-3, l);
            result+=convert3digits(s);
            l = l-3;
            if (l<=3) { // 6 digits
              s=ns.substring(0, l);
              result=convert6digits(s)+result;
            }
            if (l>3) { // 9 digits
              s=ns.substring(l-3, l);
              result=convert6digits(s)+result;
```

```
                l = l-3;
                if (l<=3) {
                    s=ns.substring(0, l);
                    result=convert9digits(s)+result;
                }
            }
        } else {
            result+=convert3digits(ns);
        }
        System.out.printf("Given number %,d is in WORDS:
\n*** %s ***",Integer.valueOf(ns),result);

    }

    /*
     * Process 3 digits
     */
    static String convert3digits(String ns) {
        String text = " ";

        // conver to number
        int n = Integer.valueOf(ns);

        // Basic numbers
        if (n<=20) {
            text+=ONES[n]+" ";
        }

        if ((n>20) && (n<=99)) {
            text+=TENS[n/10]+" ";
            if (n%10!=0){
                text+=ONES[n%10]+" ";
            }
        }

        int n1 = 0;
        if (n>99) {
            n1 = n/100;
```

```java
        if (n1<=20) {
            text+=ONES[n1]+" ";
        }
        if ((n1>20) && (n1<=99)) {
            text+=TENS[n1/10]+" ";
            if (n1%10!=0){
                text+=ONES[n1%10]+" ";
            }
        }
        text+=" HUNDRED ";
        n1 = (n-(n/100)*100);
        if (n%100!=0) {
            text+=TENS[n1/10]+ " ";
        }
        if (n%10!=0){
            text+=ONES[n1%10]+" ";
        }
    }
    return text;
}

/*
 * Process 6 digits
 */
static String convert6digits(String ns) {
    String t3 = convert3digits(ns);
    return t3+" THOUSAND ";
}

/*
 * Process 9 digits
 */
static String convert9digits(String ns) {
    String t6 = convert3digits(ns);
    return t6+" MILLION ";
}

}
```

568. Write a singleton class.

```
/**
 * SingletonCalculator.java
 * User: jmunta
 */
package com.everydayon;

import java.io.ObjectStreamException;

/**
 * @author Jagadesh Babu Munta
 *
 */
public class SingletonCalculator implements java.io.Serializable {

    /*
     * 1. Create a constant singleton object
     */
    private static final SingletonCalculator SINGLE-
TON_CALCULATOR = new SingletonCalculator();
    private static SingletonCalculator scal = null;

    /*
     * 2. Make default constructor as private so that no
object created
     *    NOTE: This step is mandatory.
     *    If you create a single object with in constructor
(like in 2nd way as below),
     *    then it will be in infinite loop as parent's default
constructor is called.
     */
    private SingletonCalculator() {      }

    /*
     * 3. Return the singleton object instance
     */
```

```java
public static SingletonCalculator getInstance() {
        return SINGLETON_CALCULATOR;
}

/*
 * 4. To avoid spurious objects and to preserve the
singleton property
 */
public Object readResolve() throws ObjectStreamEx-
ception {
        return SINGLETON_CALCULATOR;
}

// 2nd way.  to get the singleton instance
public static synchronized SingletonCalculator
getSingleInstance() {
        if (scal==null) {
                scal = new SingletonCalculator();
        }
        return scal;
}

/**
 * @param args
 */
public static void main(String[] args) {
        System.out.println("*** Singleton instance
***");
        System.out.println(" -- 1st way -- ");
        for (int i=0;i<10;i++) {
                System.out.println(SingletonCalcu-
lator.getInstance());
        }
        System.out.println(" -- 2nd way -- ");
        for (int i=0;i<10;i++) {
                System.out.println(SingletonCalcu-
lator.getSingleInstance());
        }
```

```
        }

    }


569. Write a program to demonstrate basic I/O.
    /**
     * BasicIO.java
     * User: jmunta
     */
    package com.everydayon;

    import java.io.BufferedReader;
    import java.io.Console;
    import java.io.File;
    import java.io.FileInputStream;
    import java.io.FileNotFoundException;
    import java.io.FileOutputStream;
    import java.io.FileReader;
    import java.io.FileWriter;
    import java.io.IOException;
    import java.io.InputStreamReader;
    import java.io.PrintWriter;
    import java.util.Arrays;
    import java.util.Scanner;

    /**
     * @author Jagadesh Babu Munta
     *
     */
    public class BasicIO {

        /**
         * @param args
         */
        public static void main(String[] args) {

            char [] inputChars = new char [100];
```

```java
                InputStreamReader reader = new In-
putStreamReader(System.in);
                System.out.print("1. Enter input (In-
putStreamReader):");
                try {
                        int l = reader.read(inputChars);
                        System.out.println("chars
count="+l+","+String.valueOf(inputChars));
                } catch (IOException e) {
                        e.printStackTrace();
                }


                System.out.print("2. Enter input (Scanner)
(type 'end' to end) :");
                Scanner scan = new Scanner(System.in);
                while (! scan.hasNext("end")) {
                        System.out.println(scan.next());
                }

                // read from buffer
                System.out.print("3. Enter input (Buff-
eredReader) :");
                readFromBuffer();

                // read from console
                System.out.print("4. Reading from Con-
sole...");
                readFromConsole();

                // read from file
                System.out.println("5. Reading file....");
                String fileName = System.console().read-
Line("Enter filename:");
                readFromFile(fileName);

                // write to file
                System.out.println("6. Write to file....");
                writeToFile(fileName);
```

```java
        }

        public static void readFromBuffer() {
                BufferedReader r = new Buff-
eredReader(new InputStreamReader(System.in));
                try {
                        String line = r.readLine();
                        System.out.println("Given line in-
put="+line);
                } catch (IOException e) {
                        e.printStackTrace();
                }

        }
        /**
         * Read from console
         */
        public static void readFromConsole() {
                Console c = System.console();
                String username = c.readLine("Enter user
name:");
                char [] userpwd1 = null;
                char [] userpwd2 = null;
                boolean matched = false;
                do {
                        userpwd1 = c.readPassword("En-
ter password:");
                        userpwd2 = c.readPassword("En-
ter password again:");
                        matched = Ar-
rays.equals(userpwd1, userpwd2);
                        if (!matched) {
                                System.out.println("Er-
ror:: Passwords didn't matched");
                        }
                } while (!matched);
                System.out.println("Given
```

```java
        Username:"+username +", password:"+String.val-
ueOf(userpwd1));

    }

    /**
    * Read from File
    * @param fileName
    */
    public static void readFromFile(String fileName) {
            File f = new File(fileName);

            BufferedReader r = null;
            try {
                    r = new BufferedReader(new File-
Reader(f));

                    String line = r.readLine();
                    while (line!=null) {
                            System.out.println(line);
                            line = r.readLine();
                    }

            } catch (Exception e) {
                    e.printStackTrace();
            } finally {
                    if (r!=null) { try {
                            r.close();
                    } catch (IOException e) {
                            e.printStackTrace();
                    }}
            }

    }

    /**
    * Write to File
    * @param fileName
    */
```

```java
public static void writeToFile(String fileName) {
    File f = new File(fileName);
    BufferedReader r = null;
    PrintWriter out = null;
    try {
        r = new BufferedReader(new File-
Reader(f));
        out = new PrintWriter(new File-
Writer(f+"_copy"));
        String line = null;
        while ((line = r.readLine())!=null)
{
            //System.out.println(line);
            out.println(line);

        }
    } catch (Exception e) {
        e.printStackTrace();
    } finally {
        if (r!=null) {try {
            r.close();
        } catch (IOException e) {
            e.printStackTrace();
        }}
        if (out!=null) {out.close(); }
    }

}

}
```

Selenium Samples Code

The Selenium sample code helps QA engineers in learning the browser-based website test automation using Selenium. Having examples is a good way to quickly getting into coding.

570. Write a simple selenium test to check the facebook login.

```
package com.example.tests;

import java.util.regex.Pattern;
import java.util.concurrent.TimeUnit;
import org.junit.*;
import static org.junit.Assert.*;
import static org.hamcrest.CoreMatchers.*;
import org.openqa.selenium.*;
import org.openqa.selenium.firefox.FirefoxDriver;
import org.openqa.selenium.support.ui.Select;

public class SampleFBLoginTest {
  private WebDriver driver;
  private String baseUrl;
  private boolean acceptNextAlert = true;
  private StringBuffer verificationErrors = new String-
Buffer();

  @Before
  public void setUp() throws Exception {
    driver = new FirefoxDriver();
    baseUrl = "https://www.facebook.com/";
    driver.manage().timeouts().implicitlyWait(30, TimeU-
nit.SECONDS);
  }

  @Test
```

```java
public void testSampleFBLogin() throws Exception {
    driver.get(baseUrl + "/");
    driver.findElement(By.id("email")).clear();
    driver.findElement(By.id("email")).send-
Keys("youremailid");
    driver.findElement(By.id("pass")).clear();
    driver.findElement(By.id("pass")).sendKeys("xxxx");
    driver.findElement(By.id("u_0_n")).click();
    assertEquals("Update Status", driver.findEle-
ment(By.cssSelector("span.uiIcon-
Text._5lz7")).getText());
    assertEquals("Trending", driver.findEle-
ment(By.id("u_0_1r")).getText());
    assertEquals("Name", driver.findElement(By.cssSe-
lector("span._2dpb")).getText());
    driver.findElement(By.cssSelector("div.link-
Wrap.hasCount > span")).click();
    driver.findElement(By.id("userNavigationLa-
bel")).click();
    driver.findElement(By.cssSelector("input.uiLinkBut-
tonInput")).click();
}

@After
public void tearDown() throws Exception {
    driver.quit();
    String verificationErrorString = verificationEr-
rors.toString();
    if (!"".equals(verificationErrorString)) {
        fail(verificationErrorString);
    }
}

private boolean isElementPresent(By by) {
    try {
        driver.findElement(by);
        return true;
    } catch (NoSuchElementException e) {
```

```
    return false;
  }
}


private boolean isAlertPresent() {
  try {
  driver.switchTo().alert();
  return true;
  } catch (NoAlertPresentException e) {
  return false;
  }
}


private String closeAlertAndGetItsText() {
  try {
  Alert alert = driver.switchTo().alert();
  String alertText = alert.getText();
  if (acceptNextAlert) {
    alert.accept();
  } else {
    alert.dismiss();
  }
  return alertText;
  } finally {
  acceptNextAlert = true;
  }
 }
}
```

571. Write sample code for advanced UI Elements using Sele-
     nium WebDriver such as Select, Drag-and-drop, Auto sug-
     gestion or complete. Also, take the screenshots for failed
     tests.

```
package com.everydayon.selenium.test;

import static org.testng.Assert.assertEquals;
```

```java
import java.io.File;
import java.io.IOException;
import java.text.SimpleDateFormat;
import java.util.ArrayList;
import java.util.Arrays;
import java.util.Calendar;
import java.util.List;
import java.util.concurrent.TimeUnit;

import org.apache.commons.io.FileUtils;
import org.openqa.selenium.By;
import org.openqa.selenium.Keys;
import org.openqa.selenium.OutputType;
import org.openqa.selenium.TakesScreenshot;
import org.openqa.selenium.WebDriver;
import org.openqa.selenium.WebDriverBackedSelenium;
import org.openqa.selenium.WebElement;
import org.openqa.selenium.chrome.ChromeDriver;
import org.openqa.selenium.firefox.FirefoxDriver;
import org.openqa.selenium.htmlunit.HtmlUnitDriver;
import org.openqa.selenium.ie.InternetExplorerDriver;
import org.openqa.selenium.interactions.Action;
import org.openqa.selenium.interactions.Actions;
import org.openqa.selenium.remote.DesiredCapabilities;
import org.openqa.selenium.safari.SafariDriver;
import org.openqa.selenium.support.ui.ExpectedConditions;
import org.openqa.selenium.support.ui.Select;
import org.openqa.selenium.support.ui.WebDriverWait;
import org.testng.ITestResult;
import org.testng.annotations.AfterClass;
import org.testng.annotations.AfterMethod;
import org.testng.annotations.BeforeClass;
import org.testng.annotations.DataProvider;
import org.testng.annotations.Factory;
import org.testng.annotations.Test;

import com.opera.core.systems.OperaDriver;
import com.thoughtworks.selenium.DefaultSelenium;
```

```java
/**
 * Description: Advanced UI Elements using Selenium Web-
Driver
 *   Select, Drag-and-drop, Auto suggestion or complete
 *
 * @author Jagadesh Babu Munta
 *
 */
public class AdvancedSeleniumTest {

        private WebDriver driver = null;
        private String url1 = "http://html5demos.com/drag";
        private String url2 = "http://jqueryui.com/dragga-
ble";
        private String url3 = "http://www.theautomat-
edtester.co.uk/demo2.html";
        private String url4 = "http://localhost:8000/docs/se-
lenium/dragdrop.html"; //"http://jqueryui.com/droppable";
        private String url5 = "http://localhost:8000/docs/se-
lenium/select.html"; //"http://jqueryui.com/droppable";
        private String url6 = "http://localhost:8000/docs/se-
lenium/autocomplete.html";
        private String url7 = "http://www.google.com";
        private String url8 = "http://www.monster.com";
        private String url9 = "http://www.bing.com";

        //private String url = "http://jqueryui.com/dragga-
ble"; //"http://html5demos.com/drag";
        private String browser = null;
        private static final String BROWSER_PROPERTIES
= "browsertesting.properties";
        private static final int WAIT_TIME = 10;

        @Factory(dataProviderClass=com.everydayon.sele-
nium.test.TestDataProvider.class,
                        dataProvider="testDataProvider")
        public AdvancedSeleniumTest(String browser) {
```

```
                this.browser = browser;
                System.out.println("Running with
browser="+browser);
                }


                @BeforeClass
                public void beforeClass() throws Exception{
                // Create the driver
                if ("firefox".equals(browser)) {

                        driver = new FirefoxDriver();
                        // Read properties

                        /*Properties p = new Properties();
                        //p.load(new FileReader(new
File(BROWSER_PROPERTIES)));
                        p.load(this.getClass().getResource-
AsStream(BROWSER_PROPERTIES));
                        String pName = p.getProp-
erty("firefox.profile", "default");
                        System.out.println("Using the pro-
file = "+pName);

                        // Use the profile
                        ProfilesIni profilesIni = new Pro-
filesIni();
                        FirefoxProfile profile = pro-
filesIni.getProfile(pName);

                        driver = new FirefoxDriver(pro-
file);
                        */
                } else if ("chrome".equals(browser)) {
                        System.setProperty("web-
driver.chrome.driver",
                                "C:\\seleni-
umdrivers\\chromedriver.exe");
```

```java
                driver = new ChromeDriver();
        } else if ("ie".equals(browser)) {
                System.setProperty("web-
driver.ie.driver",
                                "C:\\seleni-
umdrivers\\IEDriverServer.exe");
                DesiredCapabilities caps = new
DesiredCapabilities().internetExplorer();
                caps.setCapability("ignoreProtect-
edModeSettings", true);
                caps.setCapability("ignoreZoom-
Setting", true);
                caps.setCapability("draggable",
true);
                caps.setCapability("requireWin-
dowFocus", true);
                driver = new InternetExplorer-
Driver(caps);
        } else if ("safari".equals(browser)) {
                driver = new SafariDriver();
        } else if ("opera".equals(browser)) {
                driver = new OperaDriver();
        } else if ("htmlunit".equals(browser)) {
                driver = new HtmlUnitDriver();
        } else {
                driver = new FirefoxDriver();
        }

        //Add implicitly wait
        System.out.println("Wait time (implicit wait)
="+WAIT_TIME);
        driver.manage().timeouts().implicit-
lyWait(WAIT_TIME, TimeUnit.SECONDS);
        //driver.manage().window().maximize();
//maximize the window

        //Load the URL
        //driver.navigate().to(url);
```

```
                //driver.get(url);
        }


        @AfterClass
        public void afterClass() {
                driver.quit();
        }


        @Test(dataProvider="testData1", enabled=false)
        public void dragTest1(String src) {
                //Load the URL
                driver.navigate().to(url1);
                // Get the source element
                WebElement target = driver.findEle-
ment(By.id("bin"));
                WebElement source = driver.findEle-
ment(By.id(src));
                Actions actions = new Actions(driver);
                Action action = ac-
tions.clickAndHold(source).moveToElement(target).re-
lease(source).build();
                action.perform();
                //actions.clickAndHold().dra-
gAndDrop(source, target);
                //actions.dragAndDrop(source, target);
                //actions.perform();
        }


        //@Test(dataProvider="testData2", enabled=true)
        @Test(dataProvider="testData2", enabled=false)
        public void dragTest2(int x, int y) {
                //Load the URL
                driver.navigate().to(url2);
                driver.navigate().to(url1);
                driver.navigate().back();
                System.out.println("Locate element");
                // Get the source element
                driver.manage().timeouts().implicitlyWait(0,
```

TimeUnit.SECONDS);
          WebElement source =
                    new WebDriver-
Wait(driver,WAIT_TIME).until(ExpectedConditions.presen-
ceOfElementLocated(By.xpath("//*[@id='draggable']")));

                    System.out.println("Moving to "+x+","+y);
                    Actions actions = new Actions(driver);
                    //actions.clickAndHold(source);
                    //actions.moveByOffset(x,y);
                    //actions.release(source);
                    actions.dragAndDropBy(source,x,y);
                    actions.build().perform();
                    //actions.clickAndHold().dra-
gAndDrop(source, target);
                    //actions.dragAndDrop(source, target);
                    //actions.perform();
                    driver.manage().timeouts().implicit-
lyWait(WAIT_TIME, TimeUnit.SECONDS);
          }

          @Test (enabled=false)
          public void dragTest3() {
                    driver.navigate().to(url3);

                    WebElement source = driver.findEle-
ment(By.className("draggable"));
                    WebElement target = driver.findEle-
ment(By.className("droppable"));

                    Actions builder = new Actions(driver);
                    Action dragAndDrop =
builder.clickAndHold(source)

                    .moveToElement(target)

                    .release(source)

```
                    .build();
                    dragAndDrop.perform();


            }


            /*
             * Test drag and drop
             */
            @Test (enabled=false)
            public void dragTest4() {
                    driver.navigate().to(url4);


                    //driver.switchTo().frame(0);
                    WebElement source = driver.findEle-
ment(By.id("draggable"));
                    WebElement target = driver.findEle-
ment(By.id("droppable"));


                    Actions builder = new Actions(driver);
                    //builder.clickAndHold(source).build().per-
form();
                    Action dragAndDrop =
builder.clickAndHold(source)


                    .moveToElement(target)


                    .release(target)


                    .build();
                    dragAndDrop.perform();
                    builder.dragAndDrop(source, tar-
get).build().perform();


            }


            /*
             * Test Select
             */
```

```
@Test (enabled=false)
public void autoTest5() {
        driver.navigate().to(url5);


        //driver.switchTo().frame(0);
        /*WebElement source = driver.findEle-
ment(By.id("city"));
        source.click();
        Actions actions = new Actions(driver);
        actions.click(source).keyDown(Keys.EN-
TER).click().keyDown(Keys.ARROW_DOWN).build().per-
form();
                */
        Select selectBox = new Select(driver.findElement(By
            .cssSelector("select#city")));
        // Select 2nd option and select
        selectBox.selectByIndex(2);
        String optionValue = selectBox.getFirstSelectedOp-
tion().getText();
        assertEquals("Santa Clara", optionValue);
        // Check all options
        List<String> cityOptions = new ArrayList<String>();
        cityOptions = Ar-
rays.asList("Fremont","Sunnyvale","Santa Clara","Cuper-
tino","Newark");
        List<WebElement> options = selectBox.getOptions();
        for (WebElement option: options ) {
            System.out.println(option.getText());
            assertEquals(true,cityOptions.contains(op-
tion.getText()),"Expected City");
        }
    }


    /*
    * Test autocomplete
    */
    @Test (enabled=false)
```

```
public void autoTest6() throws Exception{
    driver.navigate().to(url6);

    WebElement tags = driver.findElement(By.cssSelec-
tor("#tags"));
    tags.sendKeys("b");
    //Thread.sleep(1000); //wait for

            driver.manage().timeouts().implicitlyWait(0,
TimeUnit.SECONDS);
    List<WebElement> newtags =
                        new WebDriver-
Wait(driver,WAIT_TIME).until(ExpectedConditions.presence-
OfAllElementsLocatedBy(By.cssSelector("[id*=\"ui\"]")));

            driver.manage().timeouts().implicit-
lyWait(WAIT_TIME, TimeUnit.SECONDS);
    Thread.sleep(1000); //wait for 1 sec to see on the screen

    newtags = driver.findElements(By.cssSelec-
tor("[id*=\"ui\"]"));
    System.out.println("Size="+newtags.size());
    assertEquals(4, newtags.size());
    for (WebElement newtag: newtags ) {
        System.out.println("Auto value="+new-
tag.getText()+";");
    }
            Actions actions = new Actions(driver);
            actions.moveToElement(new-
tags.get(2)).click().build().perform();
            Thread.sleep(500);
    String sValue = driver.findElement(By.cssSelec-
tor("#tags")).getText();
    System.out.println("Selected value="+sValue);

    // RC style
            /*DefaultSelenium sel =
```

```
                        new WebDriver-
BackedSelenium(driver,url6);
        sel.type("//*[@id='tags']", "a");
        sel.fireEvent("//*[@id='tags']", "keydown");
        */

    }
    /*
    * Test autocomplete using google search
    */
    @Test (enabled=true)
    public void autoTest7() throws Exception{
            driver.navigate().to(url7);


    WebElement tags = driver.findElement(By.cssSelec-
tor("#gs_htif0.gbqfif"));
    tags = driver.findEle-
ment(By.xpath("//*[@id='gs_htif0']|//*[@class='gbqfif']"));
    //tags.sendKeys("selenium");
    tags.sendKeys("Java Jobs in US");


    //Thread.sleep(1000); //wait for


                    driver.manage().timeouts().implicitlyWait(0,
TimeUnit.SECONDS);
    List<WebElement> newtags =
                        new WebDriver-
Wait(driver,WAIT_TIME).until(ExpectedConditions.presence-
OfAllElementsLocatedBy(By.cssSelector("[id*=\"gsr\"]")));


                    driver.manage().timeouts().implicit-
lyWait(WAIT_TIME, TimeUnit.SECONDS);
    Thread.sleep(1000); //wait for 1 sec to see on the screen
    //.//*[@id='gsr']/table/tbody/tr/td[2]/ta-
ble/tbody/tr[4]/td/div/table/tbody/tr/td[1]/span
    //newtags = driver.findElements(By.cssSelec-
tor("[id*=\"gsr\"]"));
    newtags = driver.findEle-
```

```
ments(By.xpath("//*[@id='gsr']/table/tbody/tr/td[2]/ta-
ble/tbody/tr"));
        System.out.println("Size="+newtags.size());
        for (WebElement newtag: newtags ) {
            System.out.println("Auto value="+new-
tag.getText()+";");
        }

            Actions actions = new Actions(driver);
            actions.moveToElement(new-
tags.get(2)).click().build().perform();
            Thread.sleep(500);
        String sValue = driver.findElement(By.cssSelec-
tor("#gs_tti0.gsib_a")).getText();
        System.out.println("Selected value="+sValue);


        }


        /*
        * Test autocomplete using google search
        */
        @Test (enabled=false)
        public void autoTest8() throws Exception{
            driver.navigate().to(url8);



        WebElement joinelement = driver.findEle-
ment(By.xpath("//*[@id='StaticNav']/li[1]/a"));
            joinelement.click();


        WebElement ziplabel = driver.findEle-
ment(By.xpath("//*[@id='form0']/fieldset[1]/fieldset[1]/la-
bel"));
        ziplabel.click();
        WebElement zip = driver.findElement(By.cssSelec-
tor("#UserEnteredZipName"));
        zip.sendKeys("9453");


        //Thread.sleep(1000); //wait for
```

```java
            driver.manage().timeouts().implicitlyWait(0,
TimeUnit.SECONDS);
    List<WebElement> newtags =
                    new WebDriver-
Wait(driver,WAIT_TIME).until(
                                Ex-
pectedConditions.presenceOfAllElementsLocat-
edBy(By.xpath("//*[@data-id]")));
                    driver.manage().timeouts().implicit-
lyWait(WAIT_TIME, TimeUnit.SECONDS);
    Thread.sleep(1000); //wait for 1 sec to see on the screen
    newtags = driver.findElements(By.xpath("//*[@data-
id]"));
    System.out.println("Size="+newtags.size());
    for (WebElement newtag: newtags ) {
        System.out.println("Auto value="+new-
tag.getText()+";");
    }

            Actions actions = new Actions(driver);
            actions.moveToElement(new-
tags.get(2)).click().build().perform();
            Thread.sleep(500);
    String sValue = driver.findElement(By.cssSelec-
tor("#gs_tti0.gsib_a")).getText();
    System.out.println("Selected value="+sValue);


    }


        @Test(dataProvider="testData3", enabled=false)
        public void navigateUrls(String url) {
            driver.navigate().to(url);
            try {
                Thread.sleep(100);
            } catch (Exception e) {
                    e.printStackTrace();
            }
            driver.navigate().back();
```

```
        }

        @DataProvider
        public Object[][] testData1() {
            return new Object[][]{
        {"one"},{"two"},{"three"},{"four"},{"five"}};

        }

        @DataProvider
        public Object[][] testData2() {
                //return new Object[][]{ {200,
        10},{300,50},{100,500}};
                return new Object[][]{ {200, 10}};
        }

        @DataProvider
        public Object[][] testData3() {
            return new Object[][]{
        {"http://www.google.com"},{"http://www.ya-
        hoo.com"},{"http://www.linkedin.com"}, {url8}, {url9}};

        }


        /* Take snapshot
         */
        @AfterMethod (alwaysRun=true)
        public void catchFailure(ITestResult result) {
                String dateSuffix = new SimpleDateFor-
        mat("MM_dd_yyyy_hh_mm_ss").format(
                            Calendar.get-
        Instance().getTime()).toString();
                String methodName = result.getName();
                if (!result.isSuccess()) {
                        System.out.println("Taking screent-
        shot.../failed_screens"+File.separator+methodName+"-
        "+dateSuffix+".png");
```

TakesScreenshot screenshot =
(TakesScreenshot)driver;
//assertNotNull(screenshot,"Can't
get TakesScreenshot object from driver!"+screenshot);
if (screenshot==null) {
return;
}
File srcFile =
screenshot.get-
ScreenshotAs(OutputType.FILE);
File destFile = new
File("failed_screens"+File.separator+methodName+"-
"+dateSuffix+".png");
try {
FileUtils.copyFile(srcFile,
destFile);
org.testng.Re-
porter.log(destFile.getCanonicalPath(),true);
} catch (IOException ioe) {
System.out.println("Ex-
ception while creating the snapshot file!");
}

}
}

}

572. Write a selenium program to show remote grid testing.
Also, capture the events.

*/***
* File: RemoteTest.java
*/
package com.everydayon.selenium.test;

```java
import java.io.File;
import java.io.IOException;
import java.net.URL;
import java.text.SimpleDateFormat;
import java.util.Calendar;
import java.util.concurrent.TimeUnit;

import org.apache.commons.io.FileUtils;
import org.openqa.selenium.OutputType;
import org.openqa.selenium.TakesScreenshot;
import org.openqa.selenium.WebDriver;
import org.openqa.selenium.chrome.ChromeDriver;
import org.openqa.selenium.firefox.FirefoxDriver;
import org.openqa.selenium.htmlunit.HtmlUnitDriver;
import org.openqa.selenium.ie.InternetExplorerDriver;
import org.openqa.selenium.remote.DesiredCapabilities;
import org.openqa.selenium.remote.RemoteWebDriver;
import org.openqa.selenium.safari.SafariDriver;
import org.openqa.selenium.support.events.EventFiringWebDriver;
import org.openqa.selenium.support.events.WebDriverEventListener;
import org.testng.ITestResult;
import org.testng.annotations.AfterClass;
import org.testng.annotations.AfterMethod;
import org.testng.annotations.BeforeClass;
import org.testng.annotations.DataProvider;
import org.testng.annotations.Factory;
import org.testng.annotations.Test;

import com.opera.core.systems.OperaDriver;

/**
 * Description: Listeners
 *
 *
 * @author Jagadesh Babu Munta
```

```java
 *
 */
public class RemoteTest {

        private WebDriver driver = null;
        private DesiredCapabilities caps = null;
        private EventFiringWebDriver efdriver = null;
        private String url1 = "http://www.facebook.com";
        private String url2 = "http://www.youtube.com";
        private String url3 = "http://www.google.com";

        //private String url = "http://jqueryui.com/draggable"; //"http://html5demos.com/drag";
        private String browser = null;
        private static final String BROWSER_PROPERTIES = "browsertesting.properties";
        private static final int WAIT_TIME = 10;
        private static final String HUB_URL = "http://localhost:4444/wd/hub";

        @Factory(dataProviderClass=com.everydayon.selenium.test.TestDataProvider.class,
                        dataProvider="testDataProvider")
        public RemoteTest(String browser) {
                this.browser = browser;
                System.out.println("Running with browser="+browser);
        }


        @BeforeClass
        public void beforeClass() throws Exception{
                // Create the driver
                if ("firefox".equals(browser)) {
                        caps = new DesiredCapabilities().firefox();
                        driver = new RemoteWebDriver(new URL(HUB_URL),caps);
```

```
                // Read properties

                /*Properties p = new Properties();
                //p.load(new FileReader(new
File(BROWSER_PROPERTIES)));
                        p.load(this.getClass().getResource-
AsStream(BROWSER_PROPERTIES));
                        String pName = p.getProp-
erty("firefox.profile", "default");
                        System.out.println("Using the pro-
file = "+pName);

                // Use the profile
                        ProfilesIni profilesIni = new Pro-
filesIni();
                        FirefoxProfile profile = pro-
filesIni.getProfile(pName);

                        driver = new FirefoxDriver(pro-
file);
                */
                } else if ("chrome".equals(browser)) {
                        caps = new DesiredCapabili-
ties().chrome();
                        caps.setCapability("chrome.bi-
nary",
                                "C:\\seleni-
umdrivers\\chromedriver.exe");
                        System.setProperty("web-
driver.chrome.driver",
                                "C:\\seleni-
umdrivers\\chromedriver.exe");
                        driver = new RemoteWeb-
Driver(new URL(HUB_URL),caps);
                } else if ("ie".equals(browser)) {
                        caps = new DesiredCapabili-
ties().internetExplorer();
```

```java
                System.setProperty("web-
driver.ie.driver",
                                "C:\\seleni-
umdrivers\\IEDriverServer.exe");
                caps.setCapability("ie.binary",
                                "C:\\seleni-
umdrivers\\IEDriverServer.exe");
                caps.setCapability("ignoreProtect-
edModeSettings", true);
                caps.setCapability("ignoreZoom-
Setting", true);
                caps.setCapability("draggable",
true);
                caps.setCapability("requireWin-
dowFocus", true);
                driver = new RemoteWeb-
Driver(new URL(HUB_URL),caps);
            } else if ("safari".equals(browser)) {
                caps = new DesiredCapabili-
ties().safari();
                driver = new RemoteWeb-
Driver(new URL(HUB_URL),caps);
            } else if ("opera".equals(browser)) {
                //driver = new OperaDriver();
                caps = new DesiredCapabili-
ties().opera();
                driver = new RemoteWeb-
Driver(new URL(HUB_URL),caps);
            } else if ("htmlunit".equals(browser)) {
                //driver = new HtmlUnitDriver();
                caps = new DesiredCapabili-
ties().htmlUnit();
                driver = new RemoteWeb-
Driver(new URL(HUB_URL),caps);
            } else {
                caps = new DesiredCapabili-
ties().firefox();
```

```
                    driver = new RemoteWeb-
Driver(new URL(HUB_URL),caps);
                    }


                    //Add implicitly wait
                    System.out.println("Wait time (implicit wait)
="+WAIT_TIME);
                    driver.manage().timeouts().implicit-
lyWait(WAIT_TIME, TimeUnit.SECONDS);
                    //driver.manage().window().maximize();
//maximize the window


                    // Register events
                    efdriver = new EventFiringWeb-
Driver(driver);
                    WebDriverEventListener eventListener =
new MyEventListener();
                    efdriver.register(eventListener);


                    //Load the URL
                    //driver.navigate().to(url);
                    //driver.get(url);
            }


            @AfterClass
            public void afterClass() {
                    efdriver.quit();
            }

            @Test(enabled=true)
            public void navigateTest1() throws Exception {
                    //Load the URL
                    efdriver.navigate().to(url1);
                    Thread.sleep(100); // to see the screen in-
stead of flash
                    efdriver.navigate().to(url2);
                    Thread.sleep(100);
                    efdriver.navigate().to(url3);
```

```
        Thread.sleep(100);
        efdriver.navigate().back(); //to url2
        Thread.sleep(100);
        efdriver.navigate().back(); // to url1
        Thread.sleep(100);
        efdriver.navigate().forward(); // to url2
        Thread.sleep(100);
        efdriver.navigate().forward(); // to url3

}


@DataProvider
public Object[][] testData1() {
        return new Object[][]{
{"one"},{"two"},{"three"},{"four"},{"five"}};

}


@DataProvider
public Object[][] testData2() {
        //return new Object[][]{ {200,
10},{300,50},{100,500}};
        return new Object[][]{ {200, 10}};
}


/* Take snapshot
 */
@AfterMethod (alwaysRun=true)
public void catchFailure(ITestResult result) {
        String dateSuffix = new SimpleDateFor-
mat("MM_dd_yyyy_hh_mm_ss").format(
                        Calendar.get-
Instance().getTime()).toString();
        String methodName = result.getName();
        if (!result.isSuccess()) {
                System.out.println("Taking screent-
shot.../failed_screens"+File.separator+methodName+"-
"+dateSuffix+".png");
```

```
                    TakesScreenshot screenshot =
(TakesScreenshot)driver;
                    //assertNotNull(screenshot,"Can't
get TakesScreenshot object from driver!"+screenshot);
                    if (screenshot==null) {
                        return;
                    }
                    File srcFile =
                        screenshot.get-
ScreenshotAs(OutputType.FILE);
                    File destFile = new
File("failed_screens"+File.separator+methodName+"-
"+dateSuffix+".png");
                    try {
                        FileUtils.copyFile(srcFile,
destFile);
                        org.testng.Re-
porter.log(destFile.getCanonicalPath(),true);
                    } catch (IOException ioe) {
                        System.out.println("Ex-
ception while creating the snapshot file!");
                    }


                }
            }

}


/**
 * File: MyEventListener.java
 */
package com.everydayon.selenium.test;

import org.openqa.selenium.By;
import org.openqa.selenium.WebDriver;
```

```java
import org.openqa.selenium.WebElement;
import org.openqa.selenium.support.events.WebDriverEvent-
Listener;

/**
 * @author Jagadesh Babu Munta
 *
 */
public class MyEventListener implements WebDriverEventLis-
tener{

        @Override
        public void beforeNavigateTo(String url, WebDriver
driver) {
                System.out.println("Before navigation to
"+url);
                if (url.contains("youtube.com")) {
                        System.out.println("WARNING::No
youtube please! redirecting to seleniumhq.org");
                        driver.navi-
gate().to("http://www.seleniumhq.org");
                } else if (url.contains("facebook.com")) {
                        System.out.println("WARNING::No
facebook allowed! Redirecting to linkedin.com");
                        driver.navi-
gate().to("http://www.linkedin.com");
                }
        }

        @Override
        public void afterNavigateTo(String url, WebDriver
driver) {
                System.out.println("After navigation to
"+url);
        }

        @Override
        public void beforeNavigateBack(WebDriver driver) {
```

```java
        System.out.println("Before navigation
back...");

        }

        @Override
        public void afterNavigateBack(WebDriver driver) {
            System.out.println("After navigation
back...");
        }

        @Override
        public void beforeNavigateForward(WebDriver
driver) {
            System.out.println("Before navigation for-
ward...");

        }

        @Override
        public void afterNavigateForward(WebDriver driver)
{
            System.out.println("After navigation for-
ward...");

        }

        @Override
        public void beforeFindBy(By by, WebElement ele-
ment, WebDriver driver) {
            // TODO Auto-generated method stub

        }

        @Override
        public void afterFindBy(By by, WebElement element,
WebDriver driver) {
            // TODO Auto-generated method stub
```

```java
        }

        @Override
        public void beforeClickOn(WebElement element,
WebDriver driver) {
                // TODO Auto-generated method stub
                //element.xxx()

        }

        @Override
        public void afterClickOn(WebElement element, Web-
Driver driver) {
                // TODO Auto-generated method stub

        }

        @Override
        public void beforeChangeValueOf(WebElement ele-
ment, WebDriver driver) {
                // TODO Auto-generated method stub

        }

        @Override
        public void afterChangeValueOf(WebElement ele-
ment, WebDriver driver) {
                // TODO Auto-generated method stub

        }

        @Override
        public void beforeScript(String script, WebDriver
driver) {
                // TODO Auto-generated method stub

        }
```

```java
        @Override
        public void afterScript(String script, WebDriver
driver) {
                // TODO Auto-generated method stub

        }

        @Override
        public void onException(Throwable throwable, Web-
Driver driver) {
                System.out.println("Exception
raised..."+throwable.getMessage());

        }

}


/**
 * File: TestDataProvider.java
 */
package com.everydayon.selenium.test;

import java.util.ArrayList;
import java.util.Iterator;
import java.util.List;

import org.testng.ITestContext;
import org.testng.annotations.DataProvider;

/**
 * @author Jagadesh Babu Munta
 *
 */
public class TestDataProvider {
```

```
        @DataProvider
        public static Iterator<Object[]> testDataPro-
vider(ITestContext context) {
                List<Object[]> data = new ArrayList<Ob-
ject[]>();

                //data.add(new Object[]{"firefox"});
                data.add(new Object[]{"chrome"});
                //data.add(new Object[]{"ie"});
                //data.add(new Object[]{"opera"});
                //data.add(new Object[]{"safari"});
                //data.add(new Object[]{"htmlunit"});
                return data.iterator();
        }

}


File: browsertesting.properties
# Properties
drag.url=http://jqueryui.com/draggable/
drag.source.id=bin
```

573. Write a sample code to show navigation of different links using the selenium webdriver.

```
/**
    • File: AllLinks.java
*/
package com.everydayon.selenium.test;

import java.io.File;
import java.io.IOException;
import java.text.SimpleDateFormat;
import java.util.Calendar;
import java.util.Iterator;
import java.util.List;
```

```java
import java.util.concurrent.TimeUnit;

import org.apache.commons.io.FileUtils;
import org.openqa.selenium.By;
import org.openqa.selenium.OutputType;
import org.openqa.selenium.StaleElementReferenceException;
import org.openqa.selenium.TakesScreenshot;
import org.openqa.selenium.WebDriver;
import org.openqa.selenium.WebElement;
import org.openqa.selenium.chrome.ChromeDriver;
import org.openqa.selenium.firefox.FirefoxDriver;
import org.openqa.selenium.htmlunit.HtmlUnitDriver;
import org.openqa.selenium.ie.InternetExplorerDriver;
import org.openqa.selenium.remote.DesiredCapabilities;
import org.openqa.selenium.safari.SafariDriver;
import org.testng.ITestResult;
import org.testng.annotations.AfterClass;
import org.testng.annotations.AfterMethod;
import org.testng.annotations.BeforeClass;
import org.testng.annotations.DataProvider;
import org.testng.annotations.Factory;
import org.testng.annotations.Test;

import com.opera.core.systems.OperaDriver;

/**
 * Description: Find all links
 *
 * @author Jagadesh Babu Munta
 *
 */
public class AllLinks {

    private WebDriver driver = null;

    private String browser = null;
    private static final String BROWSER_PROPERTIES
= "browsertesting.properties";
```

```
private static final int WAIT_TIME = 10;

@Factory(dataProviderClass=com.everydayon.sele-
nium.test.TestDataProvider.class,
                dataProvider="testDataProvider")
public AllLinks(String browser) {
    this.browser = browser;
    System.out.println("Running with
browser="+browser);
}



@BeforeClass
public void beforeClass() throws Exception{
    // Create the driver
    if ("firefox".equals(browser)) {

        driver = new FirefoxDriver();
        // Read properties

        /*Properties p = new Properties();
        //p.load(new FileReader(new
File(BROWSER_PROPERTIES)));
                p.load(this.getClass().getResource-
AsStream(BROWSER_PROPERTIES));
                String pName = p.getProp-
erty("firefox.profile", "default");
                System.out.println("Using the pro-
file = "+pName);

        // Use the profile
        ProfilesIni profilesIni = new Pro-
filesIni();
                FirefoxProfile profile = pro-
filesIni.getProfile(pName);

        driver = new FirefoxDriver(pro-
file);
```

```
                        */
        } else if ("chrome".equals(browser)) {
                System.setProperty("web-
driver.chrome.driver",
                        "C:\\seleni-
umdrivers\\chromedriver.exe");
                driver = new ChromeDriver();
        } else if ("ie".equals(browser)) {
                System.setProperty("web-
driver.ie.driver",
                        "C:\\seleni-
umdrivers\\IEDriverServer.exe");
                DesiredCapabilities caps = new
DesiredCapabilities().internetExplorer();
                caps.setCapability("ignoreProtect-
edModeSettings", true);
                caps.setCapability("ignoreZoom-
Setting", true);
                caps.setCapability("draggable",
true);
                caps.setCapability("requireWin-
dowFocus", true);
                driver = new InternetExplorer-
Driver(caps);
        } else if ("safari".equals(browser)) {
                driver = new SafariDriver();
        } else if ("opera".equals(browser)) {
                driver = new OperaDriver();
        } else if ("htmlunit".equals(browser)) {
                driver = new HtmlUnitDriver();
        } else {
                driver = new FirefoxDriver();
        }

        //Add implicitly wait
        System.out.println("Wait time (implicit wait)
="+WAIT_TIME);
```

```
        driver.manage().timeouts().implicit-
lyWait(WAIT_TIME, TimeUnit.SECONDS);
            //driver.manage().window().maximize();
//maximize the window


            //Load the URL
            //driver.navigate().to(url);
            //driver.get(url);
    }

    @AfterClass
    public void afterClass() {
            driver.quit();
    }

    @Test(dataProvider="testData1", enabled=true)
    public void test1(String url1) {
            //Load the URL
            driver.navigate().to(url1);
            // Find <a> elements

            List<WebElement> links = driver.findEle-
ments(By.cssSelector("* [href]"));
            System.out.println(driver.getCurren-
tUrl()+"-->"+links.size());

            Iterator<WebElement> link = links.itera-
tor();
            int totalLinks = links.size();
            for(WebElement e: links) {

            Sys-
tem.out.println("<"+e.getTagName()+">:"+e.getText()+"("+
e.getAttribute("href")+")");
                visitLink(e);
                /*
                if (! "".equals(e.getText())) {
                    try {
```

```java
                        e.click();
                        links =
driver.findElements(By.cssSelector("* [href]"));
                        }catch (StaleElemen-
tReferenceException sre) {
                                links =
driver.findElements(By.cssSelector("* [href]"));
                        }
                        totalLinks+= links.size();
                        Sys-
tem.out.println(driver.getCurrentUrl()+"-->"+links.size());
                        }

                try {
                        links = driver.findEle-
ments(By.cssSelector("* [href]"));
                        }catch (StaleElementReferenceEx-
ception sre) {
                        links = driver.findEle-
ments(By.cssSelector("* [href]"));
                        }*/
                }
                System.out.println("Grand Total #of
Links="+totalLinks);
                }

        /*
        * Visit a link
        */
        private void visitLink(WebElement e) {
                if ("".equals(e.getText())) {
                        return;
                }
                List<WebElement> links;
                try {
                        System.out.println("Before click():
<"+e.getTagName()+">: LinkText="+e.getText()+";
Link="+e.getAttribute("href"));
```

```java
                                if (e.getAttribute("href").con-
tains("#")) {
                                        System.out.println("Skip #
link");
                                        return;
                                } else {
                                        System.out.println("Click-
ing link");
                                        e.click();
                                }
                        }catch (StaleElementReferenceException
sre) {
                                System.out.println("Statelement at
"+e.getText());
                                links = driver.findEle-
ments(By.cssSelector("* [href]"));
                        }


                        links = driver.findElements(By.cssSelec-
tor("* [href]"));
                        System.out.println(driver.getCurren-
tUrl()+"-->"+links.size());
                        for (WebElement e1: links) {
                                visitLink(e1);
                        }


        }


        @DataProvider
        public Object[][] testData1() {
                //return new Object[][]{
{"http://www.nlsinc.com"},{"http://www.sjsu.edu"},{"http://w
ww.ya-
hoo.com"},{"http://www.google.com"},{"http://www.mon-
ster.com"}};
                        return new Object[][]{ {"http://www.stan-
ford.edu"}};
```

```
        }

        @DataProvider
        public Object[][] testData2() {
            //return new Object[][]{ {200,
10},{300,50},{100,500}};
            return new Object[][]{ {200, 10}};
        }

        /* Take snapshot
         */
        @AfterMethod (alwaysRun=true)
        public void catchFailure(ITestResult result) {
            String dateSuffix = new SimpleDateFor-
mat("MM_dd_yyyy_hh_mm_ss").format(
                    Calendar.get-
Instance().getTime()).toString();
            String methodName = result.getName();
            if (!result.isSuccess()) {
                System.out.println("Taking screent-
shot.../failed_screens"+File.separator+methodName+"-
"+dateSuffix+".png");

                TakesScreenshot screenshot =
(TakesScreenshot)driver;
                //assertNotNull(screenshot,"Can't
get TakesScreenshot object from driver!"+screenshot);
                if (screenshot==null) {
                    return;
                }
                File srcFile =
                    screenshot.get-
ScreenshotAs(OutputType.FILE);
                File destFile = new
File("failed_screens"+File.separator+methodName+"-
"+dateSuffix+".png");
                try {
                    FileUtils.copyFile(srcFile,
```

```
            destFile);
                                        org.testng.Re-
porter.log(destFile.getCanonicalPath(),true);
                        } catch (IOException ioe) {
                                        System.out.println("Ex-
ception while creating the snapshot file!");
                        }



                        }
                }


        }
```

Conclusion

Now, you have identified and learned the essential skills needed for becoming a good software quality and Java automation engineer. For the in-depth or expert level skills where you might want to use heavily, pick a particular book or material on those subjects.

For further software career improvement keep coding on day to day basis. Otherwise, it is easy to forget as we do many things. Also, for the cutting edge technologies and practices, search on the web and participate in the internet talks, seminars, etc. at least some time on day to day basis.

Also, share and help people who need those skills.

Once you are good at the core competencies, then learn the concepts & working knowledge around the Cloud Services, DevOps, CI-CD, Mobile, Scripting languages, Artificial Intelligence, Robotics, Advanced Ads, Developing new test frameworks, Complex integration automation techniques, etc.

In future, I will be sharing more knowledge on the above topics through books and other channels.

All the best for your dream!

References

The author used the below links for some of the references.

1. HTTP - http://www.w3.org/Protocols/rfc2616/rfc2616-sec1.html
2. Java - https://docs.oracle.com/javase
3. ANT - http://ant.apache.org
4. Maven - http://maven.org
5. Jenkins - http://www.jenkins.org
6. JUnit - http://junit.org
7. TestNG - http://testng.org
8. Git - http://github.com
9. SoapUI - https://www.soapui.org/
10. StackOverflow - http://www.stackoverflow.com
11. Wikipedia - http://www.wikipedia.com
12. Sample book on SVN at http://svnbook.red-bean.com/nightly/en/index.html

Reader's Tracking Index

In general, it is better to plan, execute and track the progress in order to achieve the goal in time. The below table can be used for completing the skills learning, review or interviews preparation.

Skill	#of Qs	Status	#of-Hrs. Spent	Start Date	Finish Date
Skill#1. Software Development Life Cycle (SDLC)	36	√			
Skill#2. Software Quality Concepts	39				
Skill#3. Object Oriented Programming & System (OOPS)	29				
Skill#4. XML	12				
Skill#5. XPath	19				
Skill#6. JSON	7				
Skill#7. Source Code Control System (SCCS)/ SCM - SVN & GIT	21				
Skill#8. Unix/Linux OS	47				
Skill#9. Java	101				
Skill#10. ANT	34				
Skill#11. Maven	36				
Skill#12. JUnit	31				
Skill#13. TestNG	21				
Skill#14. Hudson/Jenkins	24				
Skill#15. Web Applications Testing and Selenium	45				
Skill#16. Web Services (SOAP&REST API) Testing and SoapUI Tool	48				
Java Samples Code	19				
Selenium Samples Code	4				
Hands-on/Getting Started	3				

Thank you.

Learning never stops!

….. continue

-- Jagadesh Babu Munta